Network+ CoursePrep
ExamGuide/StudyGuide
Network+ Exam

D1314724

**COURSE
TECHNOLOGY**™

THOMSON LEARNING

Network +™
A CompTIA Certification Program

Australia • Canada • Mexico • Singapore • Spain • United Kingdom • United States

Network+ CoursePrep ExamGuide and Network+ CoursePrep StudyGuide are published by Course Technology.

Senior Product Manager	Lisa Egan
Managing Editor	Stephen Solomon
Senior Vice President, Publisher	Kristen Duerr
Production Editor	Kristen Guevara
Developmental Editor	Lisa Ruffolo, The Software Resource
Associate Product Manager	Laura Hildebrand
Editorial Assistants	Elizabeth Wessen, Janet Aras
Director of Product Marketing	Susan Ogar
Text Designer	Dianne Schaefer, Books By Design
Cover Designer	MaryAnn Southard

Disclaimer

Course Technology reserves the right to revise this publication and make changes from time to time in its content without notice.

For more information contact:

Course Technology

25 Thomson Place

Boston, MA 02210;

or find us on the World Wide Web at: www.course.com

For permission to use material from this text or product, contact us by

- Web: www.thomsonrights.com

- Phone: 1-800-730-2214

- Fax: 1-800-730-2215

ISBN 0-619-03522-6

ISBN 0-619-01649-3

Printed in Canada

1 2 3 4 5 WC 02 01 00 99

TABLE OF CONTENTS

The *Network+ CoursePrep ExamGuide and Network+ CoursePrep StudyGuide* are the very best tools to use to prepare for exam day. These products are intended to be utilized with the core "Guide to" book, *Network+ Guide to Networks* (ISBN 0-7600-1145-1), also written by the same author, Tamara Dean, and published by Course Technology. CoursePrep ExamGuide and CoursePrep StudyGuide provide you ample opportunity to practice, drill and rehearse for the exam!

COURSEPREP EXAMGUIDE

The *Network+ CoursePrep ExamGuide*, ISBN 0-619-03522-6, provides the essential information you need to master each exam objective. The ExamGuide devotes an entire two-page spread to each certification objective for the Network+ exam, helping you understand the objective, and giving you the bottom line information—what you *really* need to know. Memorize these facts and bulleted points before heading into the exam. In addition, there are seven practice test questions for each objective on the right-hand page. That's 700 questions total! CoursePrep ExamGuide provides the exam fundamentals and gets you up to speed quickly. If you are seeking even more opportunity to practice and prepare, we recommend that you consider our total solution, CoursePrep StudyGuide, which is described below.

COURSEPREP STUDYGUIDE

For those really serious about certification, we offer an even more robust solution—the *Network+ CoursePrep StudyGuide*, ISBN 0-619-01649-3. This offering includes all of the same quality material you get with the CoursePrep ExamGuide, including the unique two-page spread, the bulleted memorization points, and the practice questions. In addition, you receive a password valid for 6 months of practice on CoursePrep, a dynamic test preparation tool. The password is found in an envelope in the back cover of the CoursePrep StudyGuide. CoursePrep is a Web-based pool of hundreds of sample test questions. CoursePrep exam simulation software mimics the exact exam environment. The CoursePrep software is flexible, and allows you to practice in several ways as you master the material. Choose from Certification Mode to experience actual exam-day conditions or Study Mode to request answers and explanations to practice questions.

Custom Mode lets you set the options for the practice test, including number of questions, content coverage, and ability to request answers and explanation. Follow the instructions on the inside back cover to access the exam simulation software. To see a demo of this dynamic test preparation tool, go to *www.courseprep.com*.

FEATURES

The *Network+ CoursePrep ExamGuide* and *Network+ CoursePrep StudyGuide* include the following features:

List of domains and objectives taken directly from the CompTIA Web site This book is divided into two sections, each devoted to a domain of knowledge. Each section begins with a description of the domain covered on the exam. The objectives under each domain are found within the section. For more information about the Network+ Exam, visit CompTIA's Web site at *www.comptia.org*.

Detailed coverage of the certification objectives in a unique two-page spread Study strategically by really focusing in on the Network+ certification objectives. To enable you to do this, a two-page spread is devoted to each certification objective. The left-hand page provides the critical facts you need, while the right-hand page features practice questions relating to that objective. You'll find the certification objective(s) and sub-objectives(s) are clearly listed in the upper left-hand corner of each spread.

 Software Icon: This icon appears to the left of the certification objective if the objective is software related.

 Hardware Icon: This icon appears to the left of the certification objective if the objective is hardware related.

An overview of the objective is provided in the **Understanding the Objective** section. Next, **What you Really Need to Know** lists bulleted, succinct core facts, skills, and concepts about the objective. Memorizing these facts will be important for your success when taking the exam. **Objectives on the Job** places the objective in an industry perspective, and tells you how you can expect to incorporate the objective on the job. This section also provides troubleshooting information.

Practice Test Questions Each right-hand page contains seven practice test questions designed to help you prepare for the exam by testing your skills, identifying your strengths and weaknesses, and demonstrating the subject matter you will face on the exams and how it will be tested. These questions are written in a similar fashion to real Network+ Exam questions. The questions test your knowledge of the objectives described on the left-hand page and also the information in the *Network+ Guide to Networks*. Answers to the practice test questions are found on the Course Technology Web site *at www.course.com*. Search on the ISBN found on the back of your book to find the solutions quickly.

Answer Boxes: You can use the boxes to the right of the practice test questions to mark your answers, grade yourself, or write down the correct answer.

Glossary: Boldfaced terms used in the book and other terms that you need to know for the exams are listed and defined in the glossary.

For more information: This book evolved from the *Network+ Guide to Networks* (ISBN 0-7600-1145-1) also by Tamara Dean. See that book for more in-depth explanations of concepts or procedures presented here.

HOW TO USE THIS BOOK

The *Network+ CoursePrep ExamGuide and Network+ CoursePrep StudyGuide* are all you need to successfully prepare for the Network+ Certification exams if you have some experience and working knowledge of supporting and maintaining networks. This book is intended to be used with a core text, such as *Network+ Guide to Networks* (ISBN 0-7600-1145-1), also published by Course Technology. If you are new to this field, use this book as a roadmap of where you need to go to prepare for certification; use the *Network+ Guide to Networks* to give you the depth of knowledge and understanding that you need to reach your goal. Course Technology publishes a full series of network and Network+ products. For more information, visit our Web site at: *www.course.com* or contact your sales representative.

ACKNOWLEDGMENTS

I could not have completed this guide without the support and planning of the ever-capable and efficient Course Technology staff, especially Lisa Egan, Senior Product Manager, Stephen Solomon, Managing Editor, and Kristen Duerr, Publisher. Many thanks to Lisa Ruffolo, the Developmental Editor, for ensuring the clarity and consistency of the guide and to technical reviewer Cheryl Ukacar, who checked my work at every step, helping to make the guide more accurate and complete.

This domain covers the fundamentals of networking, such as the OSI model, topologies, connectivity devices, protocols, media, remote connectivity, and security. In mastering this domain you should be able to define each networking term and understand how it is used in networking.

Below are percentages of the domain and each objective reflected in the exam questions. The objectives are a percentage of the total exam, not of the domain.

Domain	Percentage of the Net+ Exam Content
I. Knowledge of Networking Technology	77% total
1. Basic Knowledge	18%
2. Physical Layer	6%
3. Data Link Layer	5%
4. Network Layer	5%
5. Transport Layer	5%
6. TCP/IP Fundamentals	16%
7. TCP/IP Suite: Utilities	11%
8. Remote Connectivity	5%
9. Security	6%

THE CHARACTERISTICS OF BUS AND RING TOPOLOGIES, THEIR ADVANTAGES AND DISADVANTAGES

UNDERSTANDING THE OBJECTIVE

Every network depends on a physical layout, or topology. The topology describes how devices are physically connected in a local-area network (LAN) or wide-area network (WAN). While most modern networks contain a combination of topologies, all combinations rely on a few fundamental topologies: bus, star, and ring, each of which has advantages and disadvantages.

WHAT YOU **REALLY** NEED TO KNOW

◆ The three fundamental network topologies are bus, star, and ring.

◆ A **bus topology** consists of a single cable connecting all nodes on a network without intervening connectivity devices. Because every node shares the same channel for data transmission, adding nodes on a bus network impairs performance.

◆ A bus topology can be considered a peer-to-peer topology because every device on the network shares the responsibility for transferring data from one point to another.

◆ Bus topologies require 50-Ohm resistors known as **terminators** at each end of the bus to prevent **signal bounce**, a phenomenon in which data travels endlessly between the two ends of the network.

◆ The bus topology is the least fault-tolerant of any topology, because one break in the cable can take down the entire network, and bus topology faults are difficult to find.

◆ A bus topology is the least expensive and simplest topology to install.

◆ In a **ring topology** each node is connected to the two nearest nodes so that the entire network forms a circle. Data is transmitted in one direction (unidirectionally) around the ring. Each workstation accepts and responds to packets addressed to it, then forwards the other packets to the next workstation in the ring.

◆ Because a ring network has no ends, and because data stops at its destination, ring networks do not require terminators.

◆ Ring topologies often use the **token passing** technique, in which a node that wants to send data picks up the constantly circling token, adds its data, sends the packet, and when the recipient accepts the packet, releases the token so that other nodes can transmit.

◆ A disadvantage of the ring topology is that one defective node can take down the network. Adding more nodes to a ring network can impair performance.

OBJECTIVES ON THE JOB

Consider topologies when designing and maintaining networks, because they influence performance, expense, ease of use, and troubleshooting. Network topologies affect the way computer rooms and work areas are cabled, the type of cabling and connectors used, and the type of NICs, hubs, routers, and other devices used.

PRACTICE TEST QUESTIONS

1. **Which of the following is the least fault-tolerant topology?**
   - a. star
   - b. ring
   - c. bus
   - d. tree

   ANSWER

2. **On a bus topology, terminators eliminate the possibility for:**
   - a. crosstalk
   - b. noise
   - c. signal bounce
   - d. EMI

   ANSWER

3. **What is the function of a token on a token passing ring network?**
   - a. It signals to the rest of the network to listen for traffic.
   - b. It signals to the rest of the network that the MAU is receiving an excessive number of errors.
   - c. It enables multiple nodes on the network to transmit data simultaneously.
   - d. It enables one node on the network to transmit data at any one time.

   ANSWER

4. **How many tokens circulate on a simple ring network?**
   - a. one
   - b. five
   - c. ten
   - d. an unlimited number

   ANSWER

5. **In which of the following topologies does the addition of more nodes detrimentally affect the network's performance?**
   - a. bus and ring
   - b. star and ring
   - c. star and bus
   - d. tree and star

   ANSWER

6. **What would happen to the entire network if one of the nodes in a bus-wired network failed?**
   - a. Performance would suffer.
   - b. nothing much
   - c. Data would no longer be transmitted.
   - d. Errors would be broadcast to every node.

   ANSWER

7. **What type of terminator is used on a bus network?**
   - a. 20-Ohm resistor
   - b. 50-Ohm resistor
   - c. 20-Ohm transistor
   - d. 50-Ohm transistor

   ANSWER

THE CHARACTERISTICS OF STAR AND MESH TOPOLOGIES, THEIR ADVANTAGES AND DISADVANTAGES

UNDERSTANDING THE OBJECTIVE

Networks are based on simple topologies, but rarely rely on them. More complex topologies not only can handle heavier traffic and traverse greater distances, but they can also improve performance and fault tolerance. The most fault-tolerant LAN topology is a star-ring hybrid. The most fault-tolerant WAN topology is a full mesh.

WHAT YOU **REALLY** NEED TO KNOW

◆ In a **star topology,** every node on the network is connected through a central device, such as a hub, in a star configuration. Each device transmits its data to the hub, which repeats the data to all other devices on the segment. The recipient then picks up the data addressed to it.

◆ Any single physical wire on a star network only connects two devices, so a cabling problem only affects two nodes. Devices such as workstations or printers transmit data to the hub, which then retransmits the data to the network segment where the destination node is located, so the destination node can pick it up.

◆ Star topologies are more fault tolerant and provide better performance than bus or ring topologies. A single cable or node fault does not immobilize a star-wired network. However, star networks require more cabling and devices, and are generally more expensive than bus or ring networks.

◆ Star networks can be easily upgraded, moved, and connected to other networks.

◆ Networks are commonly built with **hybrid topologies** that contain characteristics of more than one fundamental topology.

◆ The most common types of hybrid topologies are combinations of the star and ring or the star and bus topologies. Modern Ethernet networks typically use the star-bus hybrid topology.

◆ A location in a WAN topology is equivalent to a node in a LAN topology.

◆ A **mesh** network is one in which WAN locations are directly interconnected with multiple locations on the network. This enhances fault tolerance because the WAN location is not dependent on a single connection to the network.

◆ On a **full-mesh** network, every location on a WAN is directly connected to every other location on the WAN. On a **partial-mesh** network, only some of the locations on the WAN have multiple connections to the network.

OBJECTIVES ON THE JOB

Star and mesh topologies are both more fault tolerant than their alternatives. They are more expensive as well. But in an organization that cannot afford downtime, the more expensive topologies are worth the cost. Many organizations use the partial-mesh rather than the full-mesh topology to strike a balance between fault tolerance and expense.

PRACTICE TEST QUESTIONS

1. **Which of the following hybrid topologies uses the token passing method of data transmission?**
   a. star-bus
   b. star-star
   c. star-ring
   d. none of the above

   ANSWER

2. **What would happen to the entire network if one of the nodes in a star-wired network failed?**
   a. Performance would suffer.
   b. nothing much
   c. Data would no longer be transmitted.
   d. Errors would be broadcast to every node.

   ANSWER

3. **Which of the following is the most expensive of the simple topologies?**
   a. bus
   b. ring
   c. star
   d. tree

   ANSWER

4. **What is the function of a hub in a star-wired network?**
   a. to prevent RF emissions that may result in security breaches
   b. to increase available bandwidth by sending multiplexed signals
   c. to arbitrate addressing conflicts between sending nodes
   d. to repeat signals to all nodes on the segment

   ANSWER

5. **What type of WAN topology results when every location is directly connected to every other location on the network?**
   a. partial mesh
   b. full mesh
   c. dedicated mesh
   d. collapsed mesh

   ANSWER

6. **Which of the following is the most fault tolerant LAN topology?**
   a. ring
   b. bus
   c. tree
   d. star

   ANSWER

7. **Which of the following advantages does a partial mesh topology provide?**
   a. All nodes have multiple connections to the network.
   b. At least some nodes have multiple connections to the network.
   c. Any node can be taken down without affecting network performance.
   d. Network performance is similar, no matter what kind of link is used between nodes.

   ANSWER

THE CHARACTERISTICS OF SEGMENTS AND BACKBONES

UNDERSTANDING THE OBJECTIVE

Segments are parts of a LAN separated from other parts of the LAN (usually by intervening connectivity devices). On a segment, all nodes share the same channel. Errors on a segment can affect all nodes on that segment. Maximum segment lengths are dependent on the type of media and logical topology used. Backbones connect all the segments on the LAN.

WHAT YOU **REALLY** NEED TO KNOW

- A **segment** is a part of a LAN separated from other parts of the LAN that shares a fixed amount of bandwidth. Since a segment is shared by many nodes, errors generated by one node can affect other nodes on the same segment.

- The length of segments is limited by the type of logical topology (Ethernet or token ring) and the attenuation characteristics of the media. For example, an Ethernet 10Base2 segment can be no longer than 185 meters. An Ethernet 10BaseT segment can be no longer than 100 meters.

- To extend a network beyond the segment limit, another segment must be added using a connectivity device. On Ethernet networks, the maximum number of segments that can be connected in this manner is five.

- Every enterprise network contains a **backbone**, the cabling that connects network segments and the connectivity devices such as routers and hubs.

- Backbones must be the most reliable connections and have the greatest throughput of any part of the network.

- Backbones may be distributed, serial, collapsed, or parallel.

- A **distributed backbone** consists of hubs connected to a series of central hubs or routers in a hierarchy. This topology allows for simple expansion and limited capital outlay for growth, because additional layers of hubs can be added to existing layers.

- A **serial backbone** is the simplest type, consisting of a single connection between two connectivity devices. Serial backbones are not suitable for enterprise networks.

- The **collapsed backbone topology** uses a router or switch as the single central connection point for multiple subnetworks. In a collapsed backbone, a single router or switch is the highest layer of the backbone.

- A **parallel backbone**, in which connectivity devices are directly connected through more than one path, is the most robust type of backbone.

OBJECTIVES ON THE JOB

When planning a network, you must pay attention to the lengths of the segments you create. Remember that the cabling from a workstation to the wall jack and from the wall jack to the hub both contribute to the segment length. If you have exceeded the segment length, data errors may be intermittent and difficult to track.

PRACTICE TEST QUESTIONS

1. On any network, what part has the greatest amount of throughput?
    a. ring
    b. bus
    c. segment
    d. backbone

ANSWER

2. Which of the following is the most fault-tolerant WAN topology?
    a. star-ring
    b. collapsed backbone
    c. full mesh
    d. partial mesh

ANSWER

3. How does a WAN topology differ from a LAN topology?
    a. It is more fault tolerant.
    b. It uses different protocols.
    c. It can handle more traffic.
    d. a and b
    e. a and c

ANSWER

4. Which of the following kinds of backbones is the simplest?
    a. serial
    b. parallel
    c. collapsed
    d. distributed

ANSWER

5. Which of the following media is best for a large backbone?
    a. coaxial cable
    b. unshielded twisted pair
    c. shielded twisted pair
    d. fiber-optic cable

ANSWER

6. Which of the following is an example of a segment?
    a. the connection between two routers on a WAN
    b. the connection between a printer and a hub
    c. the connection between a workstation and a printer
    d. the connection between a router and a switch

ANSWER

7. What is the maximum segment length for a 100BaseT network using CAT 5 UTP?
    a. 10 meters
    b. 10 feet
    c. 100 meters
    d. 100 feet

ANSWER

1.2 Identify the major network operating systems, their clients, resources, and directory services

MAJOR NETWORK OPERATING SYSTEMS

UNDERSTANDING THE OBJECTIVE

On a client–server network, the network operating system runs on the server and allows clients to share file and printing resources (among other activities). There are three leading network operating systems: Windows NT (or Windows 2000), Novell NetWare, and UNIX.

WHAT YOU **REALLY** NEED TO KNOW

◆ A **network operating system (NOS)** is a software package that enables one machine to act as a server in a client-server network. Nearly all modern networks are based on the client-server model and rely on NOSs.

◆ NOSs differ in many ways, but all perform the file- and print-sharing functions, plus provide mail, remote connectivity, security, network management, and Internet services. In addition, NOSs enable a network administrator to subdivide users and resources into groups for easier management, restrict users' network access, and create, modify, and delete users and groups.

◆ While NOSs do not fit into any layer of the OSI model (they technically sit even higher than the seventh layer), some functions belong in the Application layer.

◆ When selecting a NOS, an administrator should consider how compatible it is with existing infrastructure, how much security and flexibility it provides, whether it will support all applications and future growth, its cost, vendor support, and whether the technical staff can manage it.

◆ Many LAN environments use a mix of NOSs, so you should be aware of how to integrate multiple NOSs on a single network and which clients are best to use with each NOS.

◆ On some client-server networks, the server shares the burden of application launching and processing with clients. Before choosing server hardware, determine how much of this activity the server will perform.

◆ Most networks use a server that far exceeds the minimum hardware specifications designated by the NOS vendor. Some considerations when selecting a server include how many clients and how much traffic it will support, how much storage space each user will need, what kinds of applications will run on the server (as opposed to the workstations), and what the organization can afford.

◆ All modern network operating systems support **multiprocessing**, a technique that splits tasks among multiple CPUs in the server to expedite the completion of instructions.

OBJECTIVES ON THE JOB

In many cases the choice of NOS is dictated by historical or political reasons. Knowing how NOSs work in general allows the network administrator to more easily master and effectively manage any one of the three popular network operating systems. If you are responsible for selecting the NOS for a network, research your needs and choices carefully.

PRACTICE TEST QUESTIONS

1. **What is the machine that runs the NOS called?**
   - a. controller
   - b. terminal
   - c. master
   - d. server

   ANSWER

2. **Which of the following is not necessary to consider when selecting an NOS?**
   - a. the types of applications that need to run on the server
   - b. the cost of the NOS software
   - c. the number of NICs in the server
   - d. the type of support provided by the NOS vendor

   ANSWER

3. **What can network administrators assign to groups to allow some users to view files while other users cannot?**
   - a. rights
   - b. standards
   - c. procedures
   - d. domains

   ANSWER

4. **NOSs belong to which layer of the OSI model?**
   - a. Presentation
   - b. Data
   - c. Network
   - d. none of the above

   ANSWER

5. **Which of the following applications, if running on a server, would most likely require more RAM than the minimum specified by the NOS vendor?**
   - a. MS-DOS
   - b. Telnet
   - c. MS SQL Server
   - d. Netscape Navigator

   ANSWER

6. **Which of the following were the original uses of NOSs?**
   - a. e-mail transmission and storage
   - b. file and print sharing
   - c. user authentication and encryption services
   - d. remote dial connectivity and remote control

   ANSWER

7. **What is the NOS technique that enables instructions to be completed faster on a server with many CPUs?**
   - a. multitasking
   - b. multiprocessing
   - c. multithreading
   - d. multiplexing

   ANSWER

1.2
cont.
Identify the major network operating systems, their clients, resources, and directory services

MICROSOFT WINDOWS NT

UNDERSTANDING THE OBJECTIVE

One of the most popular network operating systems is Windows NT (recently released as the Windows 2000 network operating system). This NOS grew in popularity due to its simple-to–use graphical user interface and its similarity to the Windows desktop operating system.

WHAT YOU **REALLY** NEED TO KNOW

◆ Windows NT relies on a **graphical user interface (GUI),** a pictorial representation of computer functions that makes it easy for the network administrator to manage files, users, groups, security, printers, and so on.

◆ Windows NT uses 32-bit addressing, which helps to process instructions twice as fast as 16-bit addressing, and assigns each application its own 32-bit memory area.

◆ Windows NT Server can use multiple processors, multiple NICs, and both physical and virtual memory. In order to determine what components can be used in a Windows NT server, refer to Microsoft's **Hardware Compatibility List (HCL)**. The HCL lists all the computer components proven to be compatible with Windows NT Server.

◆ To manage resources, a Windows NT network employs the domain model, in which users, groups, and resources are assigned to specific domains. A single network can have multiple domains, and resources, users, and groups can belong to multiple domains. Domains can share their users, groups, and resources by establishing trust relationships with other domains.

◆ Windows NT networks use computers on the network called **domain controllers** to manage users, groups, and privileges within the domain. Servers on the network that are not domain controllers are called **member servers**.

◆ Windows NT can support the following file systems: CDFS, FAT, FAT32, HPFS, and NTFS. Microsoft developed the **New Technology File System (NTFS)** expressly for Windows NT. NTFS integrates reliability, compression, speed, and the ability to handle large files. NTFS is the preferred file system for servers running Windows NT.

◆ A Windows NT server can communicate with almost any kind of client. Often, a network dominated by Windows NT servers uses Windows 9x or Windows NT workstations.

◆ To communicate with a NetWare server running IPX/SPX, a Windows NT server must have the Gateway Services for NetWare (GSNW) installed in addition to the IPX/SPX protocols. To communicate with a UNIX server, a Windows NT server must have the TCP/IP protocols and services installed.

OBJECTIVES ON THE JOB

Many organizations run the Windows NT network operating system, even if their network is dominated by other NOSs. Windows NT is a popular system for Web services (those running Internet Information Server) as well as file and print services.

PRACTICE TEST QUESTIONS

1. What server resource does the Windows NT NOS use for virtual memory?
   - a. hard disk
   - b. RAM
   - c. CPU
   - d. system board

   ANSWER

2. What protocol must be installed for a Windows NT server to communicate with a UNIX server?
   - a. NetBEUI
   - b. IPX/SPX
   - c. TCP/IP
   - d. ARCServe

   ANSWER

3. On a Windows NT network, which computer contains the authoritative database of all users, groups, and resources in a domain?
   - a. member server
   - b. master domain controller
   - c. master server
   - d. primary domain controller

   ANSWER

4. What is the main advantage of assigning each application its own 32-bit memory area?
   - a. The application is less likely to freeze up.
   - b. The application is less likely to interfere with other applications.
   - c. The application executes with priority over other applications.
   - d. The application can be executed from multiple workstations.

   ANSWER

5. Which of the following file systems must be present on a Windows NT server so it can communicate with Macintosh workstations?
   - a. NTFS
   - b. CDFS
   - c. HPFS
   - d. FAT

   ANSWER

6. On a Windows NT network, which computer tracks the location, availability, and identity of all shared devices?
   - a. controller
   - b. member server
   - c. domain server
   - d. browser

   ANSWER

7. What resource can you use to determine whether your server's NIC works with the Windows NT NOS?
   - a. the server resource kit
   - b. the hardware compatibility list
   - c. the Microsoft NT users forum
   - d. the emergency repair disk

   ANSWER

NOVELL NETWARE

UNDERSTANDING THE OBJECTIVE

In 1983 Novell introduced its NetWare network operating system. NetWare quickly became the standard operating system for LANs and WANs, providing reliable file-and print-sharing services to millions of users. Since then Novell has refined NetWare to include support for TCP/IP, intranet services, a graphical user interface, and better integration with other operating systems.

WHAT YOU **REALLY** NEED TO KNOW

- ◆ The original version of Novell NetWare was based on the IPX/SPX protocol. Within the last five years, Novell has expanded its compatibility with other protocols. The latest version, NetWare 5.1, is based on the TCP/IP protocol.

- ◆ Because all functions can be performed from the command line on a NetWare server, using the GUI commands and installing a pointing device are optional. Other server requirements are similar to those listed for Windows NT servers.

- ◆ Versions 4.x and higher of NetWare support multiple processors, multiple NICs, 32-bit addressing, and can use both physical and virtual memory.

- ◆ NetWare's kernel oversees all critical server functions. The program SERVER.EXE runs the kernel from a DOS prompt, and is included in the server's AUTOEXEC.BAT file.

- ◆ NetWare uses **NetWare Loadable Modules (NLMs)** to load necessary functions or applications (such as the printer console) into memory on the server.

- ◆ In NetWare versions 4.x and lower, the **server console**, a text-based menu system, is the network administrator's main interface with the server. In NetWare 5.x, administrators may use a GUI interface called **ConsoleOne**.

- ◆ An important NLM in administering a NetWare server is the **monitor module**. This provides menu access to configure and control NICs, protocols, system resources, and so on.

- ◆ In NetWare versions 4.x and higher, the **NetWare Directory System (NDS)** describes how a network's volumes, resources, users, and groups are arranged. The terms "root," "tree," and "leaf" are used to describe different elements of NDS. **NWAdmin** is used to create and administer the NDS.

- ◆ A NetWare server can accept many different types of clients, including UNIX, Macintosh, Windows 9x and Windows NT, MS-DOS, and OS/2.

- ◆ A NetWare server can connect to servers running Windows NT with the **NDS for NT** service installed. It can connect with UNIX servers via the TCP/IP protocol.

OBJECTIVES ON THE JOB

The NetWare NOS is favored by many veteran network administrators. Its history as the most popular NOS means that it still thrives in many enterprises. To succeed as a network technician or administrator in a NetWare shop, you must be especially familiar with the concepts of NDS, NWAdmin, protocols, and interconnecting with other NOSs.

PRACTICE TEST QUESTIONS

1. **What does NDS stand for?**
   a. NetWare Direct System
   b. NetWare Distributed System
   c. NetWare Digital Services
   d. NetWare Directory Services

   ANSWER

2. **From what file on a NetWare server is the SERVER.EXE program launched?**
   a. CONFIG.SYS
   b. AUTOEXEC.BAT
   c. SERVER.BAT
   d. NLM.BAT

   ANSWER

3. **On which protocol was the first version of NetWare based?**
   a. TCP/IP
   b. NetBEUI
   c. SNA
   d. IPX/SPX

   ANSWER

4. **What program is used to administer NDS?**
   a. GSNW
   b. NWAdmin
   c. NTFS
   d. NWConsole

   ANSWER

5. **A user is an example of what type of NDS object?**
   a. root
   b. branch
   c. leaf
   d. stem

   ANSWER

6. **What is the main purpose of NLMs?**
   a. to load applications or services into memory on the server
   b. to install the NetWare operating system on the server
   c. to connect NetWare servers with Windows NT servers
   d. to optimize memory usage on the server

   ANSWER

7. **What volume does NetWare create by default upon installation?**
   a. SYS
   b. VOL1
   c. USERS
   d. DATA

   ANSWER

1.2 Identify the major network operating systems, their clients, resources, and
cont. directory services

UNIX

UNDERSTANDING THE OBJECTIVE

UNIX, which grew out of a grassroots effort to create a more robust, flexible, and accessible operating system, has flourished into a standard NOS. The UNIX NOS comes in two varieties: proprietary and open source. The advantage to using a proprietary version of UNIX is in its stability and vendor support. However, open source versions are becoming more standard and more easily supported.

WHAT YOU **REALLY** NEED TO KNOW

- ◆ UNIX was developed in the 1960s with the TCP/IP protocol and was used on the first Internet host machines. UNIX still relies on the TCP/IP protocol.
- ◆ UNIX is a general term for a group of network operating systems that share similar kernels, directory structures, commands, and processing characteristics.
- ◆ UNIX versions may be proprietary (such as IBM's AIX or Sun's Solaris) or open source software. **Linux** is the most popular open source software version of UNIX.
- ◆ UNIX uses a hierarchical file system, in which the uppermost level is called the **root**. Standard directories under the root include home, dev, usr, bin, var, and lib.
- ◆ UNIX software relies on a kernel, which contains the core instruction set of the operating system. UNIX uses kernel modules to add functionality. Kernel modules are analogous to the NLMs in NetWare.
- ◆ UNIX can run on virtually any type of computer (even a workstation). However, for optimal network performance, a UNIX computer should have plenty of RAM, processing power, and hard disk capacity.
- ◆ The creators of UNIX introduced techniques for multiprocessing; thus UNIX supports multiple processors, as well as multiple NICs and virtual memory.
- ◆ UNIX servers can access FAT, NTFS, and HPFS file systems as well as shared drives on Windows NT or NetWare servers.
- ◆ The interface that accepts and runs typed commands on a UNIX server is called the **command interpreter**, or **shell**.
- ◆ The online help documents for UNIX servers are called the **man pages** and can be accessed from the command line by typing **man**.
- ◆ A UNIX server can support multiple types of clients, including Microsoft and Novell network clients, because it is based on the standard TCP/IP protocol stack.

OBJECTIVES ON THE JOB

As the oldest and arguably still the most efficient NOS, some form of UNIX is found in virtually every organization. Often, UNIX is used for HTTP, Telnet, FTP, or other Internet-related services as well as robust database servers. While some UNIX systems have GUI interfaces, most network administrators still use the command line interface, meaning they must memorize commands.

PRACTICE TEST QUESTIONS

1. **Which of the following is a true statement?**
    a. Open source versions of UNIX typically do not supply as many Internet services as proprietary versions of the software.
    b. Open source versions of UNIX are less accepted in the marketplace for use with robust applications.
    c. Open source versions of UNIX use a different file system than proprietary versions of the software.
    d. Open source versions of UNIX typically do not come with the same amount of vendor support as proprietary versions.

    ANSWER

2. **What will typing man ls and pressing Enter at the command line of a UNIX server do?**
    a. display the help text for the file list command
    b. display the server's error log
    c. display a list of users currently logged onto the system
    d. display a list of available printers

    ANSWER

3. **What is the uppermost level of a UNIX file system called?**
    a. branch
    b. leaf
    c. root
    d. tree

    ANSWER

4. **What protocol is native to the UNIX environment?**
    a. IPX/SPX
    b. NetBEUI
    c. TCP/IP
    d. SNA

    ANSWER

5. **Which of the following is a popular version of open source UNIX?**
    a. Linux
    b. VINES
    c. AIX
    d. AnyLAN

    ANSWER

6. **Which of the following is a popular use for a UNIX server, even in an environment dominated by Windows NT or NetWare?**
    a. print server
    b. graphics server
    c. authentication server
    d. HTTP server

    ANSWER

7. **What is IBM's proprietary version of UNIX called?**
    a. IBX
    b. AIX
    c. SNAX
    d. INOS

    ANSWER

INTRODUCTION TO PROTOCOLS

UNDERSTANDING THE OBJECTIVE

Protocols provide the standards for transmitting data between nodes on a network. Every type of network depends on protocols. Many networks use more than one protocol, and these networks are known as multiprotocol networks. The preferred protocols for modern networks are those that can span more than one network segment through a router, or routable protocols.

WHAT YOU **REALLY** NEED TO KNOW

◆ Many protocols are available, and organizations use more than one type on the same network. Such networks are called **multiprotocol** networks.

◆ The most popular protocol in use on modern networks is TCP/IP. Other common protocols include IPX/SPX, NetBEUI, and AppleTalk.

◆ The protocol (or protocol suite) you use depends on many factors, including existing network operating environment, technical expertise, security, and speed requirements.

◆ Protocols vary by speed, transmission efficiency, resource use, ease of setup, compatibility, and whether they can travel between one LAN segment and another.

◆ What professionals commonly term a protocol is actually a suite of **subprotocols**. For example, the TCP/IP protocol suite contains the TCP, IP, UDP, and other subprotocols. The IPX/SPX suite contains the IPX, SPX, RIP, and SAP protocols.

◆ Subprotocols perform functions—such as data translation, data handling, addressing, and error checking—that are associated with different levels of the OSI model.

◆ Protocols that carry addressing information and travel between different LAN segments via a router are called **routable**. TCP/IP, AppleTalk, and IPX/SPX are routable protocols. NetBEUI and SNA are non-routable.

◆ Protocol software comes with NOSs, but must be installed and configured on servers and workstations before two nodes on a network can communicate.

◆ Some protocols, such as NetBEUI, require little configuration, while TCP/IP requires more configuration. Often, this configuration can be automated to ease the network administrator's workload and reduce the possibility for human errors.

◆ The process of associating a protocol with a network service or an NIC is known as **binding**. A protocol does not work unless it is bound to the device's NIC. On a client, the protocol must also be bound to the client software.

OBJECTIVES ON THE JOB

Any modern LAN environment likely runs at least the TCP/IP protocol suite, because it is necessary for Internet and intranet services such as Web access and e-mail. Many LANs use additional protocols such as IPX/SPX, AppleTalk, and NetBEUI. A few LANs use outdated protocols such as SNA or DLC. A deep understanding of protocols is vital to installing, configuring, and troubleshooting a network.

PRACTICE TEST QUESTIONS

1. **A protocol that does not contain addressing information cannot be interpreted by a:**
   a. hub
   b. server
   c. router
   d. repeater

   ANSWER

2. **What protocol is most likely to be used on a NetWare 3.11 server?**
   a. TCP/IP
   b. IPX/SPX
   c. AppleTalk
   d. NetBEUI

   ANSWER

3. **Which of the following is a routable protocol?**
   a. TCP/IP
   b. AppleTalk
   c. SNA
   d. NetBEUI

   ANSWER

4. **If a newly installed server does not communicate via TCP/IP, even though the software includes the protocol, what might be the problem?**
   a. The protocol isn't the right version.
   b. The protocol isn't bound.
   c. The protocol isn't compatible with the server's hardware.
   d. The protocol isn't fixed.

   ANSWER

5. **What is a network that runs more than one protocol called?**
   a. multiprotocol
   b. semiprotocol
   c. dualprotocol
   d. ultraprotocol

   ANSWER

6. **What is the default protocol used by UNIX servers?**
   a. TCP/IP
   b. IPX/SPX
   c. AppleTalk
   d. NetBEUI

   ANSWER

7. **What protocol did Microsoft develop?**
   a. TCP/IP
   b. IPX/SPX
   c. AppleTalk
   d. NetBEUI

   ANSWER

IPX

UNDERSTANDING THE OBJECTIVE

Internetwork Packet Exchange (IPX) is a protocol belonging to the Internetwork Packet Exchange/Sequenced Packet Exchange (IPX/SPX) suite. Xerox originally designed IPX/SPX; then Novell modified it in the 1980s for its NetWare NOS. IPX contains addressing information; therefore, it belongs to the Network layer of the OSI model and is routable.

WHAT YOU **REALLY** NEED TO KNOW

- ◆ IPX operates at the Network layer of the OSI model and provides routing and inter-network services.
- ◆ IPX is a **connectionless** service. It does not require that a session be established before transmitting, and it does not guarantee that data will be delivered error-free.
- ◆ IPX uses datagrams (or packets) to transport information. An IPX datagram includes the data payload, checksum, source node, and destination node address information, plus packet length and packet type information.
- ◆ SPX belongs to the Transport layer of the OSI model and ensures that data is received whole, error-free, and in sequence.
- ◆ SPX is a **connection-oriented** protocol, meaning it must verify that a session with the destination node has been established before it transmits data.
- ◆ Because it contains addressing information, IPX/SPX is routable.
- ◆ IPX/SPX is required for Novell NetWare versions 3.x and lower. In versions 4.x and higher, IPX/SPX is optional, and often, TCP/IP is used instead.
- ◆ Other network operating systems, such as Windows NT, and workstation operating systems, such as Windows 95, can use IPX/SPX to internetwork with Novell NetWare systems. In the Windows NT Server NOS, IPX/SPX is called NWLink (for NetWare Link).
- ◆ IPX addresses contain two parts: the network address and the node address.
- ◆ The network address must be an 8-bit hexadecimal address, which means that each of its bits can have a value of either 0-9 or A-F. An example of a valid network address is 000008A2. The network address then becomes the first part of the IPX address on all nodes that use that server as their primary server.
- ◆ The IPX node address is equal to a device's MAC (or hardware) address. Because MAC addresses are burned into the NICs of every device, using IPX/SPX means a network administrator does not need to manually assign node addresses to each device.

OBJECTIVES ON THE JOB

If you are establishing or maintaining an IPX/SPX network, become familiar with the addressing conventions of this protocol. Node addresses depend on MAC addresses (which should never change). But network addresses are assigned manually. If they are improperly assigned, the server and all of its clients will be unable to communicate on the network.

PRACTICE TEST QUESTIONS

1. **What company originally designed the IPX/SPX protocol?**
   a. IBM
   b. Xerox
   c. Novell
   d. Microsoft

2. **Which of the following protocols belonging to the IPX/SPX suite ensures that data is received error-free?**
   a. IPX
   b. SPX
   c. NCP
   d. SAP

3. **Which of the following information belongs in the IPX datagram?**
   a. packet type
   b. service type
   c. media type
   d. collision type

4. **On a Windows NT server, what protocol should you install in order to connect to a NetWare 3.11 server?**
   a. GSNW
   b. NWAdmin
   c. TCP/IP
   d. NWLink

5. **Two workstations on the same network running IPX/SPX will have the same:**
   a. node address
   b. MAC address
   c. network address
   d. host address

6. **To what layer of the OSI model does IPX belong?**
   a. Presentation
   b. Session
   c. Transport
   d. Network

7. **Which of the following is not a valid network address when using the IPX/SPX protocol?**
   a. 11111111
   b. AB0045099
   c. ABCABCAB
   d. F29FF034

IP

UNDERSTANDING THE OBJECTIVE

Transmission Control Protocol/Internet Protocol (TCP/IP) is a suite of subprotocols. TCP/IP is the most popular protocol today and is used exclusively by Internet services. IP in the TCP/IP suite is similar to IPX in the IPX/SPX suite. IP contains addressing information; therefore, it belongs to the Network layer of the OSI model and is routable.

WHAT YOU **REALLY** NEED TO KNOW

◆ IP operates at the Network layer of the OSI model and provides information about how and where data should be delivered. IP is the subprotocol that enables TCP/IP to **internetwork**—that is, to traverse more than one LAN segment and more than one type of network through a router.

◆ IP is considered a **connectionless** service because it does not require that a session be established before it begins transmission, and it does not guarantee that data will be delivered in sequence or error-free.

◆ IP uses datagrams (or packets) to transport information. An IP datagram includes the data payload, checksum, source node, and destination node address information, plus packet length and protocol-type information.

◆ In the TCP/IP protocol suite, IP is the core protocol responsible for logical addressing. For this reason, addresses on TCP/IP networks are called **IP addresses**.

◆ Each IP address is a unique 32-bit number, divided into four groups of **octets**, or 8-bit bytes, that are separated by periods.

◆ IP address data is sent across the network in binary form. For example, the IP address 131.127.3.22 (in dotted-decimal notation) is the same as the binary number 10000011 01111111 00000011 00010110.

◆ All nodes on a Class A network share the first octet of their IP numbers, a number between 1 and 126. Nodes on a Class B network share the first two octets, and all their IP addresses begin with a number between 128 and 191. Class C network IP numbers share the first three octets, and their first octet is a number between 192 and 223.

◆ TCP, a connection-oriented protocol, belongs to the Transport layer of the OSI model and ensures that data is received whole, in sequence, and error-free.

◆ The IP address 127.0.0.1 is called a **loopback address**. When you try to contact this IP number, you are actually communicating with your own machine.

OBJECTIVES ON THE JOB

Since the Internet and many different applications rely on TCP/IP and probably will for a long time, the need to understand this protocol will continue to be critical. Know the addressing conventions of this protocol, as well as the addresses that have special meaning, such as the loopback address. Know how to recognize addressing conflicts and help avoid them.

PRACTICE TEST QUESTIONS

1. **Which protocol in the TCP/IP suite is responsible for addressing?**
   a. TCP
   b. IP
   c. UDP
   d. ICMP

   ANSWER

2. **At what layer of the OSI model does TCP reside?**
   a. Transport
   b. Network
   c. Presentation
   d. Session

   ANSWER

3. **Which of the following is not a valid IP address?**
   a. 127.0.0.1
   b. 10.10.10.10
   c. 199.220.37.18
   d. 392.89.32.5

   ANSWER

4. **On what class network is a workstation with an IP address of 193.12.176.55?**
   a. A
   b. B
   c. C
   d. D

   ANSWER

5. **What is a popular use of the loopback address?**
   a. troubleshooting a workstation
   b. communicating with the server
   c. checking the status of a print job
   d. initiating remote connectivity

   ANSWER

6. **Which of the following is a connection-oriented subprotocol of the TCP/IP suite?**
   a. TCP
   b. IP
   c. UDP
   d. ICP

   ANSWER

7. **Two ways of representing IP addresses include:**
   a. logical and host-centered notation
   b. network and host octet notation
   c. binary and dotted-decimal notation
   d. server and client-based notation

   ANSWER

OBJECTIVES

1.3
cont.
Associate IPX, IP, and NetBEUI with their function

NETBEUI

UNDERSTANDING THE OBJECTIVE

Network Basic Input Output System (NetBIOS) is a protocol designed by IBM to provide Transport and Session layer services for applications running on small, homogenous networks. Microsoft adopted NetBIOS as its foundation protocol, and added an application layer component on top of NetBIOS called the NetBIOS Enhanced User Interface (NetBEUI).

WHAT YOU **REALLY** NEED TO KNOW

- ◆ Microsoft adopted IBM's NetBIOS as its foundation protocol, initially for networks using LAN Manager or Windows for Workgroups, and added an application layer component on top of NetBIOS called the NetBIOS Enhanced User Interface (NetBEUI).
- ◆ NetBEUI is a fast and efficient protocol that consumes few network resources, provides excellent error correction, and requires little configuration. NetBEUI is the easiest type of protocol to set up.
- ◆ Unlike TCP/IP and IPX/SPX, neither NetBIOS nor NetBEUI provides services at all the OSI model layers, though NetBEUI roughly corresponds to the Presentation and Session layers.
- ◆ NetBEUI can only support up to 254 connections and does not allow for good security. It is therefore not appropriate for use on large networks.
- ◆ Because NetBEUI lacks a network layer (addressing information), it is not routable by itself. (If necessary, NetBEUI can be encapsulated by other protocols, then routed.)
- ◆ NetBIOS does not contain a network layer with addressing information, but to transmit data between network nodes, NetBIOS needs to know how to reach each workstation. Network administrators must assign each workstation a NetBIOS name.
- ◆ The NetBIOS name can be any combination of 16 or fewer alphanumeric characters, including special characters. (The only exception is that you cannot begin a NetBIOS name with an asterisk.)
- ◆ Once NetBIOS has found a workstation's NetBIOS name, it discovers the workstation's MAC address and uses it for further communication with the workstation.
- ◆ If you are running both TCP/IP and NetBIOS on your network, it's a good policy to make the NetBIOS name identical to the TCP/IP host name.
- ◆ On a Windows 9x client, the NetBIOS name can be viewed by choosing Control Panel – Network Properties – Identification tab. It is called the "computer name."

OBJECTIVES ON THE JOB

Today NetBEUI is most commonly used in small Microsoft–based networks to integrate legacy, peer–to–peer networks. In newer Microsoft–based networks, TCP/IP has become the protocol of choice because it is routable and more flexible and scalable than NetBEUI. Therefore, mastering NetBEUI is useful for administrators working on older Microsoft networks, but it is a skill rarely needed for administering modern networks.

PRACTICE TEST QUESTIONS

1. **What is the relationship between NetBIOS and NetBEUI?**
   a. NetBEUI encrypts NetBIOS on the network.
   b. NetBEUI enables NetBIOS to be routed.
   c. NetBEUI contains an added application layer to NetBIOS.
   d. NetBEUI is the IBM version of NetBIOS.

   ANSWER

2. **To which layers of the OSI model does NetBEUI correspond?**
   a. Physical and Network
   b. Session and Transport
   c. Transport and Network
   d. Presentation and Session

   ANSWER

3. **What does NetBEUI use to identify workstations on the network?**
   a. host name
   b. node address
   c. network address
   d. NetBIOS name

   ANSWER

4. **What company originally designed NetBIOS?**
   a. IBM
   b. Microsoft
   c. Sun
   d. Cisco

   ANSWER

5. **Why is NetBEUI not suitable for large networks?**
   a. It can only support dumb terminals.
   b. It can only support up to 254 connections.
   c. It cannot support shared devices such as printers.
   d. It can only support up to 512 NetBIOS names.

   ANSWER

6. **Under what circumstances can NetBEUI be routed?**
   a. if it's encapsulated by another protocol
   b. if it's bound to multiple NICs
   c. if it traverses LAN segments
   d. if it's assigned appropriate node addresses

   ANSWER

7. **What is the maximum number of characters in a computer name?**
   a. 8
   b. 16
   c. 32
   d. 64

   ANSWER

OVERVIEW OF FAULT TOLERANCE AND HIGH AVAILABILITY

UNDERSTANDING THE OBJECTIVE

Fault tolerance and availability are the factors that ensure data is continually accessible to users, protected from harm, and in good condition. On a network, many techniques, including physical and electronic security, virus protection, redundancy, backups, disk mirroring, and disk striping are used to ensure fault tolerance and availability.

WHAT YOU **REALLY** NEED TO KNOW

◆ **Fault tolerance** is the capacity for a system to continue performing despite an unexpected hardware or software malfunction. A **fault** is the malfunction of one component of a system. A fault can result in a failure.

◆ In broad terms, a **failure** is a deviation from a specified level of system performance for a given period of time. In other words, a failure occurs when something doesn't work as promised or planned.

◆ The aim of fault tolerance is to employ as many techniques as possible to prevent faults from becoming failures. Most of these techniques address single points of failure, or places in the network where one fault could immobilize the entire network.

◆ **Integrity** refers to the soundness of a network's programs, data, services, devices, and connections. To ensure a network's integrity, it must be protected from anything that might render it unusable.

◆ **Availability** of a file or system refers to how consistently and reliably authorized personnel can access it. To ensure availability you not only need a well-planned and configured network, but also data backups, redundant devices, and protection from hackers who could immobilize the network.

◆ A number of phenomena may compromise both integrity and availability, including: security breaches, natural disasters (tornadoes, floods, hurricanes, ice storms, etc.), malicious intruders, power flaws, and human error. Every network administrator should consider these possibilities when designing a sound network.

◆ **Redundancy** is a technique in which components or machines are used in duplicate on the network. The aim of redundancy is to eliminate single points of failure. It is often used on a network for power, cabling, server hard disks, NICs, data links, and any other component that might halt operations if it suffers a fault.

◆ Complete redundancy on a network is expensive. Therefore, a network administrator should use redundancy strategically, understanding not only where the network's single points of failure exist, but also what impact their malfunctions might have.

OBJECTIVES ON THE JOB

It isn't enough for a network administrator to implement and maintain hardware and software on a network. The network must also be continually protected from harm. Techniques such as mirroring, backups, virus protection, environmental controls, security policies, and disaster recovery are all part of protecting the network.

PRACTICE TEST QUESTIONS

1. **What is the aim of fault tolerance?**
   a. to eliminate faults
   b. to ensure that faults don't result in failures
   c. to address the least severe faults
   d. to create potential faults for testing purposes

   ANSWER

2. **Which of the following is an important environmental factor affecting availability?**
   a. heat
   b. humidity
   c. smoke
   d. all of the above

   ANSWER

3. **Which of the following components should be redundant in a fault-tolerant network?**
   a. the servers' NICs
   b. the root password
   c. the NOS software installation
   d. the SYS volume

   ANSWER

4. **Which of the following will render a network completely unusable?**
   a. failure
   b. fault
   c. redundancy
   d. security breach

   ANSWER

5. **What's one good method of securing access to a computer room?**
   a. armed guards
   b. key locks on the doors
   c. electronic badge reader
   d. voice-activated locks

   ANSWER

6. **Which of the following is the least expensive method of ensuring availability on a network of 100 nodes?**
   a. using redundant NICs on all servers
   b. using redundant fiber links to the ISP
   c. using a SONET ring to connect to the local telecommunications facility
   d. leasing off-site facilities for data backup storage

   ANSWER

7. **Which of the following is not typically a single point of failure?**
   a. a server
   b. a router
   c. a hub
   d. a workstation

   ANSWER

OBJECTIVES

1.4 Define and explain the terms that relate to fault tolerance and high availability
cont.

MIRRORING AND DUPLEXING

UNDERSTANDING THE OBJECTIVE

Mirroring is a fault–tolerance technique in which one component duplicates the transactions and data storage of another. Mirroring can occur between servers or between disks in a server. If one of the mirrored components fails, the other component can immediately assume the functions of the first.

WHAT YOU **REALLY** NEED TO KNOW

- ◆ **Server mirroring** is a fault-tolerance technique in which one server duplicates the transactions and data storage of another. The servers must be identical machines.
- ◆ Another fault-tolerance technique is **disk mirroring**, in which data from one disk is automatically copied to another disk it is written. The disks must be identical.
- ◆ Because data is continually saved to multiple locations, disk mirroring can be considered a dynamic data backup.
- ◆ A simple implementation of disk mirroring on a server is also known as **redundant array of inexpensive disks (RAID) level 1**.
- ◆ Server mirroring requires a link between the servers. It also entails software running on both servers that allows them to synchronize continually and, in case of a failure, that allows one server to take over for the other.
- ◆ In disk mirroring, when one disk in a mirrored configuration fails, the other disks automatically assume its functions. When the disk is repaired and replaced in the array, the network administrator must synchronize it with the other disks.
- ◆ In server mirroring, the other mirrored server can automatically take over for a failed server, or it might require human intervention to accomplish the transfer.
- ◆ In server mirroring, servers can occupy different physical locations.
- ◆ One potential disadvantage to mirroring is the time it takes for a mirrored component to assume the functionality of the failed component. For example, it may take 10 to 90 seconds for a mirrored disk to take over for a failed disk.
- ◆ Another disadvantage to mirroring is that network performance slows as data is copied between mirrored components. The more traffic the server has to handle, the more noticeable the impact of mirroring will be.
- ◆ The hardware costs of server mirroring are significant because one server or multiple disks within a server must be devoted to record all data.

OBJECTIVES ON THE JOB

Disk mirroring is relatively inexpensive. But server mirroring often costs more and requires more effort than an organization is willing to expend. In your network environment, you should assess how much you can spend on a redundancy solution, how much technical knowledge and time you have to support it, and how long your organization can wait for access to data on a faulty drive or server.

PRACTICE TEST QUESTIONS

1. What is required for two servers to be mirrored?
    a. software
    b. hardware
    c. a link between the servers
    d. all of the above

ANSWER

2. Which of the following statements is true?
    a. Mirrored servers must connect to the network at the same speed.
    b. Mirrored servers must have identical NICs.
    c. Mirrored servers must be in the same computer room.
    d. Mirrored servers must use the same backup scheme.

ANSWER

3. What must a network administrator do after a failed disk is re-inserted into a mirrored array?
    a. initialize the disk
    b. synchronize the disks
    c. reboot the server
    d. restore data files from backups to the disk

ANSWER

4. How much downtime can be expected while a mirrored disk assumes the role of the failed disk?
    a. 15-25 minutes
    b. 5-10 minutes
    c. 10-60 seconds
    d. 0-5 seconds

ANSWER

5. What suffers as a result of implementing mirroring on a network?
    a. security
    b. data accuracy
    c. temperature sensitivity
    d. performance

ANSWER

6. What kind of cabling is required for server mirroring?
    a. CAT5 or better
    b. CAT3 or better
    c. coax or better
    d. Any cabling will work.

ANSWER

7. How does server mirroring differ from hard disk mirroring?
    a. In server mirroring, two identical servers are mirrored, while in hard disk mirroring, two hard disks within a server are mirrored.
    b. In server mirroring, only software is necessary, while in disk mirroring, additional hardware is necessary as well.
    c. In disk mirroring, identical disk hardware is necessary, while in server mirroring, any two servers will work.
    d. In disk mirroring, a special cable is required to connect the disks, while in server mirroring, only an NOS plug-in is required to connect the servers.

ANSWER

STRIPING

UNDERSTANDING THE OBJECTIVE

Disk striping is a technique in which a computer separates data and file information and stores it on multiple disks. This technique is part of many availability strategies, including some forms of RAID (redundant array of inexpensive disks) levels 0, 3, and 5. RAID level 5 is currently the most popular form of disk striping.

WHAT YOU **REALLY** NEED TO KNOW

- ◆ **RAID level 0** is the simplest implementation of disk striping. In RAID level 0, data is written in 64K blocks equally across all disks (or partitions) in the array.
- ◆ Disk striping alone does not ensure availability because if one of the disks fails, its data will be inaccessible. Thus, RAID level 0 does not provide true redundancy.
- ◆ RAID level 0 makes good use of multiple disk partitions and improves performance by using multiple disk controllers.
- ◆ **RAID level 3** involves disk striping with a special type of ECC (error correction code) known as parity error correction code.
- ◆ The **parity** mechanism verifies data integrity by making a sum of bits in a byte equal to either an odd or even number. To accomplish parity, a parity bit (equal to zero or one) is added to the bits' sum.
- ◆ Parity bits are assigned to each data byte when it is transmitted or written to a disk. Parity is used to track the integrity of data on a disk. It has nothing to do with the data type, protocol, transmission method, or file size. The process of comparing the parity of data read from a disk with the type of parity in use by the system is known as **parity error checking**.
- ◆ RAID level 3 provides a high data transfer rate when reading from or writing to disks. Thus, RAID level 3 is well suited to applications that require speed. But in RAID 3 the parity information is on a single disk, a potential single point of failure.
- ◆ **RAID level 5** is the most common, highly fault-tolerant technique for data storage. In RAID level 5, data is written in small blocks across several disks. At the same time, parity error checking information is also distributed among the disks.
- ◆ RAID level 5 can write data faster than RAID level 3 because any of the disk controllers in the array can write the parity information. Unlike RAID level 3, RAID level 5 uses several disks for parity information, making it more fault-tolerant.

OBJECTIVES ON THE JOB

Among all the techniques that use disk striping, RAID level 5 is most commonly implemented on networks today because of its speed and high fault tolerance. You should understand how your NOS handles RAID and what kind of hardware your server requires to accomplish RAID. If you intend to use RAID on your server, it is best to order RAID to be installed by the manufacturer. That way, you are certain to get RAID components compatible with your hardware.

PRACTICE TEST QUESTIONS

1. **What is the fault-tolerance technique that uses only striping?**
   a. RAID level 0
   b. RAID level 1
   c. RAID level 3
   d. RAID level 5

   ANSWER

2. **Which of the following is most likely to be implemented on a modern network?**
   a. RAID level 0
   b. RAID level 1
   c. RAID level 3
   d. RAID level 5

   ANSWER

3. **What kind of error correction code is used in RAID levels 3 and 5?**
   a. checksum
   b. parity
   c. dotted decimal
   d. collision detection

   ANSWER

4. **In which of the following is error correction information written across multiple disks (or disk partitions)?**
   a. RAID level 0
   b. RAID level 1
   c. RAID level 3
   d. RAID level 5

   ANSWER

5. **What does the "I" in RAID stand for?**
   a. inexpensive
   b. integrated
   c. institutional
   d. internodal

   ANSWER

6. **In a RAID 0 scheme, what would be the consequence of one data disk failing?**
   a. The other disks would automatically resume its functions.
   b. A network administrator would need to command the other disks to assume the failed disk's functions.
   c. The data on the failed disk would be inaccessible, but the server would continue functioning.
   d. The server would crash.

   ANSWER

7. **What benefit do all RAID schemes share?**
   a. better performance by using multiple disk controllers
   b. true disk redundancy
   c. error correction to ensure that data is not lost
   d. the capacity to store more data than multiple disks used in serial

   ANSWER

1.4 Define and explain the terms that relate to fault tolerance and high availability
cont.

VOLUMES AND TAPE BACKUPS

UNDERSTANDING THE OBJECTIVE

A volume is a logically assigned amount of space on a physical disk. Volumes are created when the server NOS is installed, but you can modify them later for size and type. Tape backups are the most popular and inexpensive method of backing up large amounts of data. In order to ensure that data is safe, backup tapes should not be stored in the computer room.

WHAT YOU **REALLY** NEED TO KNOW

- ◆ The way volumes are created and maintained depends on the network operating system. Data and system files in volumes are often kept separated.
- ◆ Volumes are logical distinctions, while disks are physical distinctions. A single disk can hold more than one volume. Also, a single volume can be spread across multiple disks.
- ◆ Volumes are formatted with a file system. Popular types of file systems include FAT, FAT32, HPFS, NTFS, and CDFS. Some network operating systems prefer certain types of file systems. For example, Windows NT prefers NTFS, while OS/2 prefers HPFS.
- ◆ Tape backups require a tape drive connected to the network (via a system such as a file server or dedicated, networked workstation), software to manage and perform backups, and backup media.
- ◆ You can use different media, including DAT, or 8-mm cassettes, to make tape backups.
- ◆ On small networks, you can attach stand-alone tape drives to each server. On large networks, a centralized tape backup device may manage all the systems' backups.
- ◆ A backup strategy should be documented in a common area and should address at least the following questions: What kind of rotation schedule will backups follow? At what time of day or night will the backups occur? How will the accuracy of backups be verified? Where will backup media be stored? Who will be responsible for ensuring that backups occurred? How long will backups be saved? Where will backup and recovery documentation be stored?
- ◆ Once compatible backup hardware and software are purchased, you must devise a backup scheme. Some schemes include full backup (saving all data), incremental backup (saving only data that changed since the last backup was made), and differential backup (saving data that changed within the last two backup cycles).
- ◆ Incremental backup is the most popular backup scheme because it is economical and assures that all changed or new files are saved.
- ◆ For safety, store backup tapes in a location other than the building in which the computer room is located.

OBJECTIVES ON THE JOB

In choosing from the many tape backup hardware models and software packages, a network administrator must weigh the following factors: reliability, error correction, compatibility with current software, ease of use, vendor support, and cost. It is also critical to test the accuracy of backups regularly by attempting to restore data from backup tapes.

PRACTICE TEST QUESTIONS

1. **What is the most popular type of tape backup scheme?**
   a. full backup
   b. differential backup
   c. incremental backup
   d. transitional backup

ANSWER

2. **What creates volumes on a server?**
   a. HPFS
   b. NTFS
   c. the Microsoft volumes utility
   d. the network operating system

ANSWER

3. **Which of the following is a true statement?**
   a. A volume is the same as a disk.
   b. A disk can contain more than one volume.
   c. A volume can be reformatted without losing data.
   d. A volume must reside on a single disk.

ANSWER

4. **On very large networks, what is a tape backup device usually attached to?**
   a. the primary file server
   b. the secondary file server
   c. its own server
   d. the primary print server

ANSWER

5. **What kind of backup scheme saves all data in a specified volume?**
   a. incremental backup
   b. differential backup
   c. full backup
   d. exhaustive backup

ANSWER

6. **Which of the following information belongs in a good backup log?**
   a. name of the backup operator
   b. backup date
   c. type of backup software used
   d. type of tape used

ANSWER

7. **What kind of backup scheme would be used for the grandfather-father-son rotation?**
   a. full backup
   b. differential backup
   c. incremental backup
   d. transitional backup

ANSWER

1.5 Define the layers of the OSI model and identify the protocols, services, and functions that pertain to each layer

THE OSI MODEL, LAYERS 1 THROUGH 4

UNDERSTANDING THE OBJECTIVE

The Open Systems Interconnection (OSI) model is a theoretical construct that separates the functions of a network into seven layers. Each layer is associated with different protocols, hardware, or software. Layers 1 through 4 include the Physical, Data Link, Network, and Transport layers. Services that operate at these layers include electrical pulses (Physical layer), physical addressing (Data Link layer), logical addressing and routing (Network layer), and error correction (Transport layer).

WHAT YOU **REALLY** NEED TO KNOW

- ◆ The OSI model is a theoretical representation of what happens between two nodes on a network. It does not prescribe hardware or software.
- ◆ The **Physical layer** is the lowest, or first, layer of the OSI model. This layer contains the physical networking medium, such as cabling, connectors, and repeaters. Protocols at the Physical layer are responsible for generating and detecting voltage in order to transmit and receive signals carrying data.
- ◆ The Physical layer handles the data transmission rate and monitors data error rates, but does not handle error correction.
- ◆ The second layer of the OSI model, the **Data Link layer,** controls communication between the Network layer and Physical layer. Its primary function is to divide data it receives from the Network layer into distinct frames that can then be transmitted by the Physical layer.
- ◆ Bridges and switches work in the Data Link layer, because they decode frames and use the frame information to transmit data to its correct recipient.
- ◆ The primary function of the **Network layer**, the third layer, is to translate network addresses into their physical counterparts and decide how to route data from the sender to the receiver.
- ◆ The Network layer determines the best route between nodes by considering delivery priorities, network congestion, quality of service, and cost of alternative routes.
- ◆ Services that work in the Network layer include IP and IPX.
- ◆ The **Transport layer** is responsible for ensuring that data is transferred from point A to point B reliably, in the correct sequence, and without errors.
- ◆ Transport protocols also handle **flow control**, the method of gauging the appropriate rate of transmission based on how fast the recipient can accept data.
- ◆ Services that work in the Transport layer include TCP and SPX.

OBJECTIVES ON THE JOB

Knowledge of the OSI model helps you identify and fix errors on a network. It also helps you understand higher-level networking concepts such as addressing. A deep understanding of what functions occur at each layer of the OSI model helps you install, configure, and troubleshoot routers, switches, bridges, and other networking equipment.

PRACTICE TEST QUESTIONS

1. At what layer of the OSI model would a network be affected if a coaxial cable were severed?
   a. Physical
   b. Data Link
   c. Network
   d. Transport

   ANSWER

2. Which of the following functions belongs to the Network layer of the OSI model?
   a. bridging
   b. repeating
   c. routing
   d. error correction

   ANSWER

3. At what layer of the OSI model are MAC addresses interpreted?
   a. Physical
   b. Data Link
   c. Network
   d. Transport

   ANSWER

4. At what layer of the OSI model does sequencing occur?
   a. Physical
   b. Data Link
   c. Network
   d. Transport

   ANSWER

5. If a printer can interpret physical addresses but cannot interpret an IP address, at what layer is it failing?
   a. Physical
   b. Data Link
   c. Network
   d. Transport

   ANSWER

6. Which of the following is not considered when a router chooses the best path from one node to another on a network?
   a. network congestion
   b. quality of service
   c. the time to send data
   d. geographical distance between nodes

   ANSWER

7. To which layer of the OSI model do repeater hubs belong?
   a. Physical
   b. Data Link
   c. Network
   d. Transport

   ANSWER

1.5 Define the layers of the OSI model and identify the protocols, services, and
cont. functions that pertain to each layer

THE OSI MODEL, LAYERS 5 THROUGH 7

UNDERSTANDING THE OBJECTIVE

Layers 5 through 7 deal with higher-level functions such as managing traffic on a network, encoding and encrypting data, and establishing a user interface. Examples of these functions include HTTP and e-mail (the Application layer), data encryption (the Presentation layer), and session negotiation (the Session layer).

WHAT YOU **REALLY** NEED TO KNOW

◆ The **Session layer** is responsible for establishing and maintaining communication between two nodes on the network for the session's duration. Other Session layer functions include synchronizing the dialog between the two nodes, determining whether communication has been cut, and if so, where to restart transmission.

◆ The Session layer also sets the terms of communication by deciding which node communicates first and how long a node can communicate.

◆ The term **session** refers to a connection for data exchange between two parties, and is most often used in the context of terminal and mainframe communications.

◆ The Session layer is often called the traffic cop of network communications.

◆ The **Presentation layer**, the sixth layer in the OSI model, serves as a translator between the application and the network. At the Presentation layer data is formatted in a schema that the network can understand.

◆ The Presentation layer also takes care of data encryption and decryption, such as the scrambling of system passwords.

◆ The top, or seventh, layer of the OSI model is the Application layer. The **Application layer** provides interfaces to the software that enable programs to use network services, but does not refer to a particular program.

◆ Some of the services provided by the Application layer include file transfer, file management, and message handling for electronic mail.

◆ An **application program interface (API)** is a set of instructions that allows a program to interact with the operating system. APIs belong to the Application layer of the OSI model. Programmers use APIs to establish links between their code and the operating system.

◆ One API used in a network environment is **Microsoft Message Queueing (MSMQ)**. MSMQ stores messages sent between nodes in queues and then forwards them to their destination based on when the link to the recipient is available.

OBJECTIVES ON THE JOB

Problems that occur in the higher layers of the OSI model are more apt to be related to software than hardware or firmware. For example, if you have ruled out physical connectivity problems when you are unable to dial in to your ISP's modem pool, you might find a problem at the Session layer (which handles communication).

PRACTICE TEST QUESTIONS

1. **Which layer of the OSI model is also known as the traffic cop?**
    a. Transport
    b. Session
    c. Presentation
    d. Application

2. **Which of the following is a true statement?**
    a. MS Word resides at the Application layer.
    b. The MSMQ API resides at the Application layer.
    c. The network operating system resides at the Application layer.
    d. The MAC address resides at the Application layer.

3. **"Session" is a term that grew out of what kind of communication?**
    a. satellite
    b. microwave
    c. mainframe and terminal
    d. client and server

4. **At which layer of the OSI model does data encryption take place?**
    a. Transport
    b. Session
    c. Presentation
    d. Application

5. **With which layer of the OSI model is a programmer likely to be most familiar?**
    a. Transport
    b. Session
    c. Presentation
    d. Application

6. **Which layer of the OSI model takes care of synchronizing the dialog between two nodes?**
    a. Transport
    b. Session
    c. Presentation
    d. Application

7. **Which layer of the OSI model takes care of error correction?**
    a. Transport
    b. Session
    c. Presentation
    d. Application

ANSWER

ANSWER

ANSWER

ANSWER

ANSWER

ANSWER

ANSWER

COAXIAL CABLE

UNDERSTANDING THE OBJECTIVE

Coaxial cable consists of a copper wire core surrounded by an insulator, braiding, and a sheath. Coaxial cable was popular on networks through the 1980s. It provides excellent protection against noise and attenuation, but is more cumbersome to work with and more expensive than some newer forms of cabling. Coaxial cable networks use baseband transmission and rely on the bus topology. They are rarely found on modern networks.

WHAT YOU **REALLY** NEED TO KNOW

- ◆ Coaxial cable (also known as "coax") consists of a copper core surrounded by an insulator, a braided metal shielding called **braiding**, and an outer cover called the **sheath** or jacket.
- ◆ Because of its braiding, coaxial cable has a high resistance to interference from noise. It can carry signals farther than twisted-pair cabling before the signals must be amplified, though not as far as fiber-optic cabling.
- ◆ Coaxial cables come in many specifications, but you are likely to see only two or three types in use today. The significant differences among cable types lie in the materials used for their core, which influence impedance, throughput, and typical usage.
- ◆ The two most popular coaxial cable networks, Thinnet and Thicknet, rely on the bus topology. Thus, they must be terminated by a resistor at both ends to prevent signal bounce.
- ◆ Thinnet and Thicknet both rely on baseband transmission.
- ◆ **Baseband** is a transmission form in which digital signals are sent through direct current (DC) pulses applied to the wire. This direct current reserves exclusive use of the wire's capacity. Therefore, baseband systems can only transmit one signal, or one channel, at a time. Every device on a baseband system shares a single channel.

OBJECTIVES ON THE JOB

Coaxial cable is rarely found on modern networks, because coax is more expensive and more cumbersome than twisted-pair cabling. Also, the fact that they rely on bus topologies makes coaxial cable networks impractical for large organizations. However, you may find coaxial cable on older networks. You should be familiar with the different types of connectors, throughput, segment length, and handling requirements for such cable. For example, know that the bend radius for coaxial cable is greater than for twisted pair. Pay attention to the bend radius limitations for the type of cable you are installing. **Bend radius** is the radius of the maximum arc into which you can loop a cable before you will impair data transmission. Generally, a cable's bend radius is less than four times the diameter of the cable. Be careful not to exceed it.

PRACTICE TEST QUESTIONS

1. **What part of a coaxial cable protects the core from short-circuiting with the metal shielding?**
   a. braiding
   b. sheath
   c. jacket
   d. insulator

   ANSWER

2. **What part of a coaxial cable makes it resistant to noise?**
   a. braiding
   b. sheath
   c. jacket
   d. insulator

   ANSWER

3. **What LAN topology is used with coaxial cable?**
   a. bus
   b. ring
   c. star
   d. tree

   ANSWER

4. **Which of the following is the best use for coaxial cabling on a modern network?**
   a. connecting workstations to hubs
   b. connecting routers to hubs
   c. connecting two data closets on a backbone
   d. connecting servers to routers

   ANSWER

5. **In baseband transmission, how many digital signals are carried by one wire?**
   a. one
   b. two
   c. three
   d. as many as the connectivity devices can handle

   ANSWER

6. **Which of the following is true?**
   a. The type of coaxial cabling used on Ethernet networks is the same as that used for cable TV.
   b. The type of coaxial cabling used on Ethernet networks is the same as that used in SONET rings.
   c. The type of coaxial cabling used on Ethernet networks is more expensive than that used for cable TV.
   d. The type of coaxial cabling used on Ethernet networks has a different impedance requirement than that used for cable TV.

   ANSWER

7. **Because of the topology used with coaxial cable networks, how must each segment be terminated?**
   a. with transistors
   b. with resistors
   c. with voltage meters
   d. with odometers

   ANSWER

TWISTED-PAIR CABLING, IN-CLUDING CAT3, CAT5, UTP, AND STP, AND RJ45 CONNECTORS

UNDERSTANDING THE OBJECTIVE

Twisted–pair cabling consists of color–coded pairs of insulated copper wires, each with a diameter from 0.4 to 0.8 millimeters, twisted around each other and encased in plastic coating. On most modern networks, twisted–pair wire contains four wire pairs. Twisted–pair is a common choice for patch cables, horizontal wiring, and even backbone wiring.

WHAT YOU **REALLY** NEED TO KNOW

◆ Because twisted-pair cabling is less expensive and more flexible than coaxial cabling, it is the most popular form of cabling found in modern LANs.

◆ In each twisted pair of wires, one wire carries signal information while the second is grounded and absorbs interference.

◆ The more twists per inch in a pair of wires, the more noise-resistant it is. Higher-quality, more expensive twisted-pair cable contains a greater number of twists per meter or foot. This number is known as the **twist ratio**.

◆ Twisted-pair cable comes in hundreds of varieties, which vary in their twist ratio, how many wire pairs they contain, the grade of copper they use, whether they contain shielding, and what materials they use for shielding, among other things.

◆ A twisted-pair cable can contain one to 4,200 wire pairs. Modern networks use cables containing two or four wire pairs.

◆ The TIA/EIA 568 standard divides twisted-pair wiring into several categories (CATs): 1, 2, 3, 4, or 5, and soon CAT6. LANs frequently use CAT3 or CAT5 wiring.

◆ Twisted-pair cable accommodates different topologies and is often implemented in star-hybrid topologies. It can handle faster transmission rates than coaxial cable.

◆ All twisted-pair cable falls into one of two categories: shielded twisted-pair (STP) or unshielded twisted-pair (UTP).

◆ **Shielded Twisted-pair (STP)** cable consists of twisted wire pairs that are individually insulated and surrounded by a shielding made of a metallic substance such as foil. Some STP uses a braided metal shielding. STP has better noise resistance than UTP.

◆ **Unshielded Twisted-pair (UTP)** cabling consists of one or more insulated wire pairs encased in a plastic sheath. UTP does not contain additional shielding for the twisted pairs. As a result, UTP is both less expensive and less resistant to noise than STP.

◆ STP and UTP use RJ-45 connectors and data jacks, which look similar to telephone connectors and jacks.

OBJECTIVES ON THE JOB

Twisted–pair cable is ubiquitous in modern networks, so you should understand the similarities and differences among all its varieties. This understanding helps you choose and repair cabling for networks depending on their throughput and installation requirements.

PRACTICE TEST QUESTIONS

1. **How many pairs are in a twisted-pair cable?**
   a. two
   b. four
   c. eight
   d. any of the above

   ANSWER

2. **What material is used to conduct electrical signals in a twisted-pair cable?**
   a. aluminum
   b. copper
   c. steel
   d. nickel

   ANSWER

3. **Which of the following is the most popular on modern LANs?**
   a. Category 1 twisted pair
   b. Category 3 twisted pair
   c. Category 5 twisted pair
   d. Category 6 twisted pair

   ANSWER

4. **What is the purpose of a shield in twisted-pair cable?**
   a. to guard against excessive heat
   b. to minimize the impact of noise on the signal
   c. to compensate for a low twist ratio
   d. to protect the wire from physical damage

   ANSWER

5. **What is the phenomenon that occurs when a signal from one pair infringes on another pair's signal?**
   a. attenuation
   b. noise
   c. collision
   d. crosstalk

   ANSWER

6. **Which of the following is an unlikely topology for a twisted-pair network?**
   a. bus
   b. star
   c. ring
   d. star-ring

   ANSWER

7. **What standards organization sets guidelines for twisted-pair wiring?**
   a. CCITT
   b. ISO
   c. TIA/EIA
   d. IEEE

   ANSWER

FIBER OPTIC

UNDERSTANDING THE OBJECTIVE

Fiber-optic cable comes in two main varieties: single mode, in which a single frequency is used to transmit data in light pulses, and multimode, in which multiple frequencies are used to transmit light pulses. Fiber can carry more data faster and longer than copper wire, but it is overall more expensive than copper.

WHAT YOU **REALLY** NEED TO KNOW

- ◆ **Fiber-optic cable**, or simply **fiber**, contains one or several pure glass fibers in its **core**. Data is transmitted via pulsing light sent from a laser or light-emitting diode (LED) through the central fiber(s).

- ◆ Outside the fiber(s), a layer of glass called **cladding** acts as a mirror, reflecting light back to the core. This reflection allows fiber to bend around corners without losing the integrity of the light-based signal.

- ◆ Outside the cladding, a layer of plastic and a braiding of Kevlar (an advanced polymeric fiber) protect the inner core. A plastic jacket covers the braiding.

- ◆ **Single-mode fiber** carries a single frequency of light to transmit data from one end of the cable to the other end. Data can be transmitted faster and for longer distances on single-mode fiber. But single-mode fiber costs too much to be realistically considered for use on data networks.

- ◆ **Multimode fiber** carries several frequencies of light over a single or multiple fibers. This is the type of fiber-optic system typically used by data networks.

- ◆ Fiber-optic cable provides the benefits of nearly unlimited throughput, very high resistance to noise, and excellent security.

- ◆ Fiber can carry signals for longer distances than can coax or twisted-pair cable. Its overall network length benefits from not depending on repeaters or amplifiers.

- ◆ Significant drawback to using fiber are its high cost and splicing difficulty.

- ◆ Another disadvantage to fiber is that it can transmit data only unidirectionally, so one cable must contain two strands, one to send data and one to receive it.

- ◆ Fiber has proved reliable transmitting data at rates of up to 1 gigabit per second. With further improvements expected, fiber will probably surpass that limit.

- ◆ Network segments made from fiber can span 100 meters. Overall network lengths vary depending on the type of fiber-optic cable used. For multimode fiber, TIA/EIA recommends a segment limit of 2 km. For single-mode fiber, the limit is 3 km.

OBJECTIVES ON THE JOB

Because of its fast transmission rate and high resistance to noise, fiber-optic cable is used most often for backbones on LANs or WANs or for long-distance trunks provided by telecommunications carriers. Bear in mind that fiber uses different plugs and connectors than any kind of copper cabling, so special fiber patch panels and NIC ports must be used.

PRACTICE TEST QUESTIONS

1. **Which of the following is the most expensive type of transmission?**
   - a. UTP
   - b. coaxial cable
   - c. STP
   - d. fiber optic

   ANSWER

2. **How many frequencies of light are transmitted in a single-mode fiber-optic cable?**
   - a. one
   - b. two
   - c. four
   - d. six

   ANSWER

3. **What purpose does the cladding in a fiber-optic cable serve?**
   - a. It shields the cable from damage.
   - b. It shields the cable from EMI.
   - c. It acts as a mirror, reflecting the light pulses back to the core.
   - d. It acts as an insulator, protecting the light pulses from other light sources.

   ANSWER

4. **Which two of the following are advantages of fiber over copper wire?**
   - a. It can transmit data faster.
   - b. It is not susceptible to EMI.
   - c. It costs less.
   - d. It is simple to make patch cables in a pinch.
   - e. It can transmit data bidirectionally.

   ANSWER

5. **Which of the following devices would not be necessary on a purely fiber-based network?**
   - a. repeaters
   - b. bridges
   - c. switches
   - d. routers

   ANSWER

6. **What generates light pulses on a fiber-optic cable?**
   - a. voltage
   - b. magnetic field
   - c. laser
   - d. gravity

   ANSWER

7. **What is the maximum distance for a fiber segment?**
   - a. 100 meters
   - b. 1 km
   - c. 10 km
   - d. 100 km

   ANSWER

THICKNET (10BASE5) AND THINNET (10BASE2) AND THEIR CONNECTORS, INCLUDING BNC

UNDERSTANDING THE OBJECTIVE

The two major forms of coaxial cabling are Thicknet (10Base5) and Thinnet (10Base2). Both maintain the characteristics of coaxial cable (such as baseband transmission, bus topology, and so on), but have different throughput, noise resistance, and segment length specifications.

WHAT YOU **REALLY** NEED TO KNOW

◆ **Thicknet** cabling is a rigid coaxial cable, approximately 1 cm thick, used for the original Ethernet networks. Because it is often covered with a yellow sheath, it may be called "yellow Ethernet."

◆ IEEE designates Thicknet as **10Base5** Ethernet. The "10" represents its throughput of 10 Mbps, the "Base" stands for baseband transmission, and the "5" represents the maximum segment length of a Thicknet cable, 500 meters.

◆ Thicknet is less expensive than fiber-optic cable, but more expensive than twisted-pair cable and other types of coaxial cabling such as Thinnet.

◆ Thicknet requires a combination of a vampire tap to connect to a transceiver, plus a drop cable to connect network devices.

◆ Since Thicknet has high resistance to noise, it allows data to travel longer distances than other types of cabling.

◆ Thicknet can accommodate a maximum of 100 nodes per segment. Its total maximum network length is 1,500 meters.

◆ IEEE has designated **Thinnet** as **10Base2** Ethernet. The "10" represents its data transmission rate of 10 Mbps, "Base" stands for baseband transmission, and "2" represents its maximum segment length of 185, or roughly 200, meters.

◆ Thinnet's sheath is typically black and its cable diameter is approximately 0.64 cm. It's more flexible and easier to handle than Thicknet.

◆ Thinnet connects the wire to network devices with BNC T connectors. A BNC connector with three open ends attaches to the NIC at the base of the "T" while attaching to the Thinnet cable at its two sides. BNC barrel connectors (with only two open ends) are used to join two Thinnet cable segments.

◆ Thinnet can accommodate a maximum of 30 nodes per segment. Its total maximum network length is just over 550 meters.

◆ Because of its insulation and shielding, Thinnet is more resistant to noise than twisted-pair wiring. However, it is not as resistant as Thicknet.

OBJECTIVES ON THE JOB

Thicknet is almost never used on modern networks. Thinnet is occasionally used on modern networks, but more often you see it on networks installed in the 1980s. However, because twisted-pair wiring can carry more data and has come down in cost, Thinnet has become almost obsolete.

PRACTICE TEST QUESTIONS

1. **What color is typically used for the sheath of a Thinnet cable?**
   a. yellow
   b. black
   c. orange
   d. purple

   ANSWER

2. **What is the maximum distance between a workstation and a switch on a Thicknet network?**
   a. 100 meters
   b. 200 meters
   c. 500 meters
   d. 800 meters

   ANSWER

3. **In the IEEE designation 10Base2, what does the 2 represent?**
   a. 2 feet
   b. 2 Mbps
   c. 185 meters
   d. 200 yards

   ANSWER

4. **Which of the following types of cable is the most expensive?**
   a. Thicknet
   b. Thinnet
   c. UTP
   d. STP

   ANSWER

5. **What is a BNC barrel connector used for?**
   a. connecting a Thinnet workstation to the network
   b. connecting a Thicknet workstation to the network
   c. connecting two Thinnet cable segments
   d. connecting two Thicknet cable segments

   ANSWER

6. **Why is the maximum segment length for Thicknet longer than for Thinnet?**
   a. Thicknet is more noise-resistant.
   b. Thicknet is more flexible.
   c. Thicknet has a higher throughput.
   d. Thicknet is more heat-resistant.

   ANSWER

7. **What is the maximum throughput on a Thicknet network?**
   a. 1 Mbps
   b. 10 Mbps
   c. 100 Mbps
   d. 1 Gbps

   ANSWER

OBJECTIVES

Recognize and describe the characteristics of networking media and connectors

10BASET

UNDERSTANDING THE OBJECTIVE

10BaseT is an Ethernet specification that uses baseband transmission and enables data rates of up to 10 Mbps. 10BaseT networks can use unshielded or shielded twisted–pair cable, both of which use RJ–45 connectors. 10BaseT is limited to a maximum segment length of 100 meters and uses a star topology.

WHAT YOU **REALLY** NEED TO KNOW

◆ 10BaseT is the most common Ethernet cabling specification today. **10BaseT** uses baseband transmission (thus the "Base" in its name) and twisted-pair cabling (thus, the letter "T" in its name) and a star topology to transmit data at 10 Mbps.

◆ As with all Ethernet networks, 10BaseT follows communication rules called **Carrier Sense Multiple Access with Collision Detection (CSMA/CD)**. CSMA/CD allows multiple nodes to share one data channel while minimizing data collisions.

◆ 10BaseT networks use unshielded twisted-pair cabling, including Category 3, 4, and 5 cables. Unshielded twisted pair is the same kind of wiring used for telephone connections, and for this reason, 10BaseT networks historically fit well into an organization's existing physical infrastructure.

◆ One possible disadvantage to using unshielded twisted-pair cabling is that it is sensitive to electromagnetic interference caused by signals from nearby sources such as electric motors, power lines, and radars. 10BaseT technology compensates for interference through noise balancing and filtering techniques on the wire.

◆ Nodes on a 10BaseT Ethernet network connect to a central hub or repeater in a star fashion. Typical of a star topology, a single network cable only connects two devices. This characteristic makes 10BaseT networks more fault tolerant than 10Base2 or 10Base5, which use the bus topology.

◆ Since 10BaseT networks use a star topology, they are easier to troubleshoot than 10Base2 or 10Base5 networks, because you can better isolate problems.

◆ Each node on a 10BaseT network uses RJ-45 connectors to connect the network cable with the NIC at the workstation end and with the hub at the network end.

◆ The maximum distance a 10BaseT segment can traverse is 100 meters.

◆ 10BaseT networks can contain up to five sequential segments connected by four hubs or switches.

OBJECTIVES ON THE JOB

Modern networks frequently can use both 10BaseT and 100BaseT on the same network. Bear in mind that all NICs and ports on connectivity devices such as routers or hubs must be compatible with the transmission technology your network uses (such as 10BaseT). Even if your network runs only 10BaseT now, it is wise to purchase devices that can automatically sense whether the network is running 10BaseT or 100BaseT and adjust to that rate.

PRACTICE TEST QUESTIONS

1. **What type of access method does a 10BaseT network always use?**
   a. circuit switching
   b. token ring
   c. packet switching
   d. CSMA/CD

   ANSWER

2. **Which two of the following types of wiring might a 10BaseT network use?**
   a. coaxial cable
   b. CAT1
   c. CAT2
   d. CAT3
   e. CAT5

   ANSWER

3. **What is the maximum segment length for a 10BaseT network?**
   a. 100 meters
   b. 10 meters
   c. 10 feet
   d. 100 feet

   ANSWER

4. **What does the "Base" in 10BaseT represent?**
   a. Basic
   b. Baseband
   c. Baseboard
   d. Basal

   ANSWER

5. **What kind of connector is used in a 10BaseT network?**
   a. BNC barrel
   b. BNC T connector
   c. RJ-11
   d. RJ-45

   ANSWER

6. **On what topology are 10BaseT networks based?**
   a. bus
   b. tree
   c. star
   d. ring

   ANSWER

7. **What other technology can run on the same network with 10BaseT technology?**
   a. 10Base2
   b. 10Base3
   c. 10Base5
   d. 100BaseT

   ANSWER

OBJECTIVES

Recognize and describe the characteristics of networking media and connectors

100BASET, 100BASE VGANYLAN, AND 100BASE TX

UNDERSTANDING THE OBJECTIVE

100BaseT is an Ethernet transmission technology that can achieve data rates up to 100 Mbps. The most popular version of 100BaseT is the 100BaseTX specification, which can be easily added to an existing 10BaseT network and can take advantage of full duplexing. An alternative technology that also provides 100 Mbps transmission rates is 100Base–VG AnyLAN, where the "VG" stands for voice grade.

WHAT YOU **REALLY** NEED TO KNOW

◆ **100BaseT,** also known as **Fast Ethernet,** is specified in the IEEE 802.3 standard. It enables LANs to run a 100 Mbps data transfer rate, a tenfold increase from what 10BaseT provides, without requiring significant investment in new infrastructure.

◆ 100BaseT uses baseband transmission in a star-wired bus or hierarchical hybrid topology, just like 10BaseT. For best performance, it requires CAT5 or better cabling with RJ-45 data connectors. 100BaseT upgrades can be easy and inexpensive to accomplish for an organization that currently uses the popular 10BaseT technology.

◆ The length between a node and its hub for 100BaseT networks cannot exceed 100 meters.

◆ Because of the speed on a 100BaseT network, the window of time for the NIC to detect and compensate for errors is very small. To minimize undetected collisions, 100BaseT buses can only practically support a maximum of three network segments connected with two hubs.

◆ **100BaseTX** is the most popular version of 100BaseT. 100BaseTX sends signals 10 times faster than a 10BaseT network and condenses the time between digital pulses as well as the time a station is required to wait and listen in CSMA/CD.

◆ 100BaseTX requires Category 5 unshielded twisted-pair cabling.

◆ A technology related to Ethernet that also supports the 100 Mbps data transmission rate is **100Base-VG AnyLAN**. The "VG" stands for "voice grade."

◆ 100Base-VG AnyLAN is governed by IEEE standard 802.12.

◆ 100Base-VG does not use CSMA/CD, but rather an access method called Demand Priority, in which the hub arbitrates which nodes transmit data at any given time. In order to accomplish this, 100Base-VG AnyLAN networks require intelligent hubs.

◆ 100Base-VG AnyLAN uses all four wire pairs in the twisted-pair cable for unidirectional signaling; thus it cannot support **full-duplexing**. 100Base-VG AnyLAN can use the same cabling that 10BaseT networks use.

OBJECTIVES ON THE JOB

The most popular form of fast transmission technology in use today is 100BaseTX, a variation of the 100BaseT Ethernet standard. It is likely that 100BaseTX will continue to be preferred and eventually, both 100 Mbps technologies will be replaced by Gigabit Ethernet, which is capable of data transmission rates up to 1 Gbps.

PRACTICE TEST QUESTIONS

1. **How many wire pairs does the simple 100BaseT technology use?**
   - a. one
   - b. two
   - c. three
   - d. four

   ANSWER

2. **What kind of hub does a 100Base-VG AnyLAN network require?**
   - a. stackable
   - b. bridging
   - c. switching
   - d. intelligent

   ANSWER

3. **What is one reason 100BaseTX is more popular than 100Base-VG AnyLAN?**
   - a. It can transmit data faster.
   - b. It is less susceptible to data errors.
   - c. It does not require special NICs or other equipment.
   - d. It can run on CAT1 cabling.

   ANSWER

4. **Which of the following does not use CSMA/CD?**
   - a. 10BaseT
   - b. 100BaseTX
   - c. 100BaseT4
   - d. 100Base-VG AnyLAN

   ANSWER

5. **What kind of UTP does 100BaseTX require?**
   - a. CAT1
   - b. CAT2
   - c. CAT3
   - d. CAT5

   ANSWER

6. **What is the maximum number of segments that can be connected in serial on a 100BaseT network?**
   - a. two
   - b. three
   - c. five
   - d. seven

   ANSWER

7. **Which of the following technologies attempts to eliminate the possibility for data collisions?**
   - a. 10Base2
   - b. 10BaseT
   - c. 100BaseT
   - d. 100Base-VG AnyLAN

   ANSWER

FULL- AND HALF-DUPLEXING

UNDERSTANDING THE OBJECTIVE

Full–duplexing refers to a data transmission technique in which data can flow simultaneously to and from the recipient and sender. Half-duplexing refers to a transmission technique in which data can be sent in only one direction at one time. Devices such as modems and switches must be configured to allow either half-or full–duplexing (or in some cases, both).

WHAT YOU **REALLY** NEED TO KNOW

◆ **Full-duplexing** allows simultaneous data flow in both directions. To accomplish this, the connection must allow for two separate data channels. The two channels may be separate wires (or wire pairs) or multiplexed channels on the same wire.

◆ **Half-duplexing** allows data to flow in two directions, but only one direction at a time. To accomplish this, the connection must allow for at least a single channel.

◆ **Simplex** is a form of data transmission in which data can only flow in one direction. Radio broadcasts are examples of simplex transmission.

◆ Standard PSTN telephony, in which both parties can talk and hear each other simultaneously, is an example of a full-duplex system.

◆ Walkie-talkies are examples of half-duplex systems—they can transmit data in both directions, but only one party can talk while the other listens.

◆ Modern networks typically use full-duplex transmission in connections between nodes and switches and between two nodes using a crossover cable. The primary reason for using full-duplexing is that it results in much better network performance. However, if there is very little traffic on the network, the performance advantage of full-duplexing over half-duplexing may not be noticeable.

◆ While modern switches can handle either half- or full-duplexing, hubs can only use half-duplexing.

◆ The full- or half- duplexing setting may be selected in the hardware's proprietary configuration utility or by toggling a switch on the hardware's network interface card.

◆ Newer network interface cards automatically detect whether their connection is full or half-duplex, and adjust their settings accordingly. However, this auto-sensing feature is not always correct, so a manual verification may be necessary.

◆ If the auto-sense feature on a network interface card fails to detect a connection's requirements, it will choose half-duplexing (the lowest common denominator).

OBJECTIVES ON THE JOB

Problems such as inexplicably slow connections and overall poor network performance will result if a half-duplex setting is selected when full-duplex transmission is the preferred method. If full-duplex is selected when half-duplex transmission is the correct configuration, more serious problems such as repeated characters, erroneous data, and excessive collisions (possibly resulting in a drastic network slowdown) will result.

PRACTICE TEST QUESTIONS

1. **Which of the following symptoms can indicate that the port on a switch that connects it to the backbone is configured for half-duplexing while the rest of the network is using full-duplexing?**
   a. excessive collisions on the network
   b. slow network performance
   c. error messages on workstations connected to that switch
   d. error messages on hubs connected to that switch

   ANSWER

2. **Which of the following situations requires half-duplexing?**
   a. workstation-to-hub
   b. printer-to-server
   c. switch-to-workstation
   d. switch-to-switch

   ANSWER

3. **How many transmission channels must be available to accomplish full-duplexing?**
   a. one
   b. two
   c. three
   d. There is no minimum requirement for full-duplexing.

   ANSWER

4. **How might determine if your workstation's NIC is configured for full- or half-duplexing?**
   a. Consult the network operating system
   b. Consult the Windows 95 control panel
   c. Consult the NIC's configuration utility
   d. View the LED on the switch port to which your workstation is connected

   ANSWER

5. **What is the advantage of full-duplexing over half-duplexing?**
   a. Full-duplexing is more reliable.
   b. Full-duplexing allows for faster data transmission.
   c. Full-duplexing can be used with any type of network device.
   d. Full-duplexing is a more accepted standard in the industry.

   ANSWER

6. **When does the advantage of full-duplexing over half-duplexing become negligible?**
   a. when networks contain over 100 nodes
   b. when networks connect to mainframes as well as client-server hosts
   c. when networks are part of a WAN
   d. when networks carry very little traffic

   ANSWER

7. **If a workstation's NIC is capable of only half-duplexing and connects to a Catalyst 5000 switch port capable of full-duplexing, which of the following will happen?**
   a. The switch's port will sense that the NIC can only handle half-duplexing and will thereafter use half-duplexing on that port.
   b. The switch's port will attempt to communicate with the NIC using full-duplexing.
   c. The switch's port will not attempt to communicate with the NIC.
   d. The switch's will adjust its ports to half-duplexing.

   ANSWER

WAN AND LAN

UNDERSTANDING THE OBJECTIVE

LANs typically connect computers and other devices within one building, while WANs may span several buildings, a state, or the world. Because of the distance they cover, WANs use more robust connections and connectivity devices. WANs also require special attention to security, particularly when they use public networks such as the PSTN.

WHAT YOU **REALLY** NEED TO KNOW

◆ A **local-area network (LAN)** is a network of computers and other devices confined to a small area such as an office or a single building.

◆ A **wide-area network (WAN)** is a network of computers that spans multiple locations. A WAN can connect two or more LANs. The Internet is an example of a complex WAN.

◆ The main purpose of both LANs and WANs is for multiple users to share data, storage devices, and peripherals inexpensively. Both also enable multiple workstations and hosts to communicate, even though they are not directly attached.

◆ WANs and LANs are similar in that they use many of the same protocols, transmission methods (for example, Ethernet or token ring), and types of connectivity devices.

◆ LANs and WANs differ in their topologies, media, methods of user access, and methods of security. For example, while modern LANs use coaxial or twisted-pair wiring to connect clients and servers, a WAN may use PSTN, T-carriers, ISDN, DSL, cable, fiber optic, X.25 (frame) networks, satellite, or other means of connecting clients and servers.

◆ A WAN link is typically described as **point-to-point** because it connects one site to only one other site, as opposed to connecting one site to several other sites as a hub connects many workstations on a LAN.

◆ WAN links that use a **dedicated line**, or a connection that is continuously available, have better network performance than WAN links using public lines such as the PSTN.

◆ For the best redundancy, a WAN should use the full- or partial-mesh topology. LANs do not use mesh topologies.

◆ Many WANs use public transmission systems and therefore require more security considerations than LANs, which are limited to local, dedicated connections. Encryption is a popular way of securing data transmitted on a WAN.

◆ Because they cover smaller distances and use dedicated cabling, LANs can generally achieve much better network performance than WANs.

OBJECTIVES ON THE JOB

Knowing the difference between a LAN and a WAN is a basic networking concept. However, knowing how these differences affect data transmission and ultimately users, requires more analysis. A performance problem on a LAN may have a completely different cause (for example, a faulty hub) than a performance problem on a WAN (for example, a downed link between one national carrier and another).

PRACTICE TEST QUESTIONS

1. **Which three of the following could a LAN and WAN have in common?**
    a. They use TCP/IP.
    b. They use a full-mesh topology.
    c. They use a router.
    d. They use CSMA/CD.
    e. They use the PSTN.

    ANSWER

2. **Which of the following is used when a 56K modem dials into a remote access server?**
    a. DSL
    b. PSTN
    c. T-1
    d. SONET

    ANSWER

3. **Which of the following will affect network performance over WAN links?**
    a. a faulty patch cable
    b. a jamming workstation NIC
    c. a misconfigured hub
    d. a failed gateway router

    ANSWER

4. **Which two of the following are considered dedicated?**
    a. PSTN
    b. DSL
    c. Ethernet
    d. T-3

    ANSWER

5. **What is the world's largest WAN also known as?**
    a. Internet
    b. Arpanet
    c. Darpanet
    d. ARCNet

    ANSWER

6. **Which of the following protocols would be used only for a WAN?**
    a. HTTP
    b. BGP
    c. RARP
    d. FTP

    ANSWER

7. **In what instance is the one-to-many type of link used?**
    a. between multiple locations on a WAN
    b. between multiple servers and workstations on a LAN
    c. between a switch and multiple devices on a LAN
    d. between a switch and another switch on a WAN

    ANSWER

SERVER, WORKSTATION, AND HOST; SERVER-BASED NETWORKING AND PEER-TO-PEER NETWORKING

UNDERSTANDING THE OBJECTIVE

In the client-server model, servers are dedicated to managing resources while workstations have limited responsibility for processing applications or storing files. In peer-to-peer networking, all machines connected to the network can act as clients and servers.

WHAT YOU **REALLY** NEED TO KNOW

◆ A **server** is a computer on the network that runs network operating software (such as Windows NT Server, Novell NetWare, or UNIX) and manages data, programs, users, groups, security, printers, and other elements in the client-server model.

◆ A **workstation** is the most common form of client, and contains its own hard disk, memory, CPU, monitor, keyboard, and NIC. In server-based networking, workstations depend on servers to supply and manage shared resources.

◆ In server-based networking, servers are more powerful computers than workstations. In order to run several programs for multiple clients, they must possess greater memory, CPU, and hard disk resources.

◆ Server-based networking is also known as client-server networking.

◆ Clients on a server-based network may also run applications and store data. However, to share files with other clients, they use the server as an intermediary.

◆ In **peer-to-peer networking**, all computers are connected via a single cable, and any computer on the network can act as both server and client. The advantage to this model is that it is simple and inexpensive to set up. However, this model doesn't scale well and presents difficult challenges to maintaining security. Peer-to-peer networking is used only for small LANs.

◆ The advantages of server-based networking over peer-to-peer networking include centralized management of user-level and share-level security, optimization of processing power within a central computer, and the ability to handle more complex topologies and a greater number of clients with ease.

◆ The term host may have different meanings depending on the context in which it's used. A **host** on a TCP/IP-based network may be any machine with a valid IP address. In broader terms, a host is a type of server that supplies shared resources to remote clients. For example, when you connect to a Web site on the Internet, you are downloading data from a host.

OBJECTIVES ON THE JOB

Most organizations use server-based networking, rather than peer-to-peer networking. Only small, older, cost-conscious environments will use the latter. Server-based networking requires more complex network operating software and typically uses more complex topologies than peer-to-peer networking.

PRACTICE TEST QUESTIONS

1. Which of the following organizations is most likely to use a peer-to-peer network?

    a. a multinational insurance company with 4,000 users

    b. a recently established local arts foundation with 20 users

    c. a family-owned lumber company with 10 users

    d. a local ISP

ANSWER

2. Which three of the following would be clients on a server-based network?

    a. a computer running NetWare 5.0

    b. a computer running Windows 95

    c. a computer running Macintosh OS 8.0

    d. a computer running Red Hat Linux

    e. a computer running Windows NT Server 4.0

ANSWER

3. Which of the following is an advantage to peer-to-peer networking over server-based networking?

    a. It's less complex to configure.

    b. It's more powerful.

    c. It can use multiple protocols.

    d. It scales well.

    e. It provides excellent security.

ANSWER

4. Which of the following does a server on a server-based network not typically perform?

    a. application license management

    b. data storage

    c. virus detection on floppy disks

    d. print queue management

ANSWER

5. What is the most popular topology for a modern client-server LAN?

    a. bus

    b. star

    c. ring

    d. star-bus hybrid

ANSWER

6. What do all hosts have in common?

    a. They all have a valid IP address.

    b. They all have a valid IPX address.

    c. They all serve files to the Web.

    d. They all manage shared files.

ANSWER

7. What is the most popular topology for a peer-to-peer LAN?

    a. bus

    b. star

    c. ring

    d. star-bus hybrid

ANSWER

OBJECTIVES

Identify the basic attributes, purpose, and function of the following network elements

CABLE, NIC, AND ROUTER

UNDERSTANDING THE OBJECTIVE

Cables form the foundation of the network at the Physical layer. They carry data (in the form of electrical pulses) to and from each node on the network. NICs (network interface cards) also function at the Physical layer, providing the connection between a device and the cable. Finally routers, which function at the Network layer of the OSI model, determine the pathways for data according to their destination addresses.

WHAT YOU **REALLY** NEED TO KNOW

◆ A **cable** is one form of transmission media, the method by which data is transferred from one node on the network to another. Popular types of cable are coaxial, unshielded twisted pair, shielded twisted pair, and fiber optic.

◆ A **patch cable** is a relatively short cable that acts as an intermediate connection between nodes. For example, a patch cable would connect a workstation to a wall jack.

◆ A **crossover cable** is a type of patch cable in which the transmit and receive wire pairs are reversed in one of the two RJ-45 connectors. It can be used to cascade hubs or to connect two nodes without an intervening hub.

◆ NICs are connectivity devices that enable a network node (such as a workstation, server, printer, router, switch, etc.) to receive and transmit data over the network media. NICs are also sometimes called **network adapters**.

◆ NICs belong to the Physical layer of the OSI model and transmit data signals to the cable.

◆ NICs come in a variety of types depending on network transport system (Ethernet vs. token ring), network transmission speed connector interfaces type of system board or device they suit, and of course, manufacturer.

◆ A **router** is a multiport device that can connect dissimilar networks, interpret Layer 3 addressing information, determine the shortest, fastest path between two nodes, and reroute traffic if a primary path is down but another path is available. Routers operate at the Network layer (Layer 3) of the OSI model.

◆ A typical router has an internal processor, its own memory and power supply, input and output jacks for different types of network connectors (depending on the network type), and usually, a management console interface.

◆ Network administrators usually configure and manage routers by telnetting to the router's IP address and using text-based commands at the prompt.

OBJECTIVES ON THE JOB

You should be able to identify whether a data transmission problem lies with the cable, NIC, or connectivity device (such as a router). You should also be able to construct patch and crossover cables. Finally, you should be experienced with installing, configuring, and troubleshooting NICs from various manufacturers in various devices.

PRACTICE TEST QUESTIONS

1. **To which layer of the OSI model do routers belong?**
   - a. Physical
   - b. Data Link
   - c. Transport
   - d. Network

   ANSWER

2. **Which of the following is the least expensive type of cabling?**
   - a. fiber optic
   - b. coaxial cable
   - c. UTP
   - d. STP

   ANSWER

3. **Which three of the following functions do routers perform?**
   - a. determine the fastest path between two nodes on a network
   - b. interpret MAC addresses
   - c. interpret IP addresses
   - d. assign IPX addresses
   - e. filter broadcast transmissions

   ANSWER

4. **What type of cable connects a hub to a patch panel?**
   - a. crossover cable
   - b. patch cable
   - c. plenum cable
   - d. transverse cable

   ANSWER

5. **Which two of the following will affect what type of NIC you should purchase for a client?**
   - a. CPU
   - b. cabling
   - c. memory
   - d. network speed
   - e. authentication method

   ANSWER

6. **To what layer of the OSI model do NICs belong?**
   - a. Physical
   - b. Transport
   - c. Network
   - d. Presentation

   ANSWER

7. **What TCP/IP utility is used to manage a router?**
   - a. PING
   - b. NETSTAT
   - c. ARP
   - d. TELNET

   ANSWER

BROADBAND AND BASEBAND

UNDERSTANDING THE OBJECTIVE

A network may use one of two types of signaling: broadband or baseband. Most LANs rely on baseband transmission since it uses digital pulses, which are more precise and can be repeated without also amplifying noise. Baseband also has the advantage of allowing two–directional signaling on one wire. Broadband transmission uses analog signals and allows unidirectional signaling on one wire.

WHAT YOU **REALLY** NEED TO KNOW

- ◆ **Baseband** transmission sends digital signals through direct current (DC) pulses applied to the wire. This direct current reserves exclusive use of the wire's capacity. Therefore, baseband systems can only transmit one signal, or one channel, at a time.

- ◆ Baseband transmission supports bidirectional signal flow, which means that computers can both send and receive information on the same length of wire.

- ◆ Baseband transmission is susceptible to attenuation. Baseband systems use repeaters to regenerate and amplify the signal so that data can travel beyond the maximum segment length of the cabling.

- ◆ Ethernet is an example of a baseband system.

- ◆ **Broadband** is a form of transmission in which signals are modulated as radio frequency (RF) analog pulses that use different frequency ranges.

- ◆ Though broadband isn't digital, using multiple frequencies enables a broadband system to use several channels on the wire, and thus carry much more data than a baseband system. A cable TV connection, which is broadband, can carry at least 25 times the data that a typical baseband system (like Ethernet) carries.

- ◆ In broadband systems, signals travel only in one direction. Therefore, broadband cabling must provide separate wires for transmission and receipt of data.

- ◆ Broadband transmission is generally more expensive than baseband transmission because of the extra hardware involved. On the other hand, broadband systems can span longer distances before amplification than baseband.

- ◆ Broadband signals, like baseband, are susceptible to attenuation. Broadband systems use amplifiers to boost the signal.

- ◆ "Broadband" has two meanings in networking. The broadband described in this section, was the original meaning of broadband. In a discussion of WANs, the term "broadband" refers to networks that use digital signaling and have very high transmission rates, such as Asynchronous Transfer Mode (ATM).

OBJECTIVES ON THE JOB

You almost always work with baseband signals in the field of networking. Therefore, you should be familiar with the need for such signals to be repeated, and further, how many feet (or meters) a baseband segment can extend before a repeater is necessary.

PRACTICE TEST QUESTIONS

1. **Ethernet is an example of what type of transmission?**
   a. baseband
   b. broadband
   c. wideband
   d. switched

   ANSWER

2. **What do baseband and broadband have in common?**
   a. Both can transmit signals bidirectionally.
   b. Both are susceptible to attenuation.
   c. Both use multiple frequencies to transmit several channels of data simultaneously.
   d. Both use digital signals.

   ANSWER

3. **Which two of the following are capable of distorting a baseband signal?**
   a. dust
   b. fluorescent lights
   c. loud noises
   d. electric motors
   e. sunspots

   ANSWER

4. **What is the main difference between an amplifier and a repeater?**
   a. An amplifier regenerates a signal while a repeater boosts a signal.
   b. An amplifier doubles the signal while a repeater simply boosts the signal.
   c. An amplifier boosts a signal while a repeater regenerates a signal.
   d. There is no difference.

   ANSWER

5. **On an Ethernet network, how many signals can be transmitted simultaneously on the wire?**
   a. one
   b. two
   c. any multiple of two
   d. any number

   ANSWER

6. **In baseband transmission, what creates binary signals on the wire?**
   a. heat
   b. RF
   c. AC
   d. DC

   ANSWER

7. **Which of the following can support the longest segment length?**
   a. baseband
   b. broadband
   c. wideband
   d. narrowband

   ANSWER

GATEWAY

UNDERSTANDING THE OBJECTIVE

Gateways connect two systems that use different formatting, communications protocols, or architecture. To accomplish this, gateways must be able to operate at multiple layers of the OSI model. They must communicate with an application, establish and manage sessions, translate encoded data, and interpret logical and physical addressing data.

WHAT YOU **REALLY** NEED TO KNOW

◆ In general, a **gateway** is a computer running special software or a connectivity device that acts as a translator between two dissimilar systems. It may connect networks running different protocols, architecture, or formatting.

◆ Gateways operate at multiple layers of the OSI model, including Application, Session, Transport, and Network. They repackage incoming information so the destination network can read it. They may also perform security and filtering functions.

◆ Gateways can exist on servers, microcomputers, or mainframes. In the case of connecting two large networks, a gateway may be a specialized router.

◆ Gateways are much slower than bridges or normal routers because of the complex translations they conduct. Because they are slow, gateways have the potential to cause extreme network congestion.

◆ The most common type of gateway is the e-mail gateway, which translates messages from one type of system to another. An e-mail gateway would allow people who use Eudora e-mail to correspond with people who use GroupWise e-mail. This type of gateway is typically software running on a server.

◆ An Internet gateway allows and manages access between LANs and the Internet. An Internet gateway can restrict the kind of access LAN users have to the Internet and vice versa. This type of gateway typically runs on a router.

◆ When configuring clients for Internet access, the IP address of the gateway needs to be specified in the TCP/IP parameters.

◆ A LAN gateway allows segments of a LAN running different protocols or different network models to communicate with each other. A router or server may act as a LAN gateway.

◆ The LAN gateway category might also include remote access servers that allow dial-up connectivity to a LAN.

OBJECTIVES ON THE JOB

During your networking career you will most likely hear gateways discussed in the context of Internet connectivity. When configuring servers and clients on a LAN that connects to the Internet, you must know the gateway TCP/IP address so the network can use it to connect to outside systems.

PRACTICE TEST QUESTIONS

1. **Why are gateways slower than bridges?**
   a. because they must read the source and destination MAC addresses
   b. because they must manage sessions, translate encoded data, and interpret logical and physical addresses
   c. because they must assign new IP addresses to every packet
   d. because they must interpret application programming interface output

   ANSWER

2. **Typically, what is the last octet in an Internet gateway IP address?**
   a. 1
   b. 10
   c. 100
   d. 255

   ANSWER

3. **What type of gateway would connect token ring and Ethernet networks within one building?**
   a. e-mail gateway
   b. IBM host gateway
   c. Internet gateway
   d. LAN gateway

   ANSWER

4. **Which two of the following could be considered gateways?**
   a. router
   b. firewall
   c. switch
   d. bridge

   ANSWER

5. **Which two of the following could host an e-mail gateway?**
   a. PC
   b. switch
   c. printer
   d. server

   ANSWER

6. **When acting as an e-mail gateway, in which OSI model layers does a gateway perform most of its functions?**
   a. Data Link and Physical
   b. Transport and Network
   c. Transport and Session
   d. Application and Presentation

   ANSWER

7. **Why are gateways necessary?**
   a. because different NIC vendors may use different MAC address naming conventions
   b. because different routers may follow different forwarding protocols
   c. because different LANs may use different protocols or architectures
   d. because different LANs may use different cabling media

   ANSWER

2.1 Given an installation, configuration, or troubleshooting scenario, select an appropriate course of action if a client workstation does not connect to the network after installing or replacing a network interface card

KNOWLEDGE OF HOW THE NETWORK CARD IS USUALLY CONFIGURED, INCLUDING EPROM, JUMPERS, AND PLUG AND PLAY SOFTWARE

UNDERSTANDING THE OBJECTIVE

Several elements contribute to the proper installation and configuration of a network interface card. The manufacturer encodes some of the configuration information in the EPROM chip on the NIC's circuit board. The computer's BIOS, if it is Plug and Play compatible, assigns more information such as the IRQ, DMA channel, and I/O address.

WHAT YOU **REALLY** NEED TO KNOW

◆ **Firmware** is a combination of hardware and software. A NIC's firmware contains information about its transmission speed capabilities, its preferred IRQ, I/O port address, and duplexing capabilities, among other things. In many cases, you do not need to change the NIC's firmware.

◆ The hardware component of firmware is a read-only memory (ROM) chip that stores data established at the factory; it may be changed by configuration utilities that come with a NIC. More specifically, since this type of ROM's data can be erased, then changed, it is called **erasable programmable read-only memory (EPROM).**

◆ A **jumper** is a small pin on a circuit board. A piece of metal covered with plastic can be placed over a pair of jumpers to complete a circuit between the two pins. Closing a connection between two jumpers instructs the hardware to act differently. For example, jumpers can indicate the NIC's network speed.

◆ Better firmware and circuitry (to detect options such as network speed) have largely replaced jumpers on NICs. Jumpers on NICs are nearly obsolete.

◆ **Plug and Play (PnP)** technology, implemented by Microsoft beginning with its Windows 95 operating system, that attempts to automatically configure newly inserted devices such as NICs, monitors, sound cards, etc. In order for PnP to work, the BIOS, hardware, and operating system must all be PnP-compatible.

◆ Plug and Play technology can assign IRQ addresses, DMA channels, and I/O addresses. However, even if PnP is used, device drivers (the software unique to each component) must still be installed and configured properly through the operating system.

◆ Plug and Play technology does not work with older hardware or operating systems.

◆ Occasionally Plug and Play technology does not work with newer components, though the manufacturer and operating system indicate that it should. In this case, it may be necessary to disable Plug and Play capability through the computer's BIOS.

OBJECTIVES ON THE JOB

While software and hardware manufacturers have attempted to make installation as simple as possible, their methods do not always work. At that point, knowledge of changing jumpers, manually configuring IRQ and other settings, and modifying BIOS settings will help you connect a device to the network. Older devices and operating systems require more manual configuration than newer systems.

PRACTICE TEST QUESTIONS

1. Which of the following is a setting that enables a NIC to communicate with the system board?
    a. BIOS
    b. jumper
    c. IRQ
    d. IP address

2. What is created when a pair of jumpers is covered with a small, metal and plastic bracket?
    a. an electrical circuit
    b. a network connection
    c. an instruction to the network
    d. a command to bypass configuration

3. After approximately what year is it safe to assume that hardware and operating systems fully adopted Plug and Play technology?
    a. 1990
    b. 1992
    c. 1994
    d. 1996

4. Which two of the following parameters will Plug and Play technology assign to a newly discovered device?
    a. IRQ
    b. MAC address
    c. IP address
    d. port number
    e. I/O address

5. What company popularized the use of Plug and Play technology?
    a. IBM
    b. Microsoft
    c. Cisco
    d. HP

6. Which of the following is an IRQ frequently used for NICs?
    a. 11
    b. 4
    c. 6
    d. 1

7. What stores configuration information about a NIC from the manufacturer?
    a. RAM
    b. EPROM
    c. BIOS
    d. device driver

2.1
cont. Given an installation, configuration, or troubleshooting scenario, select an appropriate course of action if a client workstation does not connect to the network after installing or replacing a network interface card

USE OF NETWORK CARD DIAGNOSTICS, INCLUDING THE LOOPBACK TEST AND VENDOR-SUPPLIED DIAGNOSTICS

UNDERSTANDING THE OBJECTIVE

All network interface cards are shipped from the manufacturer with a diagnostics program, usually on a floppy disk. This diagnostics program can perform multiple tests on the NIC's hardware and operation, and it can also enable a network technician to change some of the parameters written into the NIC's EPROM chip.

WHAT YOU **REALLY** NEED TO KNOW

◆ The network card diagnostic program is a utility that can check and modify the configuration of the NIC, including parameters established in the EPROM. It is supplied by the NIC manufacturer and shipped with the NIC on a floppy disk.

◆ Although each manufacturer supplies a proprietary version of a diagnostic program, many have similar interfaces and commands.

◆ A NIC diagnostic program can perform up to a dozen tests on the NIC to determine whether its hardware is functioning correctly and what its settings are.

◆ A NIC's diagnostic program also enables you to easily change properties of the EPROM chip on the NIC.

◆ Besides testing the functionality of the hardware, common uses for a NIC diagnostic program include modifying the NIC's full- vs. half-duplex setting, specifying a 10- or 100-Mbps transmission rate, specifying a media type, or modifying the NIC's I/O address or IRQ.

◆ Even the NIC's MAC address can be changed through a diagnostic program. However, since this address is guaranteed to be unique, it should never be changed.

◆ One of the diagnostic utilities that comes with the NIC software performs a loopback test on the NIC to make sure it can transmit and receive data properly. This test requires a loopback plug or cable. A **loopback plug** is a connector that plugs into a port, and crosses over the transmit line to the receive line so that outgoing signals can be redirected back into the computer for testing.

◆ A NIC's diagnostic program can also perform an echo test. In this test, two NICs (one of them known to be good) are required. The good NIC acts as an echo server while the questionable NIC acts as the echo client. The echo client sends a packet to the echo server, and the echo server bounces the packet back to the echo client. If the packet is received without errors, the echo test was successful.

◆ Perform all of the tests that come with the NIC diagnostic software, except the echo test, while the NIC is not attached to the network. Perform the echo test when only the two participating NICs are connected to the network. A malfunctioning NIC may cause errors on the network.

OBJECTIVES ON THE JOB

Most problems with NICs result from incorrect protocol configuration, incorrectly installed device drivers, or hardware failure. The last problem is the one that the NIC diagnostics software can help detect. A NIC diagnostics disk for every make and model of NIC should be readily available to technical staff who support clients and servers.

PRACTICE TEST QUESTIONS

1. Which two of the following can be changed using a NIC's diagnostic software?
   a. the NIC's IP address
   b. the NIC's host name
   c. the NIC's use of full duplex or half duplex
   d. the NIC's network speed
   e. the NIC's hub port

   ANSWER

2. In addition to the NIC diagnostic software, what is required to perform a loopback test on a 10Base2 network?
   a. a BNC T connector
   b. a BNC barrel connector
   c. a 50-Ohm resistor
   d. a transceiver

   ANSWER

3. After installing a NIC on a workstation, you discover that it is being recognized by the operating system and the proper devices are installed, but it cannot find the network. Before running the network diagnostics tests, what do you check?
   a. whether the NIC is firmly seated in the system board
   b. whether the NIC is experiencing an IRQ conflict
   c. whether the NIC is properly connected to the network
   d. whether the NIC has the proper jumpers selected

   ANSWER

4. Which of the following should never be changed through the NIC diagnostic program?
   a. MAC address
   b. IP address
   c. media type
   d. network speed

   ANSWER

5. When does it make the most sense to perform a NIC diagnostics test?
   a. when a NIC can communicate with IPX devices but not with IP devices
   b. when a NIC is properly configured but cannot successfully ping the loopback address
   c. when a NIC is properly configured but transmits data at an extremely slow rate
   d. when a NIC is properly installed and configured but cannot transmit data past the firewall

6. Why is it wise to disconnect the NIC from the network before performing diagnostics?
   a. the diagnostic test generates a small voltage that may damage other devices
   b. the diagnostics test may cause a faulty NIC to generate errors on the network
   c. the test results will not be accurate if other devices are present on the network
   d. if the NIC is faulty, the test searches for another NIC

   ANSWER

7. How will you know if the diagnostic program has discovered problems with a NIC?
   a. at least one of the tests will be marked "failed"
   b. at least one of the tests will continue to repeat until you stop the program
   c. a Windows error message indicates that the diagnostics program aborted
   d. a NIC diagnostics error will appear indicating that the NIC must be replaced

   ANSWER

OBJECTIVES

2.1
cont.

Given an installation, configuration, or troubleshooting scenario, select an appropriate course of action if a client workstation does not connect to the network after installing or replacing a network interface card

THE ABILITY TO RESOLVE HARDWARE RESOURCE CONFLICTS, INCLUDING IRQ, DMA, AND I/O BASE ADDRESS

UNDERSTANDING THE OBJECTIVE

All devices in a computer, including its NIC, must have IRQs, I/O base addresses, memory address ranges, and sometimes DMA addresses assigned. Each of these resources contributes to the system board, memory, or CPU's ability to communicate with the device. Sometimes, two devices may attempt to reserve the same resource, resulting in a conflict. In the case of a NIC, the most obvious sign of a resource conflict is an inability to connect to the network.

WHAT YOU **REALLY** NEED TO KNOW

◆ An **Interrupt Request Line (IRQ)** is the means by which a device can request attention from the CPU. IRQs are identified by numbers from 0 to 15. Some computer devices reserve IRQ numbers; for example, a floppy disk controller takes IRQ 6. Additional devices such as sound cards, graphics cards, modems, and NICs must contend for the remaining IRQs.

◆ The **I/O base address** setting specifies, in hexadecimal notation, which area of memory acts as a channel for moving data between the NIC and the CPU. Like its IRQ, a device's I/O base address cannot be used by any other device.

◆ The **Direct Memory Address (DMA) channel** provides a method for devices to directly communicate with the computer's memory, improving the performance of that device. DMAs are not required and are not used by every device.

◆ The **memory address range** indicates, in hexadecimal notation, the area of memory that the NIC and CPU use for exchanging, or buffering, data. As with IRQs, some memory ranges are reserved for specific devices, most notably the system board. Reserved address ranges can never be selected for new devices.

◆ The BIOS attempts to assign free resources to devices. But the BIOS can be wrong, and in such cases, conflicts may occur.

◆ If two devices choose the same IRQ, I/O base address, memory address range, or DMA channel, operational and performance problems will result.

◆ If conflicts occur with these settings, you need to manually set a device's resources rather than accept the default. You can either enter the CMOS menu and change the settings, or, in the case of a Windows 9x client, choose Control Panel – System and select the device's properties from the Device Manager tab.

OBJECTIVES ON THE JOB

Resolving resource conflicts takes patience and persistence. Often, a NIC continually tries to choose the same resource although it is in use by another device. Rather than trial-and-error modifications, you may find preferred resource settings in the manufacturer's documentation for the product. When all else fails, it may be necessary to remove the conflicting device (such as a sound card) and reinstall the NIC.

PRACTICE TEST QUESTIONS

1. If you are troubleshooting a NIC problem on a Windows 95 workstation and you suspect that a resource conflict is causing the problem, where can you look to verify your hunch?
    a. Control Panel – Network Properties – Adapter
    b. Control Panel – Network Properties – Addressing
    c. Control Panel – System – Device Manager
    d. Control Panel – System – Hardware Profiles

    ANSWER

2. If an IRQ resource conflict exists with a NIC, which of the following devices is most likely to be reserving the same IRQ?
    a. floppy disk drive
    b. CD-ROM
    c. display adapter
    d. sound card

    ANSWER

3. Which two of the following symptoms might appear if a client is experiencing a resource conflict that includes its NIC?
    a. It may not be able to connect to the network.
    b. It may not be able to read floppy disks.
    c. It may not be able to accept any new devices.
    d. It may experience errors in transmitting and receiving data.

    ANSWER

4. Which of the following is a valid I/O base address?
    a. 03F
    b. T61
    c. 200PFF1
    d. 3FK0333

    ANSWER

5. Which two of the following can be changed in the CMOS utility?
    a. IRQs
    b. memory ranges
    c. IP addresses
    d. MAC addresses
    e. slot numbers

    ANSWER

6. The DMA channel provides a device with a direct connection to which of the following resources?
    a. hard disk
    b. system board
    c. disk controller
    d. memory

    ANSWER

7. What does the I in IRQ stand for?
    a. information
    b. interrupt
    c. integrated
    d. intelligent

    ANSWER

HUBS AND MAUS

UNDERSTANDING THE OBJECTIVE

Hubs are simple repeaters that connect multiple devices to a network's backbone on an Ethernet network. MAUs perform the same function on a token ring network, and because of the star-ring topology that they typically support, have a different design than hubs. A hub is essentially a multiport repeater that retransmits incoming data to all its other ports.

WHAT YOU **REALLY** NEED TO KNOW

◆ At its most primitive, a **hub** is a multiport repeater containing one port that connects to a network's backbone and multiple ports that connect to a group of workstations (or a patch panel). Hubs come in many different varieties.

◆ In addition to connecting Macintosh and PC workstations, hubs may connect print servers, switches, file servers, or other devices to a network.

◆ Hubs typically support a star or star-hybrid topology on an Ethernet network.

◆ Some hubs also allow for multiple media connector types and/or multiple data transmission speeds.

◆ On a hub, the **uplink port** is the receptacle used to connect one hub to another hub in a daisy chain or hierarchical fashion. An uplink port may look like any other port, but it should only be used to interconnect hubs.

◆ On a hub, the **backbone port** is the receptacle used to connect a hub to the network's backbone. For 10BaseT networks this type of connection is often made with short lengths of Thinnet coaxial cabling.

◆ The **link LED** is the light on a port that indicates whether it is in use. If a connection is live, this light should be solid green.

◆ On token ring networks, hubs are called **Multistation Access Units (MAUs)**. On modern token ring networks, the star-ring hybrid topology is most common. The MAU completes the ring internally with a Ring In/Ring Out port at either end of the unit. These ports allow the MAU to make a ring topology with other devices.

◆ Token ring networks can easily be expanded by connecting multiple MAUs through their Ring In/Ring Out ports. Unused ports on a MAU, including Ring In and Ring Out ports, have self-shorting data connectors that internally close the loop.

◆ The self-shorting feature of token ring MAU ports makes token ring highly fault-tolerant. For example, if you discover a faulty NIC on the network, and remove that workstation's cable from the MAU, the MAU's port will close the ring internally.

OBJECTIVES ON THE JOB

You should understand how to identify a faulty hub port, either through testing or by looking at the link LED. Faulty hub ports are not unusual, particularly on less expensive equipment, and should always be suspected when a device cannot communicate with the network, once the NIC and the device itself have been ruled out as the problem's cause.

PRACTICE TEST QUESTIONS

1. **What is the main difference between a hub and a MAU?**
    a. Hubs can extend a network while MAUs cannot.
    b. MAUs can be used in a star-bus topology while hubs cannot.
    c. Hubs are typically used with Ethernet networks while MAUs are used with token ring networks.
    d. Hubs are more fault-tolerant than MAUs.

    ANSWER

2. **What can you view to determine whether a hub port is receiving information from a workstation's NIC?**
    a. the backbone port
    b. the uplink LED
    c. the link LED
    d. the Ring In LED

    ANSWER

3. **Which of the following characteristics do MAUs and hubs share?**
    a. Both connect multiple workstations to the network backbone.
    b. Both interpret IPX and IP addressing information.
    c. Both forward or filter frames based on their network segment.
    d. Both interpret MAC addresses to determine where to send data.

    ANSWER

4. **What does the M in MAU stand for?**
    a. media
    b. maximum
    c. multiple
    d. multistation

    ANSWER

5. **Which of the following is probably the least expensive device?**
    a. switch
    b. MAU
    c. router
    d. hub

    ANSWER

6. **What is used to connect one hub to another hub in a daisy chain fashion?**
    a. their uplink ports
    b. their backbone ports
    c. their Ring In ports
    d. their Ring Out ports

    ANSWER

7. **Which two of the following are used to connect one MAU to another?**
    a. their uplink ports
    b. their downlink ports
    c. their Ring Out ports
    d. their Ring In ports
    e. their backbone ports

    ANSWER

SWITCHING HUBS, REPEATERS, AND TRANSCEIVERS

UNDERSTANDING THE OBJECTIVE

Repeaters and transceivers are simple devices that belong to the Physical layer of the OSI model and retransmit analog or digital signals. A repeater, in addition to retransmitting the signal, amplifies or regenerates the signal, respectively, depending on whether it is analog or digital. This is necessary because attenuation causes a signal to weaken as it moves farther across the network. Switching hubs are more intelligent devices than repeaters or transceivers. Switching hubs can interpret the addresses of the data packets they receive and, based on those addresses, direct the data to the proper port for transmission.

WHAT YOU **REALLY** NEED TO KNOW

- A **switching hub** can interpret the addresses of incoming data and, based on those addresses, forward data to the appropriate port on the hub.

- Traditional hubs, in contrast, simply rebroadcast incoming data to all of their ports and allow the destination node to pick it up. Since switching hubs forward packets only to one port, they provide better performance than traditional hubs.

- Newer switching hubs can support both 10BaseT and 100BaseT Ethernet transmission. They may also support load balancing, in which the hub automatically determines which port should be assigned to each LAN segment based on traffic ports.

- Digital and analog signals on a network are subject to attenuation. As a consequence, they must be amplified and regenerated in order to travel longer distances. **Repeaters** are the connectivity devices that perform the regeneration and amplification of an analog or digital signal.

- Repeaters belong to the Physical layer of the OSI model, and therefore have no means of interpreting the data they are retransmitting. For example, they cannot improve or correct a bad or erroneous signal; they can only repeat it.

- A repeater contains one input port and one output port, so it is capable of receiving and repeating only one data stream.

- The word "transceiver" is derived from a combination of the words "transmitter" and "receiver". A **transceiver** is a device that receives and transmits signals. In most modern networks, a transceiver can only be found in NICs. Transceivers also belong to the Physical layer of the OSI model.

OBJECTIVES ON THE JOB

Depending on what type of network you support, you may work with hubs (Ethernet) or MAUs (token ring). Switching hubs are useful on Ethernet networks when greater speed and efficiency in transmitting data is desired. As hubs become more and more sophisticated, you will have to rely on the documentation that ships with the equipment, rather than any prior assumptions you may have about hubs being simplistic. Some hubs have management consoles similar to a router's and can monitor their traffic through every port.

PRACTICE TEST QUESTIONS

1. **What is the difference between a transceiver and a repeater?**
   a. A transceiver can interpret addressing information while a repeater cannot.
   b. A repeater can interpret addressing information while a transceiver cannot.
   c. A repeater can amplify signals while a transceiver cannot.
   d. A transceiver can determine the best path for data between network nodes while a repeater cannot.

2. **Which of the following is most like a bridge?**
   a. a transceiver
   b. a switching hub
   c. a repeater
   d. a modular hub

3. **In which of the following situations would a repeater be the most appropriate selection?**
   a. when you are attempting to connect two LAN segments and extend the maximum network length
   b. when you are attempting to connect two LAN segments and provide load balancing between the segments
   c. when you are attempting to extend the length of a network segment
   d. when you are attempting to optimize the speed with which data is transmitted between subnets

4. **On modern networks, where is a transceiver usually found?**
   a. in the file server's NOS
   b. in the NIC
   c. in the modem
   d. in the client software

5. **Which of the following belongs to the Physical layer of the OSI model?**
   a. switch
   b. brouter
   c. bridge
   d. transceiver

6. **Which two of the following can interpret address information?**
   a. bridge
   b. repeater
   c. transceiver
   d. modem
   e. switching hub

7. **Which of the following can improve the accuracy of a data transmission?**
   a. transceiver
   b. repeater
   c. router
   d. hub

BRIDGES, WHAT THEY ARE AND WHY THEY ARE USED

UNDERSTANDING THE OBJECTIVE

Bridges are devices that connect two LANs or LAN segments using one port per segment. Bridges listen to all network traffic and, based on the packets' MAC addresses, determine whether to forward the packets to another segment or to discard them. Bridges keep track of which MAC addresses should be forwarded to which port in a filtering database.

WHAT YOU **REALLY** NEED TO KNOW

- ◆ **Bridges** are devices that move frames between two LANs or LAN segments.
- ◆ Bridges are similar to repeaters in that they do not modify the contents of a packet. But they are more sophisticated than repeaters, because they interpret addressing information and filter packets.
- ◆ Because they can selectively filter packets, bridges can be useful for separating LAN segments, thus reducing the possibility that errors on one segment will affect transmission on the other segment.
- ◆ Like repeaters, bridges can extend the physical distance limitation of a network.
- ◆ Bridging occurs at the Data Link layer of the OSI model, which encompasses flow control, error handling, and physical addressing.
- ◆ Bridges read the destination MAC address of each frame and decide whether to forward (retransmit) the packet to another segment on the network or, if it belongs to the same segment as the source address, filter (discard) it.
- ◆ As nodes on a network transmit data through the bridge, the bridge establishes a **filtering database** of known MAC addresses and their location on the network. (This filtering database is also known as a **forwarding table**.) The bridge uses its filtering database to determine whether a packet should be forwarded or filtered.
- ◆ A bridge does not immediately know which workstations are associated with its various ports. After it is installed, the bridge polls the network to discover the destination address for each packet it handles. Next, it records the destination node's MAC address and the port it belongs to in its filtering database. Over time, it will discover all nodes on the network and have database entries for each.
- ◆ Because bridges cannot interpret Network layer information, they do not distinguish between different protocols passing through. Because they are protocol-ignorant, bridges can move data faster than traditional routers.

OBJECTIVES ON THE JOB

Since bridges operate at the Data Link layer, they cannot interpret Network layer information as routers do. They can, however, connect LANs that use different transmission methods (for example, Ethernet and token ring), and they can extend the length of a network. In general, bridges are used less than routers or switches because they lack flexibility and because routers and switches have dropped in price.

PRACTICE TEST QUESTIONS

1. Which of the following do bridges and repeaters have in common?
   a. Both can interpret IP addresses.
   b. Both can interpret MAC addresses.
   c. Both maintain a filtering database.
   d. Both can extend the maximum length of a LAN.

   ANSWER

2. At what layer of the OSI model does bridging occur?
   a. Application
   b. Session
   c. Network
   d. Data Link

   ANSWER

3. Which of the following is associated with a MAC address in a bridge's filtering database?
   a. port number
   b. IP address
   c. protocol
   d. subnet mask

   ANSWER

4. Why is a bridge faster than a traditional router?
   a. because it does not interpret Network layer information
   b. because it does not acknowledge data transmission errors
   c. because it is connectionless
   d. because it cannot connect LANs running different protocols

   ANSWER

5. Under what conditions will a bridge filter a packet?
   a. when it detects an incorrect checksum
   b. when it detects a damaged header
   c. when the packet's destination MAC address belongs to the port on which the bridge received it
   d. when the packet's source MAC address belongs to the port on which the bridge received it

   ANSWER

6. What IEEE standard describes bridging?
   a. 802.1
   b. 802.2
   c. 802.3
   d. 803.5

   ANSWER

7. If a bridge connects two segments on the same LAN, how many ports will be in use on the bridge?
   a. one
   b. two
   c. four
   d. six

   ANSWER

THE 802 SPECS, INCLUDING THE TOPICS COVERED IN 802.2, 802.3, AND 802.5

UNDERSTANDING THE OBJECTIVE

Everything in the networking field, from the hardware to the protocols, relies on standards so components from different manufacturers can be easily integrated. IEEE is the body that sets standards at the Physical and Data Link layers of the OSI model for computer networking. The most well-known IEEE standards are those set by the 802 committee.

WHAT YOU **REALLY** NEED TO KNOW

◆ The **Institute of Electrical and Electronic Engineers (IEEE)**, or "I-triple-E," is an international society composed of engineering professionals. It maintains a standards board that establishes its own standards for the electronics and computer industry and contributes to other standards-setting bodies such as ANSI.

◆ IEEE's committees set standards at different layers of the OSI model. The IEEE 802 (committee) standards specify how Ethernet and token ring networks handle data.

◆ IEEE developed these standards before the OSI model was standardized by ISO, but IEEE's 802 standards can be applied to the Physical or Data Link layers of the OSI model.

◆ The 802.2 standards apply to the Logical Link Control layer, a sublayer of the Data Link layer of the OSI model.

◆ Ethernet 802.2 is the default frame type for Novell's IntraNetWare network operating system. The defining characteristics of its data portion are the source and destination service access points that belong to the Logical Link Control layer.

◆ The 802.3 standards define the MAC layer elements, including the cabling and interfaces, of networks using the CSMA/CD (carrier sense multiple access/collision detection) transmission methods (Ethernet and Gigabit Ethernet). 802.3 is the most popular networking standard today.

◆ Ethernet 802.3 is the original NetWare frame type and the default for networks running NetWare versions lower than 3.12. It only supports the IPX/SPX protocol.

◆ Ethernet 802.3 is sometimes also called 802.3 "raw," because its data portion contains no control bits. Its fields match those of Ethernet 802.2, minus the Logical Link Control layer information.

◆ The 802.5 standards define the MAC layer elements, including the cabling and interfaces, of networks using the token ring transmission method.

◆ Token ring networks transmit data at either 4 Mbps or 16 Mbps over shielded or unshielded twisted-pair wiring.

OBJECTIVES ON THE JOB

You should be familiar with the two best-known IEEE standards, 802.3 and 802.5, which specify standards for Ethernet and token ring, respectively. 802.3 Ethernet is the most common network in use today and will continue to be the favorite choice among network administrators.

PRACTICE TEST QUESTIONS

1. **Which IEEE standard governs token ring networking?**
   - a. 802.1
   - b. 802.2
   - c. 802.3
   - d. 802.5

   ANSWER

2. **Which IEEE standard governs flow control on CSMA/CD networks?**
   - a. 802.1
   - b. 802.2
   - c. 802.3
   - d. 802.5

   ANSWER

3. **The 802.2 standards apply to what sublayer of the Data Link layer?**
   - a. the MAC sublayer
   - b. the Logical Link Control sublayer
   - c. the Access Method sublayer
   - d. the Network Transmission sublayer

   ANSWER

4. **To which other standards body does IEEE contribute its recommendations?**
   - a. ISO
   - b. OSI
   - c. ITU
   - d. ANSI

   ANSWER

5. **Which IEEE working group is developing standards for wireless networking?**
   - a. 802.6
   - b. 802.8
   - c. 802.11
   - d. 802.12

   ANSWER

6. **In what year was the IEEE 802 committee formed?**
   - a. 1980
   - b. 1990
   - c. 1995
   - d. 1998

   ANSWER

7. **Which IEEE standard governs Metropolitan Area Networks (MANs)?**
   - a. 802.1
   - b. 802.5
   - c. 802.6
   - d. 802.9

   ANSWER

THE FUNCTIONS AND CHARACTERISTICS OF MAC ADDRESSES

UNDERSTANDING THE OBJECTIVE

A MAC address is the unique hexadecimal number assigned to a NIC and hardcoded on its circuit board at the manufacturer's factory. The MAC address operates in the MAC sublayer of the Data Link layer of the OSI model. It provides the interface between the Physical layer and the Logical Link Control sublayer of the Data Link layer.

WHAT YOU **REALLY** NEED TO KNOW

◆ The second layer of the OSI model, the **Data Link layer,** controls communication between the Network layer and the Physical layer. Its primary function is to divide data it receives from the Network layer into distinct frames that can then be transmitted by the Physical layer.

◆ The Data Link layer is subdivided into the Logical Link Control and the MAC sublayers.

◆ The **MAC sublayer** appends the physical address of the destination to the data frame, thus creating a connection between the Physical layer and the Logical Link Control sublayer of the Data Link layer.

◆ **Data Link layer addresses** are fixed numbers associated with the networking hardware and are usually assigned and hardcoded into the network adapter at the factory. These addresses are also called **MAC addresses,** after the Media Access Control (MAC) sublayer, or physical addresses.

◆ MAC addresses are hexadecimal numbers guaranteed to be unique because industry standards govern what numbers each manufacturer can use.

◆ As an example, NICs manufactured by the 3Com Corporation begin with the following sequence of six characters: 00608C. The part of the MAC address unique to a particular vendor is called the **block ID**. The remaining six characters in the sequence are added at the factory, based on the NIC's model and manufacture date, and together are called the **device ID**. An example of a device ID assigned by a manufacturer might be 005499. Together, this block ID and device ID would result in a unique MAC address of 00608C005499.

◆ MAC addresses are used by some connectivity devices to direct data on a network.

◆ The block IDs assigned to manufacturers are publicly available.

◆ You can view the MAC address of a device or client's NIC through the NIC diagnostic utility or, on a Windows device, through the WINIPCFG or IPCONFIG utilities. It may also be printed on the NIC's circuit board.

OBJECTIVES ON THE JOB

MAC addresses, which are key pieces of information in troubleshooting, should never be changed (and it is difficult to do so). For example, you need to know how to recognize and interpret MAC addresses to resolve other addressing conflicts (such as IP or IPX conflicts).

PRACTICE TEST QUESTIONS

1. **Which of the following is an example of a valid MAC address?**
    a. 128.7.99.24
    b. AE:09:33:00:23:B5
    c. 92:CG:50:28:K3:48
    d. 247.34.188.203

ANSWER

2. **What part of a MAC address would all like-model Ethernet NICs have in common?**
    a. bound ID
    b. host ID
    c. node ID
    d. block ID

ANSWER

3. **Which of the following devices depends on MAC addresses to forward packets?**
    a. modem
    b. repeater
    c. bridge
    d. router

ANSWER

4. **How can an end user discover a Windows 98 workstation's MAC address?**
    a. by checking the TCP/IP properties
    b. by running WINIPCFG /all at the MS DOS prompt
    c. by running IPCONFIG /all at the MS DOS prompt
    d. by checking the network adapter properties in the Devices tab of the System properties dialog box

ANSWER

5. **Which two of the following terms are used interchangeably with "MAC address"?**
    a. physical address
    b. Data Link layer address
    c. logical address
    d. virtual address
    e. media address

ANSWER

6. **What does MAC stand for?**
    a. median axis channel
    b. multiple access carrier
    c. media access control
    d. multiple arbitrator channel

ANSWER

7. **Which of the following occurs at the MAC sublayer?**
    a. Data is framed for transmission via the Physical layer.
    b. Checksum data is added to the data packet.
    c. Flow control data is added to the data packet.
    d. Packets are padded if they do not meet the minimum packet size.

ANSWER

ROUTING OCCURS AT THE NETWORK LAYER AND THE DIFFERENCE BETWEEN A ROUTER AND A BROUTER

UNDERSTANDING THE OBJECTIVE

Routers use Network layer addressing information to intelligently route data between LANs. A brouter is a device that combines the features of a bridge and a router. Its main advantage is that it can accept and forward nonroutable protocols such as SNA or NetBEUI.

WHAT YOU **REALLY** NEED TO KNOW

- ◆ The primary function of the Network layer, the third layer in the OSI model, is to translate network addresses into their physical counterparts and decide how to route data from the sender to the receiver.
- ◆ When used in networking, to **route** means to intelligently direct data based on addressing, patterns of usage, quality of service, and network availability.
- ◆ Since the Network layer handles routing, **routers** belong in it. Routers are devices that connect network segments and intelligently direct data. A router has multiple ports and can connect dissimilar LANs and WANs running at different transmission speeds and using a variety of protocols.
- ◆ The Network layer protocols also compensate for disparities in the capabilities of the devices they are transmitting data to, through, and from. To accomplish this, they employ segmentation and reassembly of packets.
- ◆ Unlike bridges, routers are protocol-dependent. They must be designed or configured to recognize protocols on the network.
- ◆ A typical router has an internal processor, its own memory and power supply, input and output jacks for different types of network connectors (depending on the network type), and usually, a management console interface.
- ◆ To determine the best path between two nodes, routers communicate with each other through **routing protocols**.
- ◆ The networking industry has adopted the term **bridge router**, or **brouter**, for routers that take on some characteristics of bridges. The advantage of crossing a router with a bridge is that you can forward nonroutable protocols, such as NetBEUI, plus connect multiple network types through one device.
- ◆ A brouter offers support at Layers 2 and 3 of the OSI model. It intelligently handles any packets that contain Layer 3 addressing information and simply forwards the rest.

OBJECTIVES ON THE JOB

Routers are one of the most common devices used to connect two different LANs. They are sophisticated and flexible. However, the more sophisticated the device, the more complex it is to install, configure, and maintain. Careful thought must be put into designing a network with routers.

PRACTICE TEST QUESTIONS

1. **What is one of a router's primary functions?**
   a. to determine the best path for forwarding data to its destination
   b. to regenerate attenuated signals
   c. to separate groups of network devices into broadcast domains

   ANSWER

   d. to filter traffic according to subnet

2. **Which of the following addresses could a router interpret?**
   a. 506.78.34.110
   b. 128.92.35.117
   c. AE:09:35:00:BF:34

   ANSWER

   d. AA:01:01:46:34:29:80

3. **What is the function of a routing protocol?**
   a. to enable communications between routers
   b. to facilitate translation between the Network and Transport layers of the OSI model
   c. to convert nonroutable protocols into routable protocols

   ANSWER

   d. to ensure that encapsulated protocols are routed properly

4. **Which two of the following factors do routers consider when selecting the best path for data to travel between two nodes?**
   a. network transmission type
   b. network congestion
   c. protocol
   d. data priority

   ANSWER

   e. packet size

5. **In which layers does a brouter function?**
   a. layers 1 and 2
   b. layers 2 and 3
   c. layers 3 and 4

   ANSWER

   d. layers 4 and 5

6. **A brouter combines features of a router and what else?**
   a. bridge
   b. switch
   c. broadcast domain

   ANSWER

   d. firewall

7. **Which of the following cannot forward NetBEUI packets?**
   a. repeater
   b. hub
   c. bridge

   ANSWER

   d. router

DIFFERENCE BETWEEN ROUTABLE AND NONROUTABLE PROTOCOLS AND THE CONCEPT OF DEFAULT GATEWAYS AND SUBNETWORKS

UNDERSTANDING THE OBJECTIVE

A routable protocol carries Network layer addressing information that can be interpreted by a router and used to direct the data to its destination on the network. Gateways are a method of connecting two dissimilar LANs or subnetworks. Subnetworks are groupings of devices on a LAN that share some portion of their logical address.

WHAT YOU **REALLY** NEED TO KNOW

◆ Tasks at each layer of the OSI model are carried out by network protocols. In the networking industry, the term "protocol" is often used to refer to a group, or suite, of individual protocols that work together. The protocols within a suite are assigned different tasks, such as data translation, data handling, error checking, and addressing, and correspond to different layers of the OSI model.

◆ Protocols vary by speed, transmission efficiency, utilization of resources, ease of setup, compatibility, and whether they are routable.

◆ Protocols that can span more than one LAN segment are **routable**, because they carry network layer and addressing information that can be interpreted by a router.

◆ IPX/SPX, TCP/IP, and AppleTalk are routable protocols, while SNA and NetBEUI are nonroutable. Nearly all modern networks, and any network that must connect with the Internet, runs routable protocols.

◆ A **subnetwork**, or subnet, is a part of a network in which the nodes share the network portion of their logical addresses.

◆ The division of a large LAN into subnetworks can simplify logical address management, reduce the likelihood of a rogue device incapacitating the entire network, and in some cases, improve network performance.

◆ **Gateways** are a combination of software and hardware that enable two different network segments to exchange data. Since one device on the network cannot send data directly to a device on a different subnet or network, gateways must intercede and pass the information between subnets or networks.

◆ Gateways that connect two subnets are usually routers or interfaces on routers.

◆ Nodes that rely on gateways must identify their gateway's IP address in their TCP/IP settings. Gateway IP addresses typically end with a .1 octet.

OBJECTIVES ON THE JOB

Nearly all networks use routable protocols, and more specifically, TCP/IP. Because of the need to interconnect and communicate between LANs, the importance of having a routable protocol cannot be overemphasized. Gateways and subnetworks are also very common, even on small LANs.

PRACTICE TEST QUESTIONS

1. What is one characteristic that all routable protocols share?
   a. They can traverse more than one LAN segment.
   b. They can determine the best path between two nodes.
   c. They can exchange Physical layer information.
   d. They can translate API information.

   ANSWER

2. Which of the following pairs of devices belong to the same subnetwork?
   a. 155.09.80.225
   b. 155.09.80.207
   c. 255.255.255.255
   d. 105.90.88.207

   ANSWER

3. Which two of the following are routable protocols?
   a. TCP/IP
   b. SNA
   c. NetBEUI
   d. IPX/SPX

   ANSWER

4. A routable protocol contains addressing information from what layer of the OSI model?
   a. Physical
   b. Transport
   c. Network
   d. Data Link

   ANSWER

5. What device is used to connect an internal LAN with the Internet?
   a. subnetwork
   b. gateway
   c. firewall
   d. bridge

   ANSWER

6. Which two of the following devices can be used to connect two subnetworks on the same LAN?
   a. a modem
   b. a switch
   c. a router
   d. a server
   e. a NIC

   ANSWER

7. What digit(s) usually makes up the last octet of a default gateway address?
   a. 0
   b. 255
   c. 10
   d. 1

   ANSWER

REASON FOR EMPLOYING UNIQUE NETWORK IDS

UNDERSTANDING THE OBJECTIVE

IP and IPX are Network layer protocols. Thus, they are associated with the logical IDs assigned to each device on a routed network. These IDs must be unique or else the devices that share logical addresses will experience critical transmission problems. Conventions govern the assignment of both IPX and IP addresses. To work on the Internet, IP addresses have to be registered and obtained from the Internet authority, InterNIC.

WHAT YOU **REALLY** NEED TO KNOW

- ◆ Just as you have a distinct street address to ensure reliable delivery of your bills and magazines, every device on a routed network has a unique Network layer address to ensure reliable delivery of data.
- ◆ The two most popular types of Network layer protocols are IP and IPX. The logical addresses that these protocols contain are called IP addresses and IPX addresses.
- ◆ Network layer addresses adhere to conventions to ensure that devices such as routers can interpret them and properly route data.
- ◆ Each Network address is divided into two parts: network and host (or node). The network portion is common to all nodes on one network, while the host (node) portion is unique to each device.
- ◆ Network addresses can be manually assigned. However, no two devices can share the same logical address. If this occurs, other nodes on the network cannot reliably respond to requests from either device.
- ◆ In TCP/IP networking, a service called DHCP can automatically assign IP addresses to devices. Among other things, DHCP ensures that no two nodes on the same TCP/IP network have the same IP address.
- ◆ Whether IP addresses are assigned manually or automatically, the network administrator must ensure that IP addresses are assigned consistently according to a plan and within the boundaries of an organization's valid IP address range. InterNIC is the central authority on Internet addresses and names. By requiring organizations to register with them for ranges of IP addresses, InterNIC ensures that no two hosts on the Internet share the same address.
- ◆ In IPX addressing, the address 00000000 is a null value and cannot be used as the network portion of the address. FFFFFFFF is a broadcast address and therefore cannot be assigned either.

OBJECTIVES ON THE JOB

If you have witnessed the problems that occur when two devices attempt to use the same logical address, you understand the importance of assigning unique addresses to each device on a network. In the best case, shared logical addresses can make a few infrequently used workstations display garbage on their screens or occasionally be unable to send data to the network.

PRACTICE TEST QUESTIONS

1. **Which of the following is a valid IPX address?**
   - a. 000008A2:0060973E97F3
   - b. 00000100:G0684038
   - c. 245BD9723:3490C4008443FF1
   - d. FFFFFFFF:085C3450B3C2

   ANSWER

2. **What is the method whereby IP addresses can be automatically assigned from a server?**
   - a. SMTP
   - b. POP3
   - c. DHCP
   - d. FTP

   ANSWER

3. **Which two of the following symptoms may indicate that two Windows 9x workstations on a network are assigned the same IP address?**
   - a. Strange noises emanate from the machines.
   - b. Applications freeze up on one or more of the workstations.
   - c. The workstations lose power.
   - d. One or more workstations are unable to communicate with the network.
   - e. One or more workstations show resource conflicts in the Device Manager window.

   ANSWER

4. **Which part of an IPX address is the same as a device's MAC address?**
   - a. network
   - b. subnetwork
   - c. node
   - d. suffix

   ANSWER

5. **Where is the network portion of an IPX address determined?**
   - a. at the server
   - b. at the router
   - c. at the gateway
   - d. at the workstation

   ANSWER

6. **What authority assigns unique ranges of IP addresses to organizations who request them?**
   - a. IEEE
   - b. IETF
   - c. TIA/EIA
   - d. InterNIC

   ANSWER

7. **What command allows you to find out what IPX address your workstation is using?**
   - a. NETSTAT
   - b. TRACERT
   - c. NLIST /user
   - d. IPXCONFIG

   ANSWER

DIFFERENCE BETWEEN STATIC AND DYNAMIC ROUTING

UNDERSTANDING THE OBJECTIVE

Static routing is a technique in which a network administrator programs a router to use specific paths between nodes. Since it does not account for occasional network congestion, failed connections, or device moves, static routing is not optimal. Dynamic routing, however, automatically calculates the best path between two nodes and accumulates this information in a routing table.

WHAT YOU **REALLY** NEED TO KNOW

- ◆ Routers are devices that connect multiple LANs or LAN segments and direct data between nodes using the best possible route.
- ◆ The best path between nodes on a network depends on the number of hops between nodes, the current network activity, unavailable links, varying network transmission speeds, and topology.
- ◆ In **static routing**, a router contains routing tables (instructions on how to forward packets) that are manually programmed by a network administrator. Since the location of devices on a network and the best paths between them can change often, static routing is not a flexible or efficient technique.
- ◆ In **dynamic routing**, a router calculates the best path between nodes and automatically updates its routing tables if it detects network congestion or failures. Dynamic routing is faster and more reliable than static routing.
- ◆ Most modern routers support both dynamic and static routing. Often, network administrators will instruct the router to use primarily dynamic routing but insert some manual instructions (static routing techniques). One example is manually specifying a router of last resort, the router that accepts all packets deemed unroutable.
- ◆ To determine the best path, routers communicate through **routing protocols**. Routing protocols are used between routers only to collect data about network status and contribute to selection of best paths. From this data, routers create routing tables to use for future packet forwarding.
- ◆ In addition to its ability to find the best path, a routing protocol is often characterized by its **convergence time**, the time it takes for a router to recognize the best path if a change or outage occurs, and its **bandwidth overhead**, the burden placed on the underlying network to support the routing protocol.
- ◆ The most common routing protocols are RIP, OSPF, EIGRP, and BGP.

OBJECTIVES ON THE JOB

Because of their flexibility and multitude of options, routers are not simple to install. Typically, a technician or engineer must be very familiar with routing technology to know how to best place and configure a router.

PRACTICE TEST QUESTIONS

1. **Which of the following is not a routing protocol?**
   a. BGP
   b. EIGRP
   c. ISP
   d. RIP

   ANSWER

2. **What is one advantage of dynamic routing over static routing?**
   a. It is more reliable.
   b. It is more flexible.
   c. It does not require any configuration.
   d. It can interpret both IP and IPX addresses.

   ANSWER

3. **In what kind of situation might static routing be useful?**
   a. to avoid congested links on the network
   b. to avoid downed links on the network
   c. to assign a router of last resort for unroutable packets
   d. to isolate troublesome machines from the rest of the network

   ANSWER

4. **What contains information about best paths on a router?**
   a. filtering database
   b. WINS table
   c. DHCP configuration
   d. routing table

   ANSWER

5. **Which two of the following conditions cause a dynamic router to change its best path designations?**
   a. network congestion
   b. a flurry of unroutable traffic
   c. a security breach
   d. a workstation move
   e. significant Internet use

   ANSWER

6. **What must a network administrator do after a server is moved from one LAN segment to another on a network whose routers use static routing?**
   a. Modify the routing table to indicate the new best path to that server.
   b. Change the router designation in the server's TCP/IP properties.
   c. Reboot the router to allow it to detect the new best path to that server.
   d. Reconfigure the router to accept packets from more than one LAN segment.

   ANSWER

7. **What manufacturer makes the most popular routers today?**
   a. IBM
   b. Microsoft
   c. Hewlett-Packard
   d. Cisco

   ANSWER

DISTINCTION BETWEEN CONNECTIONLESS AND CONNECTION-ORIENTED TRANSPORT

UNDERSTANDING THE OBJECTIVE

A connection-oriented protocol ensures accurate data delivery by using acknowledgments, checksums, and flow control. A connectionless protocol does not guarantee accurate delivery or even delivery of data.

WHAT YOU **REALLY** NEED TO KNOW

- ◆ A **connection-oriented protocol** requires a connection to be established and verified before it will exchange data. This is the type of connection the telephone system uses.
- ◆ A connection-oriented protocol that resides at the Transport layer of the OSI model is the Transmission Control Protocol (TCP). TCP forms the basis for many other, higher-layer TCP/IP protocols, including FTP and TELNET. Thus, FTP and TELNET both require a connection to be established before they begin transmitting data.
- ◆ Connection-oriented protocols are good for long, steady data transmissions and when the source node requires monitoring or verification of the transmission.
- ◆ A **connectionless protocol** does not require a connection to be established before it exchanges data. It simply sends data to the destination without first verifying a connection.
- ◆ User Datagram Protocol (UDP) is a connectionless protocol which resides at the Transport layer of the OSI model. It offers no assurance that packets will be received in the correct sequence. In fact, this protocol does not guarantee that the packets will be received at all. Furthermore, it provides no error checking or sequence numbering.
- ◆ In some situations, connectionless protocols are more appropriate than connection-oriented protocols because they can transmit data faster. For example, they are appropriate for short bursts of traffic.
- ◆ One instance in which connectionless protocols provide an advantage over connection-oriented protocols is in the transmission of live video data. In these cases, TCP, with its acknowledgments, checksums, and flow control mechanisms, would add too much overhead to the transmission and bog it down.
- ◆ The IP protocol is connectionless, and thus, the Internet is one large WAN that depends on connectionless communication. However, in cases that require assured delivery of data, TCP is used atop IP.

OBJECTIVES ON THE JOB

The difference between connection-oriented and connectionless protocols can be a significant factor in troubleshooting. If a router accepts some but not all traffic, you can check whether the accepted traffic is consistently connectionless and the rejected data is consistently connection-oriented. This could indicate a configuration problem with the router.

PRACTICE TEST QUESTIONS

1. **Which of the following relies on a connectionless protocol?**
   - a. BOOTP
   - b. TELNET
   - c. FTP
   - d. SNMP

   ANSWER

2. **Which two of the following fields does a TCP datagram contain?**
   - a. reverse lookup
   - b. sequence number
   - c. acknowledgment number
   - d. socket address
   - e. time to live

   ANSWER

3. **Which of the following fields does a UDP datagram contain?**
   - a. padding
   - b. acknowledgment
   - c. sequence number
   - d. destination port

   ANSWER

4. **What Transport layer protocol is used by POP3?**
   - a. IP
   - b. IPX
   - c. TCP
   - d. UDP

   ANSWER

5. **For which of the following applications is a connectionless protocol well suited?**
   - a. live video transmission
   - b. network device monitoring
   - c. file transfer
   - d. login authorization

   ANSWER

6. **What kind of network is the Internet?**
   - a. connection-oriented
   - b. connectionless
   - c. IPX-based
   - d. TCP-based

   ANSWER

7. **What is the function of an ACK?**
   - a. to confirm the receipt of data
   - b. to establish and verify a connection
   - c. to control the flow of data
   - d. to ensure that datagrams arrive in sequence

   ANSWER

PURPOSE OF NAME RESOLUTION, EITHER TO AN IP/IPX ADDRESS OR A NETWORK PROTOCOL

UNDERSTANDING THE OBJECTIVE

While the network understands IP and IPX addresses, humans are more comfortable with names. If humans use names to identify machines, then the network needs to know how to translate those names into addresses. On a TCP/IP network this is the function of the DNS server. On an IPX/SPX network, this is accomplished by servers on the network's backbone.

WHAT YOU **REALLY** NEED TO KNOW

◆ People prefer to associate names with networked devices, rather than remember IPX or IP addresses. For this reason, mechanisms to translate IP and IPX addresses into easily remembered names were developed shortly after the advent of networks.

◆ On a TCP/IP network, each device is assigned a host name that is associated with its IP address. Together with its domain name, a host name uniquely identifies that device to other devices on the TCP/IP network.

◆ The **Domain Name System (DNS)** is a method of automatically translating domain names into IP addresses. Every TCP/IP network that wants to communicate with the Internet must have a DNS server at its disposal (whether it is local or remote).

◆ DNS is organized hierarchically for the worldwide Internet. If an organization's DNS server does not know the IP address of a requested host, it queries a higher-level DNS server. If that DNS server also doesn't know the IP address of the host, it queries a higher-level DNS server, and so on.

◆ The DNS database is distributed over several key computers across the Internet to prevent catastrophic failure if one or a few computers go down.

◆ DNS is a TCP/IP service that belongs to the Application layer of the OSI model.

◆ IPX name resolution is accomplished at the network server. Each client is manually assigned an IPX name, and the server translates this name into its IPX address.

◆ Strictly adhering to IPX naming conventions is particularly important when attempting to run IPX over IP links.

◆ Naming devices is useful not only for making them more memorable but for establishing how the LAN is organized. For example, a marketing and an accounting department may share the same TCP/IP segment and the network ID 132.65.88.24, but to distinguish them, they may be assigned host names such as client1.mktg.abccorp.com and client1.acctg.abccorp.com.

OBJECTIVES ON THE JOB

If your organization has no naming conventions, consider reassigning names to follow a convention. Although this requires time and adjustment on the part of end users, it leads to easier troubleshooting and maintenance. The most important thing in naming is to never assign the same name to two different devices.

PRACTICE TEST QUESTIONS

1. **Which two of the following can a DNS server interpret?**
   a. IPX address
   b. IP address
   c. routing table
   d. filtering table
   e. domain name

   ANSWER

2. **Why are machines named?**
   a. so the network can identify them
   b. so humans can more easily identify them
   c. so they can receive data addressed to their name
   d. so no two devices will have the same address

   ANSWER

3. **Where does IPX name resolution occur?**
   a. on the DNS server
   b. on the router
   c. on the firewall
   d. on the IPX/SPX server

   ANSWER

4. **Which of the following must understand IPX/SPX addresses without translation?**
   a. a Novell 3.12 server
   b. a Windows NT server
   c. a Red Hat LINUX server
   d. a Cisco firewall

   ANSWER

5. **If you are the network administrator at a large corporation with multiple departments in multiple locations, and you need to determine how to name devices on the network, which runs TCP/IP, what kind of scheme might you devise?**
   a. Assign unique, top-level domain names to each department.
   b. Assign unique host names to each department.
   c. Assign unique portions of the fully qualified host names to each department.
   d. Assign unique domain names to each location.

   ANSWER

6. **Where does the global DNS database reside?**
   a. on the core DNS server
   b. It is distributed among many DNS servers.
   c. on each TCP/IP client
   d. on the default IP gateway

   ANSWER

7. **What is the function of a primary DNS server?**
   a. to service all IP address resolution requests
   b. to service IP address resolution requests only if the default gateway is down
   c. to service IP address resolution requests only if the proxy server is down
   d. to service all IP address and IPX address resolution requests

   ANSWER

THE CONCEPT OF IP DEFAULT GATEWAYS

UNDERSTANDING THE OBJECTIVE

On TCP/IP networks, the gateways that connect subnets are called default IP gateways. These gateways are usually interfaces on routers that are assigned a special IP address. This IP address must be specified in the TCP/IP configuration of devices that need to use the IP default gateway to communicate with other subnets.

WHAT YOU **REALLY** NEED TO KNOW

◆ Gateways are a combination of software and hardware that enable two different network segments to exchange data. In the context of IP addressing, a gateway facilitates communication between different IP networks or subnets.

◆ Since one device on the network cannot send data directly to a device on another subnet, it requires a gateway to intercede and pass the information from one subnet or network to another. Gateways that connect two subnets or networks are usually routers or interfaces on routers.

◆ Every device on a TCP/IP network that connects to other networks has a **default gateway**, the gateway that first interprets its outbound requests to other subnets and last interprets its inbound requests from other subnets.

◆ In the TCP/IP configuration of every device, the address of a default gateway has to be specified before the device can communicate with devices on other TCP/IP networks.

◆ Each default gateway is assigned its own IP address. Typically, the IP address of a default gateway contains only the number "1" in its last octet.

◆ Default gateways may connect more than one internal network, or connect an internal network with external networks such as WANs or the Internet.

◆ Routers in an internetworking situation must maintain a routing table to determine where to forward information. Since IP default gateways are routers (or more specifically, interfaces on routers), these gateways must also maintain routing tables.

◆ The Internet contains a vast number of routers and gateways. Each gateway only handles a relatively small amount of addressing information, which it uses to forward data to another gateway that knows more about the data's destination.

◆ As with routers on an internal network, Internet gateways also maintain default routes to known addresses to expedite data transfer. The gateways that make up the Internet backbone are called **core gateways**. Core gateways are operated by the Internet Network Operations Center (INOC).

OBJECTIVES ON THE JOB

In troubleshooting TCP/IP networks, you can isolate a problem that lies with the IP gateway if you find that TCP/IP traffic travels properly within a subnet, but not outside the subnet. Conversely, if traffic travels beyond the subnet (but has problems elsewhere), you can assume that the problem lies outside the IP default gateway.

PRACTICE TEST QUESTIONS

1. **Which of the following IP addresses probably belongs to an IP default gateway?**
   a. 161.57.89.110
   b. 161.57.89.10
   c. 161.57.89.0
   d. 161.57.89.1

   ANSWER

2. **In which two of the following situations would an IP default gateway be necessary?**
   a. A printer with an IP address of 159.45.22.144 receives a print job from a server with an IP address of 159.45.22.39.
   b. A client with an IP address of 144.92.104.82 sends an e-mail message to a client with an IP address of 144.92.39.82.
   c. A client with an IP address of 144.92.104.56 downloads a Web page from an HTTP server with an IP address of 10.12.10.13.
   d. A client with an IP address of 144.92.104.56 retrieves a file from a Windows NT server with an IP address of 144.92.104.20.

   ANSWER

3. **In a post office analogy of data routing, the IP default gateway would be most like:**
   a. the mail carrier
   b. the mail truck
   c. the letter writer
   d. the post office

   ANSWER

4. **Which of the following best describes an IP default gateway?**
   a. an interface on a router
   b. an interface on a server
   c. a firewall
   d. a switch

   ANSWER

5. **What kinds of gateways connect smaller IP gateways to form the Internet backbone?**
   a. backbone gateways
   b. central gateways
   c. core gateways
   d. serial gateways

   ANSWER

6. **How many gateways are necessary to transfer information across the Internet from a client with the IP address 122.09.83.67 to a client with the IP address 155.67.28.30?**
   a. at least two
   b. at least four
   c. at least six
   d. at least eight

   ANSWER

7. **Where can a user discover the IP address of his or her default gateway?**
   a. in the network adapter settings
   b. from his or her organization's Web page
   c. in the PC manufacturer's documentation
   d. in the TCP/IP settings

   ANSWER

THE PURPOSE AND USE OF DHCP

UNDERSTANDING THE OBJECTIVE

DHCP replaced BOOTP as an easier and more accurate method of assigning IP addresses to clients on a network. Both arose from the need to streamline the IP addressing process when networks became large and relied mostly on TCP/IP. DHCP is ubiquitous on modern networks, and because of its popularity, the software that controls DHCP is part of all network operating systems and client software.

WHAT YOU **REALLY** NEED TO KNOW

- ◆ **Dynamic Host Configuration Protocol (DHCP)** is an automated means of assigning a unique IP address to every device on a network.
- ◆ DHCP centrally manages IP allocation from a DHCP server on the network. It leases IP addresses to a client when the client requests a DHCP response via UDP broadcast.
- ◆ DHCP leases last for a time period that the network administrator specifies, from minutes to forever. The IP address assigned to a node will remain in effect (even after rebooting) until the lease has expired.
- ◆ DHCP leases can be manually forced to expire or renew at any time from either the client's TCP/IP configuration or the server's DHCP configuration. In Windows terms, terminating a DHCP lease is called a **release**.
- ◆ The network administrator in charge of IP address management must install and configure DHCP on a server whose network operating system (such as Windows NT Server, NetWare 4.11 or higher, or UNIX) can run DHCP.
- ◆ DHCP reduces the possibility for error in IP assignment. With DHCP there is no possibility that a workstation will be assigned an invalid address, and *almost* no possibility for two workstations to try to use the same IP address and cause network errors.
- ◆ DHCP limits the amount of time that networking staff have to spend managing IP addresses. The opposite of DHCP, static addressing, requires someone to manually configure an IP address on each node.
- ◆ DHCP enables users to move their workstations and printers without having to change their TCP/IP configuration. As long as a workstation is configured to obtain its IP address from a central server, the workstation can be attached anywhere on the network and receive a valid address.

OBJECTIVES ON THE JOB

Because it can be easily established and managed, DHCP is a popular method of IP address allocation on large and small networks alike. Client and server operating systems make DHCP even easier by making it part of their TCP/IP software. In fact, DHCP is typically selected as the default method of obtaining IP addresses on client machines. But despite its ease of use, DHCP is not foolproof. Occasionally the DHCP server assigns duplicate addresses and causes errors for some clients. And DHCP should not be used for servers or other devices whose IP addresses need to remain static. For example, a Web server's IP address needs to be known by the rest of the Internet so the DNS can find it; therefore, it should not change.

PRACTICE TEST QUESTIONS

1. **By what means does a newly connected client find the DHCP server?**
    a. It issues a TCP request to which the DHCP server responds.
    b. It issues an ARP request to which the DHCP server responds.
    c. It issues a UDP broadcast to which the DHCP server responds.
    d. It issues a NETSTAT request to which the DHCP server responds.

    ANSWER

2. **What older TCP/IP utility does DHCP replace?**
    a. NBTSTAT
    b. NETSTAT
    c. RARP
    d. BOOTP

    ANSWER

3. **What is the best course of action if a Windows 95 client receives a message upon booting up, indicating that another workstation has reserved the IP address it previously leased from the DHCP server?**
    a. Click OK and ignore the error.
    b. Click OK, click Release, and then click Renew in the TCP/IP Properties dialog box.
    c. Write down the MAC address of the other workstation and reboot that workstation before continuing.
    d. Click OK, then select Release All in the TCP/IP Properties dialog box.

    ANSWER

4. **Which two of the following are advantages to using DHCP over older IP addressing methods?**
    a. DHCP uses fewer server resources.
    b. DHCP requires less time to manage.
    c. DHCP reduces the possibility for duplicate addresses.
    d. DHCP requires a much shorter host file.

    ANSWER

5. **What is the opposite of DHCP?**
    a. static addressing
    b. limited term addressing
    c. octet addressing
    d. physical addressing

    ANSWER

6. **Which of the following is made easier because of DHCP?**
    a. workstation naming
    b. subnetting
    c. cabling
    d. client moves

    ANSWER

7. **If not manually terminated, how long does a DHCP lease last?**
    a. up to two days
    b. one week
    c. as long as the network administrator specifies
    d. infinitely

    ANSWER

THE PURPOSE AND USE OF DNS

UNDERSTANDING THE OBJECTIVE

The Domain Name System (DNS) associates IP addresses with domains on the Internet to allow clients to more easily transfer information. DNS, which replaces the older method of resolving names via a single host file, is a hierarchical system in which multiple servers across the Internet share the burden of finding machines belonging to specific domains.

WHAT YOU **REALLY** NEED TO KNOW

◆ Every TCP/IP host is associated with a **domain**, a group of computers that belong to the same organization and have part of their IP addresses in common.

◆ A domain is identified by its **domain name**. Usually, a domain name is associated with a company or other type of organization, such as a university or military unit. For example, IBM's domain name is ibm.com.

◆ The Internet naming authority, InterNIC, has established conventions for domain naming in which certain suffixes apply to every type of organization that uses the Internet. This suffix is known as a **Top-Level Domain (TLD)**. The TLD for a business is .com, while the TLD for an educational institution is .edu.

◆ Once an organization reserves a domain name, the rest of the world's computers know to associate the domain name with that organization, and no other organization can legally use it.

◆ In the mid-1980s a new, hierarchical way of tracking domain names and their addresses, called the **Domain Name System (DNS)**, was developed. The DNS database does not rely on one file or even one server, but is distributed over several key computers across the Internet to prevent catastrophic failure if one or a few computers go down.

◆ DNS is a TCP/IP service that belongs to the Application layer of the OSI model.

◆ While some organizations use only one name server, large organizations often maintain two—a primary and secondary name server—to help ensure Internet connectivity.

◆ Each device on the network relies on the name server and therefore must know how to find it. The IP address of the client's primary and secondary DNS servers must be specified in the client's TCP/IP properties, so the client knows what machine to query when looking up a name.

◆ To more efficiently route traffic, DNS is divided into three components: resolvers, name servers, and name space.

OBJECTIVES ON THE JOB

Every client on the network must be able to find the primary DNS server to resolve Internet names to addresses. A problem with a DNS server will cut off a network from the Internet. Because the Internet is critical to many organizations, a secondary DNS server is typically used, so that if the primary DNS server fails, clients can still connect to the Internet.

PRACTICE TEST QUESTIONS

1. **Which two of the following domain names could belong to a business?**
   a. ferrari.edu
   b. ferrari.mil
   c. ferrari.com
   d. ferrari.it
   e. ferrari.gov

   ANSWER ▢

2. **What best describes the relationship between a primary and secondary DNS server?**
   a. A primary DNS server automatically assumes the duties of a secondary DNS server if the secondary DNS server fails.
   b. A secondary DNS server handles DNS lookup requests when the primary DNS server is too busy.
   c. A secondary DNS server automatically assumes the duties of a primary DNS server if the primary DNS server fails.
   d. A primary DNS server balances the DNS request load between itself and the secondary DNS server.

   ANSWER ▢

3. **Which two of the following are included in a fully qualified host name?**
   a. DNS server address
   b. domain name
   c. host name
   d. host file name
   e. machine name

   ANSWER ▢

4. **What is a significant difference between using DNS and using a host file?**
   a. DNS is hierarchical, while a host file is flat.
   b. A host file is easier to maintain than DNS.
   c. A host file is more efficient than DNS.
   d. DNS represents a single point of failure while a host file ensures redundancy.

   ANSWER ▢

5. **How many different organizations can use the same domain name?**
   a. one
   b. no more than two
   c. no more than two, as long as they are located in the same country
   d. no more than four

   ANSWER ▢

6. **Which of the following best describes the relationship between IP addresses and domains?**
   a. Each domain is associated with a single IP address.
   b. Each IP address is associated with a single domain.
   c. Each domain is associated with a range of IP addresses.
   d. Each IP address is associated with a group of domains.

   ANSWER ▢

7. **To what layer of the OSI model does DNS belong?**
   a. Application
   b. Presentation
   c. Session
   d. Transport

   ANSWER ▢

THE PURPOSE AND USE OF WINS AND HOST FILES

UNDERSTANDING THE OBJECTIVE

Although the Internet outgrew the host file system, the concept of host files remains useful on internal networks to associate device host names with IP addresses. Similarly, the Windows Internet Naming Service (WINS) can be used to associate NetBIOS names to IP addresses on an internal network.

WHAT YOU **REALLY** NEED TO KNOW

◆ Every device on the Internet is technically known as a host. Every host can take a **host name**, a name that describes the device.

◆ In its early days, the Internet was used by fewer than 1,000 hosts. The entire Internet relied on one ASCII text file called HOSTS.TXT to associate domain names with IP addresses. This file was generically known as a **host file.**

◆ The growth of the Internet made a host file impossible to maintain—the file required constant changes, polling the file strained the Internet's bandwidth capacity, and if the file were accidentally deleted, the whole Internet would have failed.

◆ The use of a host file for Internet name resolution was replaced in the 1980s by the Domain Name System (DNS).

◆ Within an organization, host files still serve to associate internal host names with their IP addresses.

◆ The first line of a host file begins with a pound sign followed by comments.

◆ On a UNIX-based computer, the host file is called /etc/hosts. On a Windows NT or Windows 9x computer, this file is called lmhosts.

◆ A host file contains a line identifying each host's name, IP address, and alias. An **alias** is a nickname for the host within an organization.

◆ The **Windows Internet Naming Service (WINS)** provides a means of resolving NetBIOS names with IP addresses. WINS provides for the NetBIOS protocol what DNS provides for the TCP/IP protocol.

◆ While DNS runs on multiple servers, WINS runs on a single server.

◆ WINS can be implemented on servers running Windows NT Server version 3.5 or above. The WINS server maintains a database that accepts requests from Windows or DOS clients to register with a particular NetBIOS name.

◆ WINS does not assign names or IP addresses; it only keeps track of NetBIOS names and their addresses.

OBJECTIVES ON THE JOB

While a host file is no longer used for the Internet, it can be a powerful tool within an organization to assign machine aliases and allow internal devices to quickly communicate with each other. Host files can be maintained on a central server or on each client on a network.

Ship returns to:

COURSE TECHNOLOGY
DISTRIBUTION CENTER
7625 EMPIRE DRIVE
FLORENCE, KY 41042

The enclosed materials are sent to you for your review by
L.WADE/D.BARNES/D.VUJEVIC 800 6487450

SALES SUPPORT

SHIP TO: OBERTA SLOTTERBECK
HIRAM COLLEGE
MATH & COMPUTER SCIENCE DEPT
5525 ALLYN ROAD
HIRAM OH 44234

WAREHOUSE INSTRUCTIONS

SLA: 7   BOX: Staple

LOCATION	QTY	ISBN	AUTHOR/TITLE
K-26F-003-03	1	0-619-01521-7	MEADORS LAB MNL:NETWK+ GDE TO NTWRKS 1
K-34F-000-10	1	0-619-03522-6	DEAN NETWORK+ COURSEPREP EXAMGDE 1

INV# 41683953SM
PO# 30498545
DATE: 09/18/01
CARTON: 1 of 1
ID# 3571710

PRIME-INDCT-GROUP

VIA: UP

PAGE 1 OF 1

BATCH: 1241460
015/025

PRACTICE TEST QUESTIONS

1. **What character is used in a host file to indicate a comment?**
   - a. comma
   - b. semicolon
   - c. forward slash
   - d. pound sign

   ANSWER

2. **Where on a client workstation is WINS configured?**
   - a. in the network adapter properties
   - b. in the modem settings
   - c. in the TCP/IP properties
   - d. in the Microsoft client settings

   ANSWER

3. **What is the name of a host file found on a Windows 95 workstation?**
   - a. hosts
   - b. etc/hosts
   - c. hostfile
   - d. lmhosts

   ANSWER

4. **Which one of the following is most likely to use WINS?**
   - a. a Windows 3.11 workstation
   - b. a Linux server
   - c. a Novell server
   - d. a Windows 2000 workstation

   ANSWER

5. **What is a short name for a client specified in a host file used on an internal network?**
   - a. host
   - b. alias
   - c. domain
   - d. NetBIOS name

   ANSWER

6. **Which of the following should be used on hosts contained in a host file?**
   - a. DHCP
   - b. static IP addressing
   - c. WINS
   - d. PING

   ANSWER

7. **To what layer of the OSI model does WINS belong?**
   - a. Application
   - b. Presentation
   - c. Session
   - d. Transport

   ANSWER

THE IDENTITY OF THE MAIN PROTOCOLS THAT MAKE UP THE TCP/IP SUITE, INCLUDING TCP AND UDP

UNDERSTANDING THE OBJECTIVE

TCP and UDP are two of the core subprotocols of the TCP/IP suite. They both operate at the Transport layer, but differ in that TCP is connection-oriented (it verifies that a connection has been established before transmitting) while UDP is connectionless (it transmits without previously verifying a connection).

WHAT YOU **REALLY** NEED TO KNOW

◆ The **Transport Control Protocol (TCP)** belongs to the Transport layer of the TCP/IP suite and provides reliable data delivery services.

◆ TCP is a **connection-oriented** subprotocol, which means it requires that a connection be established between communicating nodes before it transmits data.

◆ TCP sits on top of the IP subprotocol and makes up for IP's reliability deficiencies with its checksum, flow control, and sequencing information. If an application relied only on IP to transmit data, IP would send packets indiscriminately, without checking whether the destination node is offline, for example, or whether the data becomes corrupt during transmission.

◆ A TCP segment contains several components that ensure data reliability, including acknowledgment, code, urgent pointer, and flow control fields.

◆ The **User Datagram Protocol (UDP)**, like TCP, also sits in the Transport layer of the OSI model and relies on IP. Unlike TCP, UDP is a connectionless transport service. UDP offers no assurance that packets will be received in the correct sequence. In fact, this protocol does not guarantee that the packets will be received at all.

◆ UDP's lack of sophistication is an advantage in situations where data must be transferred quickly, such as live audio or video transmissions over the Internet. In these cases, TCP, with its acknowledgments, checksums, and flow control mechanisms, would add too much overhead to the transmission and bog it down.

◆ In contrast to the TCP segment's ten fields, the UDP header contains only four fields: source port, destination port, length, and checksum.

OBJECTIVES ON THE JOB

The most important things to understand about TCP and UDP are that they both reside in the Transport layer and depend on the IP subprotocol. In optimizing and troubleshooting networks, it is critical to understand that TCP is connection-oriented while UDP is connectionless. Different higher-level TCP/IP subprotocols (for example, FTP and HTTP) rely on either TCP or UDP, using UDP when efficiency is their primary criterion or TCP when reliability is more important. For example, TCP should never be used by an application attempting to send live video feeds over the Internet, because its error-correction and flow control mechanisms will cause severe data transmission delays.

PRACTICE TEST QUESTIONS

1. **What Transport layer subprotocol does FTP use?**
    a. TCP
    b. UDP
    c. ARP
    d. IP

    ANSWER

2. **What Transport layer subprotocol does SNMP use?**
    a. TCP
    b. UDP
    c. ARP
    d. IP

    ANSWER

3. **Which two of the following fields do UDP and TCP datagrams have in common?**
    a. Acknowledgment Number
    b. Source Port
    c. Sequence Number
    d. Destination Port
    e. Flow Control

    ANSWER

4. **What is an advantage of using UDP over TCP?**
    a. It is more reliable.
    b. It is more secure.
    c. It is better understood.
    d. It is more efficient.

    ANSWER

5. **How can you specify that an Application layer protocol, such as HTTP, uses TCP or UDP?**
    a. by changing TCP/IP configuration settings
    b. by modifying the router protocol preferences
    c. by specifying one or the other in the preface to a destination URL
    d. You cannot specify this information.

    ANSWER

6. **What is the function of the Acknowledgment field in the TCP datagram?**
    a. It confirms receipt of the data in a return message to the sender.
    b. It confirms the size of the datagram to the recipient.
    c. It confirms the sequence of the data to the sender.
    d. It confirms the length of the datagram's header.

    ANSWER

7. **What Network layer protocol do both UDP and TCP rely on?**
    a. IPX
    b. IP
    c. ICMP
    d. POP

    ANSWER

OBJECTIVES

6.1
cont.
Demonstrate knowledge of TCP/IP fundamentals

THE IDENTITY OF THE MAIN PROTOCOLS THAT MAKE UP THE TCP/IP SUITE, INCLUDING POP3 AND SMTP

UNDERSTANDING THE OBJECTIVE

Together, POP3 and SMTP form the routine that enables clients to pick up e-mail from a server. While SMTP transfers mail between servers, POP3 accepts the mail from SMTP and holds it until e-mail clients retrieve it. POP3 and SMTP depend on each other to deliver mail between networks. A newer subprotocol, Internet Mail Access Protocol (IMAP), is replacing POP3 in some places.

WHAT YOU **REALLY** NEED TO KNOW

- ◆ The **Simple Mail Transfer Protocol (SMTP)** moves messages from one e-mail server to another over TCP/IP-based networks. SMTP is a simple subprotocol of the TCP/IP suite.
- ◆ SMTP provides the basis for Internet e-mail service and relies on higher-level programs for its instructions. Services such as the UNIX sendmail software provide a more friendly and sophisticated mail interface while using SMTP for transport.
- ◆ Requests to receive and send mail go through port 25 on SMTP servers.
- ◆ The **Post Office Protocol (POP)** relies on SMTP. POP is a subprotocol of the TCP/IP suite that provides centralized storage for e-mail messages. POP also assigns error messages in the case of undeliverable mail.
- ◆ The current and most widely used version of POP is POP3.
- ◆ A POP server is necessary to store messages because users are not always logged on to the network and available for receiving messages from the SMTP server.
- ◆ Both SMTP and a service such as POP3 are necessary for a mail server to receive, store, and forward messages.
- ◆ When configuring clients to use Internet e-mail, the SMTP and POP3 server names must be specified within the e-mail client.
- ◆ A small organization can use one POP server for all its users' mail. Very large corporations can have several POP servers, one for each department. Internet service providers typically have one large POP server for all their clients.
- ◆ POP3 does not let users keep the mail on the server after they retrieve it, which can be a disadvantage for users who move from machine to machine. A newer protocol that is replacing POP3, **Internet Mail Access Protocol (IMAP),** does let users read messages and keep them on the mail server.
- ◆ Network administrators with limited disk space might prefer POP3 to IMAP precisely because POP3 does not allow users to keep mail on the server once it is read.

OBJECTIVES ON THE JOB

If a company's SMTP server is down, mail cannot leave the organization, but can be exchanged within the organization. If a POP3 server is down, clients cannot pick up mail because the SMTP server cannot transfer mail to it. Most companies have a single SMTP server and one or more POP3 servers for storing mail.

PRACTICE TEST QUESTIONS

1. If all users in a multinational organization can send and receive mail to and from colleagues, except for those in the Marketing department, what is likely the source of the problem?
    a. the company's SMTP server
    b. the company's POP server
    c. the Marketing department's SMTP server
    d. the Marketing department's POP server

    ANSWER

2. Comparing protocols to the postal service, SMTP is like:
    a. the mail sorting machine
    b. the mail sender
    c. the mail delivery person
    d. the post office

    ANSWER

3. What is one advantage of POP over IMAP?
    a. It requires fewer resources on the server.
    b. It allows clients to save unread messages on the server.
    c. It allows clients to selectively delete messages on the server before downloading them.
    d. It is more reliable.

    ANSWER

4. What does the S in SMTP stand for?
    a. system
    b. selective
    c. simple
    d. secure

    ANSWER

5. Where must a client identify its SMTP server to properly send and receive mail?
    a. within the e-mail client software
    b. within the TCP/IP configuration
    c. within the hardware device settings
    d. within the Control Panel – Modem settings

    ANSWER

6. In the analogy with the postal service, POP would be like:
    a. the mail carrier
    b. the post office
    c. the mail truck
    d. the mail sender

    ANSWER

7. Which protocol is responsible for interpreting the following type of address: *user@mailserver.com*?
    a. SMTP
    b. POP
    c. IMAP
    d. SNMP

    ANSWER

OBJECTIVES

6.1 Demonstrate knowledge of TCP/IP fundamentals
cont.

THE IDENTITY OF THE MAIN PROTOCOLS THAT MAKE UP THE TCP/IP SUITE, INCLUDING SNMP AND FTP

UNDERSTANDING THE OBJECTIVE

SNMP is the underlying mechanism through which network devices and connections are managed. It can detect whether a device is responding under certain predefined conditions. FTP is the basic file transfer utility used most often to download programs and data from the Internet, and to upload data to Web pages or other TCP/IP hosts.

WHAT YOU **REALLY** NEED TO KNOW

◆ The **Simple Network Management Protocol (SNMP)** collects information (such as up/down status) about devices on the network. Network administrators rely on SNMP to monitor and manage networks.

◆ As its name implies, SNMP is a very simple subprotocol. Its functionality is limited to determining whether a device is responding under specified conditions.

◆ SNMP relies on the Transport layer subprotocol UDP; therefore, it does not verify that a connection has been established before it attempts to discover information about a device.

◆ Information gathered via SNMP is stored in a **Management Information Base (MIB)** by a network management system. MIBs are then interpreted by sophisticated network management software packages such as H-P OpenView.

◆ The **File Transfer Protocol (FTP)** is an Application layer protocol in the TCP/IP suite that enables a client and server to directly exchange data through a series of commands. FTP manages file transfers between TCP/IP hosts.

◆ At the Transport layer, FTP depends on the TCP protocol, and is therefore connection-oriented.

◆ FTP is a popular way to distribute files over the Internet. Some software sites allow users to download programs through a process called "anonymous FTP" in which their FTP host does not require a secure log-on.

◆ FTP transfers are separated into two channels: one for data and one for control information. FTP data is exchanged over TCP port 20 and the FTP control commands are sent and received through TCP port 21.

◆ Although FTP is simple, it lets you show file and directory structures, manage files and directories, send data in binary or ASCII format, compress files, and append files.

OBJECTIVES ON THE JOB

Network administrators often use SNMP to determine the health of the network. For example, a Web server's HTTP port can be monitored through SNMP to determine if it is responding. If SNMP doesn't detect a response, a program can use that information to alert the network administrator that the Web page is down. Thanks to SNMP, problems can be detected and addressed quickly.

PRACTICE TEST QUESTIONS

1. On which of the following Transport layer subprotocols does SNMP rely?

    a. TCP

    b. UDP

    c. IPX

    d. IP

    ANSWER

2. To connect to the Netscape FTP site from an MS DOS prompt on a Windows 98 workstation, what command would you use?

    a. ftp netscape.com

    b. ftp open ftp.netscape.com

    c. ftp ftp.netscape.com

    d. open ftp.netscape.com

    ANSWER

3. What stores information collected by the SNMP protocol?

    a. MIP

    b. MIB

    c. SMIP

    d. SMB

    ANSWER

4. What port is used for FTP data transfer?

    a. 20

    b. 21

    c. 23

    d. 25

    ANSWER

5. Which two of the following programs could be considered network management systems?

    a. Netscape Navigator

    b. MS SQL Server

    c. NetHealth

    d. H-P OpenView

    ANSWER

6. In addition to detecting whether a device is running, what other two functions can SNMP help provide?

    a. LAN topology mapping

    b. traffic route optimization

    c. broadcast transmission filtering

    d. notification of network problems

    e. collision detection

    ANSWER

7. What can you type at the FTP prompt to see a list of available commands?

    a. ?

    b. query

    c. list commands

    d. commands/q

    ANSWER

THE IDENTITY OF THE MAIN PROTOCOLS THAT MAKE UP THE TCP/IP SUITE, INCLUDING HTTP AND IP

UNDERSTANDING THE OBJECTIVE

IP and HTTP are fundamental TCP/IP subprotocols required for connections to the Web. IP is a Network layer subprotocol that contains addressing information and is necessary for data to traverse different network segments in a TCP/IP environment. HTTP is an Application layer protocol that translates to and from Web servers.

WHAT YOU **REALLY** NEED TO KNOW

◆ **Hypertext Transport Protocol (HTTP)**, an Application layer protocol, is the language that Web clients and servers use to exchange commands and control information.

◆ When a Web user types the Uniform Resource Locator (URL) or IP number of a Web page in the Web browser's address field, HTTP transports the information about the request to the Web server and returns the Web server's information in **Hypertext Markup Language (HTML)**, the Web document formatting language.

◆ HTTP is also the mechanism that connects users to links after clicking them.

◆ The original version of HTTP, HTTP/0.9, was released in 1990. This version provided only the simplest means of transferring data over the Internet. Since then, HTTP has been improved to make Web client/server connections more efficient, reliable, and secure.

◆ Simple HTTP information is not secured in transit. To make the HTTP exchange secure, a version of HTTP called S (Secure)-HTTP must be used. Alternatively, regular HTTP can be used with an encryption program such as SSL (Secure Sockets Layer).

◆ The **Internet Protocol (IP)** belongs to the Network layer of the OSI model and is one of the core subprotocols in the TCP/IP suite.

◆ IP contains logical addressing information and therefore is the subprotocol that enables TCP/IP to **internetwork**—that is, to traverse more than one LAN segment and more than one type of network through a router.

◆ IP is an unreliable, **connectionless-oriented** protocol, which means it does not guarantee delivery of data. But higher-level protocols of the TCP/IP suite use IP information to ensure that data packets are delivered to the right addresses.

◆ The IP portion of a data frame is called an **IP datagram**. The IP datagram acts as an envelope for data and contains information necessary for routers to transfer data between subnets.

OBJECTIVES ON THE JOB

You should understand the differences between HTTP and HTML for troubleshooting purposes. In addition, you should understand the security limitations of HTTP in case your clients are attempting to transmit secure data. You must understand IP, one of the core TCP/IP subprotocols, before practicing more advanced networking functions such as network planning and architecture, network optimization, monitoring, and troubleshooting.

PRACTICE TEST QUESTIONS

1. To which layer of the OSI model does HTTP belong?
    a. Network
    b. Transport
    c. Session
    d. Application

ANSWER

2. Which two of the following are valid IP addresses?
    a. 188.17.0.34
    b. 267.12.11.89
    c. 5.0.2.8
    d. 255.0.0.0.0

ANSWER

3. Which of the following is a valid HTTP address?
    a. 205.23.118.89:80
    b. 5.0.2.8:23
    c. 256.34.77.112:25
    d. 45.90.11.343:23

ANSWER

4. In what year was HTTP first released?
    a. 1989
    b. 1990
    c. 1991
    d. 1993

ANSWER

5. Which three of the following can be interpreted by HTTP (and result in the display of a Web page)?
    a. *http://www.whitehouse.gov*
    b. *html://www.ibm.net*
    c. *tcp://www.loc.gov*
    d. *www.microsoft.net*
    e. *ftp://ftp.netscape.com*

ANSWER

6. Which two of the following protocols could not function without IP?
    a. IPX
    b. SNMP
    c. POP3
    d. SPX
    e. NetBEUI

ANSWER

7. Which of the following fields would not be found in an IP header?
    a. ACK
    b. Destination port
    c. Source port
    d. Checksum

ANSWER

THE IDEA THAT TCP/IP IS SUPPORTED BY EVERY OS AND MILLIONS OF HOSTS WORLDWIDE

UNDERSTANDING THE OBJECTIVE

TCP/IP was not the first protocol used on LANs, but it was the first protocol used on the Internet. Because of its flexibility (it works on almost any server or client), its ease of use, and its adherence to open standards rather than proprietary ones, TCP/IP has become the most popular protocol on computers across the world. The use of the Internet grows exponentially each year, and this growth is predicted to continue for at least the next five years.

WHAT YOU **REALLY** NEED TO KNOW

- ◆ The precursor to TCP/IP was developed by the United States Department of Defense for its Advanced Research Projects Agency network (ARPAnet) in the late 1960s.
- ◆ Because of its low cost, ease of use, and ability to communicate among a multitude of dissimilar platforms, TCP/IP has become extremely popular. TCP/IP is now a de facto standard on the Internet and is fast becoming the default protocol on LANs.
- ◆ TCP/IP has always been the protocol of choice for UNIX-based systems and networks. More recently, it has become the protocol of choice for NetWare and Windows-based networks as well.
- ◆ Every modern type of network client now supports TCP/IP, including not only workstations and their operating systems, but also printers and other peripherals.
- ◆ One of the greatest advantages to using TCP/IP is that it is a routable protocol, which means it carries network addressing information that can be interpreted by routers.
- ◆ Hosts worldwide depend on the TCP/IP protocol, including all devices that connect to the Internet. The number of these devices grows exponentially each year and probably exceeds several million.
- ◆ Because of the growing use of TCP/IP hosts on the Internet, the threat of running out of unique IP numbers for every host looms.
- ◆ The Internet Engineering Task Force (IETF) continues to work on improving TCP/IP's capabilities. The current version of the protocol used throughout the Internet is called IP version 4. The newest version, IPV6, contains many improvements over IPV4, including a 16-byte address space (compared to the 16-bit address space in IPV4).
- ◆ IPV6 promises to help alleviate the concern of running out of unique IP addresses. However, IPV6 is not backward compatible with IPV4, a limitation that might be hampering its acceptance.

OBJECTIVES ON THE JOB

Every networking situation involves TCP/IP, so knowledge of TCP/IP is valuable. Not only is the Internet, which is based on TCP/IP, becoming a critical component in business and education success, but these organizations rely on TCP/IP to run their internal networks. TCP/IP is used and understood worldwide, and is thus a universal language. Mastering the setup, maintenance, and troubleshooting of TCP/IP may be the most valuable skill to bring to a job.

PRACTICE TEST QUESTIONS

1. **For what organization was TCP/IP originally developed?**
   a. The University of Pennsylvania
   b. Georgetown University
   c. AT&T
   d. The U.S. Defense Department

   ANSWER

2. **What is one major limitation of IPV4?**
   a. It cannot be routed through more than one default gateway.
   b. It can only run on 10- or 100-Mbps connections.
   c. Its address space is limited to 16 bits.
   d. It is not compatible with BGP routing.

   ANSWER

3. **Which two of the following are significant advantages of TCP/IP over NetBIOS?**
   a. TCP/IP is routable.
   b. TCP/IP is more compatible with Windows-based networks.
   c. TCP/IP is less expensive to run.
   d. TCP/IP is more widely accepted and used.

   ANSWER

4. **Which two of the following protocols carry network-addressing information?**
   a. TCP/IP
   b. IPX/SPX
   c. NetBEUI
   d. SNA

   ANSWER

5. **Why hasn't IPV6 been widely implemented?**
   a. It is still in development.
   b. It does not operate as efficiently as IPV4.
   c. It is not backward compatible with IPV4.
   d. It is not compatible with existing connectivity devices.

   ANSWER

6. **What organization has been responsible for developing IPV6?**
   a. IEEE
   b. TIA/EIA
   c. The U.S. Defense Department
   d. IETF

   ANSWER

7. **What percentage of hosts on the Internet can understand TCP/IP?**
   a. 10%
   b. 25%
   c. 50%
   d. 100%

   ANSWER

THE PURPOSE AND FUNCTION OF INTERNET DOMAIN NAME SERVER HIERARCHIES (HOW E-MAIL ARRIVES IN ANOTHER COUNTRY)

UNDERSTANDING THE OBJECTIVE

DNS uses a distributed hierarchy of name servers to efficiently determine how to find domains and machines on the Internet. In general, the zones in this hierarchy are based on geography. If a name server in one DNS zone cannot resolve a requested name to its IP address, the server forwards the request to a higher-level name server until the requested name is recognized by a name server.

WHAT YOU **REALLY** NEED TO KNOW

◆ DNS is divided into three components: resolvers, name servers, and name space.

◆ **Resolvers** are hosts on the Internet that need to look up domain name information.

◆ **Name servers** contain databases of names and their associated IP addresses. A name server supplies a resolver with the information it requires. If the name server cannot resolve the IP address, the query is passed to a higher-level name server.

◆ Each name server manages a group of devices, collectively known as a **zone**, which in turn is responsible for distributing naming information.

◆ Many name servers across the globe cooperate to keep track of IP addresses and their associated domain names. The Internet and DNS rely on hierarchical zones of name servers. The hierarchies are roughly arranged by geography.

◆ **Name space** refers to the actual database of Internet IP addresses and their associated names.

◆ Name space is not a database that can be opened and viewed like a store's inventory database. It is an abstract concept that describes how name servers share DNS information. However, pieces of it are tangible and stored on a name server in a **resource record**.

◆ Resource records are organized into approximately 20 different types. Each contains a name field to identify the domain name of the machine to which the record refers, a type field to identify the type of resource record, a class field to identify the class to which the record belongs (usually "IN," or "Internet"), a time to live field, a data length field, and the actual record data.

◆ A **root server** is a name server maintained by InterNIC that acts as the ultimate authority on how to contact top-level domains, such as those ending with .com, .edu, .net, and .us. InterNIC maintains 13 root servers around the world.

OBJECTIVES ON THE JOB

As a network administrator, you need to know how to set up resource records for machines handled in your DNS zone, and how to communicate with higher-level DNS name servers. Because resource records are often entered manually on a DNS server, human error can cause at least a localized network bottleneck if the DNS concepts are not well understood.

PRACTICE TEST QUESTIONS

1. **Which two of the following fields would be found in a resource record?**
   a. data length
   b. source address
   c. socket number
   d. time to live

   ANSWER

2. **What is the database of machine names and their associated IP numbers called?**
   a. root space
   b. name server system
   c. domain name records
   d. name space

   ANSWER

3. **In which situation would the zone hierarchy of DNS servers matter?**
   a. a user in Detroit sends a file across the company WAN to a user in Los Angeles
   b. a user in Oslo at ABC Corporation sends a file to a user in Virginia at XYZ Corporation
   c. a user in Marketing at ABC Corporation sends a file to a user in Accounting at ABC Corporation
   d. a user in Frankfurt at ABC Corporation prints to a printer in London at ABC Corporation over a dedicated link

   ANSWER

4. **A large, prosperous Internet retailer has four offices on its WAN which uses public transmission media to exchange all types of data, both internally and externally. Which of the following is the best solution for the number and placement of name servers in this company?**
   a. one, at the corporation's headquarters
   b. one at the corporation's headquarters and one at a second location
   c. at least two at the corporation's headquarters and at least one at every other location
   d. at least two at the corporation's headquarters and at least two at every other location

   ANSWER

5. **When a home Internet user dials into his ISP and attempts to retrieve the Yahoo home page, which DNS server is the first to handle the client's request to resolve *www.yahoo.com*?**
   a. the ISP's primary DNS server
   b. the ISP's gateway server
   c. the zone's DNS server
   d. the closest Internet root server

   ANSWER

6. **What provides the highest level of DNS authority?**
   a. root servers
   b. core routers
   c. zone servers
   d. backbone servers

   ANSWER

7. **Which domain suffixes are used in the e-mail address of a U.S. senator?**
   a. .mil
   b. .com
   c. .us
   d. .gov

   ANSWER

THE A, B, AND C CLASSES OF IP ADDRESSES AND THEIR DEFAULT SUBNET MASK NUMBERS

UNDERSTANDING THE OBJECTIVE

Most IP addresses used on modern LANs belong to either a Class A, B, or C network. To efficiently use a limited number of IP addresses, the concept of subnetting was devised in the 1980s. Subnetting separates networks into smaller subnets that can use more IP addresses, as long as a subnet mask is specified.

WHAT YOU **REALLY** NEED TO KNOW

- An IP address is 32 bits in size. In dotted decimal notation, every IP address is grouped into four 8-bit octets that are separated by decimal points.
- Each IP address is divided into two parts: network and host. The network portion is common to all nodes on a network, while the host portion is unique to a device.
- The network portion of an address indicates whether the device belongs to a Class A, B, C, D, or E network.
- Most IP addresses on a network belong to one of three network classes: A, B, or C.
- An IP address whose first octet is 1-126 belongs to a Class A network. All the IP addresses for devices on a Class A segment share the same first octet.
- An IP address whose first octet is 128-191 belongs to a Class B network. All the IP addresses for devices on a Class B segment share the first two octets.
- An IP address whose first octet is 192-223 belongs to a Class C network. All the IP addresses for devices on a Class C segment share the first three octets.
- **Subnetting** is the process of subdividing a single class of network into multiple, smaller networks. It results in a more efficient use of limited IP addresses.
- In subnetting, one of the address's octets is used to indicate how the network is subdivided. Rather than consisting simply of network and host information, a subnetted address consists of network, subnet, and host information.
- Devices in a subnetted network are assigned a **subnet mask**, a special 32-bit number that, combined with a device's IP address, tells the rest of the network the network class to which the device is attached.
- If a subnet mask is not specified, the default subnet mask for a Class A network is 255.0.0.0. For a Class B network, the default subnet mask is 255.255.0.0, and for a Class C network, the default subnet mask is 255.255.255.0.

OBJECTIVES ON THE JOB

Most organizations obtain a block of IP addresses from their Internet service provider. Typically, these are Class B or C IP addresses. ISPs often provide a limited number of addresses because they, too, have a limited number. To make better use of precious IP addresses, organizations often implement subnetting.

PRACTICE TEST QUESTIONS

1. **What is the default subnet mask for a Class B network?**
    a. 0.0.0.0
    b. 255.0.0.0
    c. 255.255.0.0
    d. 255.255.255.255

    ANSWER

2. **How many octets in their IP addresses do two devices on the same Class A network have in common?**
    a. one
    b. two
    c. three
    d. four

    ANSWER

3. **What is the main purpose for subnetting a network?**
    a. to create a more systematic way of tracking addresses on the network
    b. to more equitably allocate addresses to all devices on a network
    c. to make more efficient use of a limited number of addresses
    d. to make TCP/IP client and server configuration easier

    ANSWER

4. **What types of information are contained in the IP address of a device on a network that has not been subnetted?**
    a. host, subnet, and network
    b. host, server, and network
    c. protocol and network
    d. host and network

    ANSWER

5. **To what type of network does the default subnet mask 255.255.255.0 belong?**
    a. Class A
    b. Class B
    c. Class C
    d. Class D

    ANSWER

6. **For what purpose is a Class D address used?**
    a. broadcasting
    b. multicasting
    c. subnetting
    d. filtering

    ANSWER

7. **To what class of network does the device with an IP address of 192.34.56.109 belong?**
    a. Class A
    b. Class B
    c. Class C
    d. Class D

    ANSWER

USE OF PORT NUMBERS (HTTP, FTP, SMTP) AND PORT NUMBERS COMMONLY ASSIGNED TO A GIVEN SERVICE

UNDERSTANDING THE OBJECTIVE

Sockets depend on the assignment of port numbers to different processes. When one computer attempts to communicate with another, it alerts the socket address of the desired process on the other computer. The second computer recognizes the request and establishes the virtual circuit between the two to begin exchanging data.

WHAT YOU **REALLY** NEED TO KNOW

- ◆ A **socket** is a logical address assigned to a specific process running on a host computer. It forms a virtual connection between the host and client.
- ◆ A **port** is a number assigned to a process running on a host. Port numbers can have any value. Some software programs that choose their own port numbers by default.
- ◆ The socket's address is a combination of the host computer's IP address and the port number associated with a process. For example, the Telnet service on a Web server with an IP address of 10.43.3.87 might have a socket address of 10.43.3.87:23, where 23 is the standard port number for the Telnet service.
- ◆ A port number is expressed as a number following a colon that follows an IP address. The port number is not considered an additional octet in the socket address.
- ◆ The default port numbers for commonly used TCP/IP services generally have values lower than 255.
- ◆ Default port numbers for common services are as follows: Telnet - 23, HTTP - 80, FTP - 20 for data transfer and 21 for commands, SMTP - 25, POP3 - 101.
- ◆ The use of port numbers simplifies TCP/IP communications. When a client requests communications with a server and specifies port 23, for example, the server knows immediately that the client wants a Telnet session. No extra data exchange is necessary to define the session type, and the server can initiate the Telnet service without delay. The server connects to the client's Telnet port, which by default is also port 23, and establishes a virtual circuit.
- ◆ Port numbers can be configured through software. Most servers maintain a text-based file of port numbers and their associated services, which is editable. Changing a default port number is not usually a good idea, though, because it goes against the standard. However, some network administrators who are preoccupied with security may change their servers' port numbers in an attempt to confuse potential hackers.

OBJECTIVES ON THE JOB

You most often use port numbers when networking with the Internet. For example, if you install Web server software, you must identify some ports on that server. You can then leave ports at their defaults (for example, port 80 for the HTTP server) or change them to another number not already reserved by a process.

PRACTICE TEST QUESTIONS

1. Which of the following two port numbers are used for FTP?
    a. 20
    b. 21
    c. 22
    d. 23
    e. 25

ANSWER

2. Which of the following is a valid port number for HTTP?
    a. 80
    b. 800
    c. 808
    d. 888
    e. any of the above

ANSWER

3. The socket address 204.113.19.80:23 probably belongs to which of the following services?
    a. FTP
    b. HTTP
    c. SNMP
    d. Telnet
    e. TRACERT

ANSWER

4. In which of the following situations does it make sense to use a port number other than the default assigned by the software?
    a. when configuring an FTP server for users of freeware to download a patch
    b. when configuring a Web server that hosts an online clothing store
    c. when configuring an FTP server for employees within an organization to download their payroll information
    d. when configuring the SNMP interface on a server inside an organization's firewall

ANSWER

5. A socket allows two computers to establish what kind of circuit?
    a. virtual
    b. closed
    c. transitory
    d. application

ANSWER

6. Which of the following processes probably uses the socket address 135.67.99.118:80?
    a. HTTP
    b. Telnet
    c. FTP
    d. SNMP
    e. TRACERT

ANSWER

7. How many ports can be assigned on one server?
    a. only one
    b. no more than 10
    c. no more than 100
    d. There is no limit.

ANSWER

DEFINITION OF IP PROXY AND WHY IT IS USED

UNDERSTANDING THE OBJECTIVE

A proxy service is one that acts on behalf of another service. Typically, a proxy server is used in networking at the border between an internal LAN and an outside WAN (such as the Internet). A proxy server can filter outgoing and incoming requests for data (by URL, protocol type, or IP address, for example), cache frequently used Web pages, and obscure the specific IP addresses of devices on an internal LAN. These functions provide some measure of security, but a proxy server alone is not enough to secure a network. Proxy servers are typically used in conjunction with a firewall.

WHAT YOU **REALLY** NEED TO KNOW

- ◆ In networking, the term **proxy** means a device or service that acts on behalf of another device or service.
- ◆ Using a proxy for a server or network device can improve security and the performance of servers, or simplify addressing on a local network.
- ◆ Proxy servers situated between internal LAN clients and the Internet can improve performance by caching requests and saving them on local disks for future retrieval. This saves subsequent clients who request the same data from having to connect to a remote host on the Internet, thus expediting the retrieval.
- ◆ A proxy device may determine what type of traffic can be exchanged between clients on an internal LAN and the Internet. The proxy may filter requests to the Internet, for example, or allow only specific IP addresses to send traffic through while denying transmission attempts from other IP addresses.
- ◆ A proxy server also acts as a way to obscure internal IP addresses. After a client sends its data to the proxy server, the proxy server repackages the data frames that make up the message so that, rather than the workstation's IP address being the source, the proxy server inserts its own IP address as the source.
- ◆ A proxy server may also allow or deny transmission requests depending on the type of protocol. For instance, a proxy server can prevent outside clients from reaching a server's FTP service, but allow outside clients to access its HTTP service.
- ◆ If a network uses a proxy server for Web access, each client's browser must be configured to point to the proxy server. All major Internet browser programs contain a space for the proxy server's IP address in their properties or preferences options.
- ◆ While proxy servers do provide some measure of security, they are usually placed on the network together with a firewall.

OBJECTIVES ON THE JOB

The IP proxy, or proxy server, is a critical component for many LANs that connect to the Internet. It is frequently used to improve the performance and security of Internet connectivity on behalf of clients behind a firewall. To use a proxy server, clients must be configured to point to the server. This is accomplished by entering a parameter into the client's Web browser. All network operating systems can supply some type of proxy server software, either as part of their program or as an add-on program.

PRACTICE TEST QUESTIONS

1. **How does a proxy server improve Web performance for clients on a private LAN?**
   a. It can assist incoming data to clients because of its IP addressing proxy.
   b. It enables incoming requests to bypass the firewall.
   c. It can hold Web requests in a cache so that subsequent requests for those pages can be fulfilled locally.
   d. It enables users to save frequently used bookmarks in a shared location.

2. **Which two of the following can a proxy server use as criteria to filter incoming traffic?**
   a. IP address
   b. MAC address
   c. checksum
   d. protocol
   e. TTL

3. **Which of the following IP ranges is most likely to be found on a small, private network that uses a proxy server?**
   a. 10.09.1.1 – 10.10.10.10
   b. 124.89.33.1 – 124.89.33.230
   c. 222.45.112.1 – 222.45.113.1
   d. 188.30.10.1 – 188.30.10.10

4. **Which of the following is a disadvantage to Web caching?**
   a. It takes more time to initially retrieve the Web pages for the cache.
   b. It requires clients to configure an additional parameter in their Web browsers.
   c. It does not guarantee that the cached Web pages are the most current.
   d. It is difficult to configure.

5. **What device is usually found near a proxy server on the network?**
   a. modem
   b. firewall
   c. switch
   d. protocol analyzer

6. **If a client on a local LAN uses an IP address of 100.100.10.2 and the LAN's proxy server uses an IP address of 205.66.127.88, when the client connects to a remote host on the Internet, what will the remote host regard as the client's IP address?**
   a. 100.100.10.2
   b. 100.100.10.1
   c. 205.66.127.1
   d. 205.66.127.88

7. **Where in Netscape Navigator could you enter the IP address of a proxy server?**
   a. Edit – Preferences – Advanced – Proxies
   b. Tools – Options – Proxies
   c. Tools – Options – Servers – Proxy
   d. Edit – Preferences – Advanced – Cache

ANSWER

ANSWER

ANSWER

ANSWER

ANSWER

ANSWER

ANSWER

THE IDENTITY OF NORMAL CONFIGURATION PARAMETERS FOR A WORKSTATION, INCLUDING IP ADDRESSES, DNS, DEFAULT GATEWAY, IP PROXY CONFIGURATION, WINS, DHCP, HOST NAME, AND INTERNET DOMAIN NAME

UNDERSTANDING THE OBJECTIVE

Every node on a TCP/IP network refers to parameters to send and receive data from other nodes. The most important parameters include the IP address, DNS server, and default gateway. If DHCP is used, it assigns at least an IP address to each client.

WHAT YOU **REALLY** NEED TO KNOW

◆ All nodes on a TCP/IP network have a unique IP address. The IP address, which resides at the Network layer of the OSI model, helps the network determine the source and destination of data.

◆ Domain Name System (DNS) assigns host names based on an international hierarchy of names. On a TCP/IP network, a DNS server translates domain names into IP addresses.

◆ Before a node on a TCP/IP network can exchange data with a node that has a host and domain name, the node must contain the name or IP address of the DNS server on the DNS Configuration tab of the TCP/IP Properties dialog box.

◆ A default gateway interprets outbound and inbound requests between an internal LAN and other subnets or networks. Default gateways are typically interfaces on routers, which are assigned a unique IP address. To communicate beyond their subnet, nodes must specify their default gateway in their TCP/IP configuration.

◆ An IP proxy is a server or device that acts as an intermediary between an internal and external LAN to filter requests, cache Web pages, or prevent unauthorized access to a network. If an IP proxy server is used, it must be specified in the client software.

◆ WINS translates NetBIOS names into IP addresses, and is only used on NetBIOS networks. If WINS is used, the IP address of the WINS server must be specified on the WINS Configuration tab of the clients' TCP/IP Properties dialog box.

◆ DHCP automatically assigns IP addresses to clients on a TCP/IP network. To use DHCP, select "Obtain IP address automatically" on the IP Address tab of the clients' TCP/IP Properties dialog box.

◆ If DHCP is used, you do not have to identify the IP address or subnet mask on the client.

◆ A host name is the unique name of a TCP/IP node. You can specify it on the DNS Configuration tab of the TCP/IP Properties dialog box.

◆ A domain name is the name assigned to a group of hosts on the same network. Specify the domain name to which a client belongs on the DNS Configuration tab of the TCP/IP Properties dialog box.

OBJECTIVES ON THE JOB

When configuring or troubleshooting clients on a network, you must know the TCP/IP parameters each client should specify. Because many of the TCP/IP settings are entered manually, human error can prevent connectivity. For the same reason, end users should not be allowed to access TCP/IP settings.

PRACTICE TEST QUESTIONS

1. **Which of the following settings allows a client on a TCP/IP network to communicate with hosts on the Internet?**
   - a. DHCP
   - b. proxy server
   - c. firewall
   - d. default gateway

ANSWER

2. **Which of the following settings enables a TCP/IP client to use DHCP?**
   - a. WINS server specification
   - b. DNS server specification
   - c. "Obtain IP address automatically" selected
   - d. default gateway specification

ANSWER

3. **If a workstation belongs to a Class C network, what should its default subnet mask be?**
   - a. 255.0.0.0
   - b. 255.255.0.0
   - c. 255.255.255.0
   - d. 255.255.255.255

ANSWER

4. **Which of the following is a fully qualified host name?**
   - a. Tester
   - b. Tester.angle.com
   - c. Tester@angle.com
   - d. tester.com

ANSWER

5. **How can an organization reserve a domain name?**
   - a. by entering it into their DNS server's etc/hosts file
   - b. by listing it with an Internet directory service
   - c. by purchasing the rights to the domain via the U.S. Copyright office
   - d. by registering it with InterNIC

ANSWER

6. **What is the function of a WINS server?**
   - a. translates NetBIOS names into IP addresses
   - b. translates TCP/IP host names into IP addresses
   - c. translates domain names into IP addresses
   - d. translates MAC addresses into IP addresses

ANSWER

7. **Which two of the following can be specified in the TCP/IP Properties – IP Address tab?**
   - a. whether the client uses WINS
   - b. whether the client uses DHCP
   - c. the client's subnet mask
   - d. the address of the client's default gateway
   - e. the client's host name

ANSWER

7.1 Explain how and when to use TCP/IP utilities to test, validate, and troubleshoot IP connectivity

ARP AND TELNET

UNDERSTANDING THE OBJECTIVE

ARP is a utility that can obtain the MAC address of a device on a TCP/IP network based on its IP address. ARP broadcasts a packet containing the IP address to all nodes on the network, and the machine whose IP address matches responds with its MAC address. Telnet is a popular terminal emulation utility that enables clients to log on to TCP/IP hosts and perform tasks as if the user were sitting at the device's console.

WHAT YOU **REALLY** NEED TO KNOW

◆ **Address Resolution Protocol (ARP)** is a TCP/IP protocol that translates IP addresses into MAC (physical) addresses.

◆ ARP accomplishes this translation by broadcasting a packet to the entire network. This packet contains the IP address of the host for which the MAC address needs to be known. When the host whose IP address is being broadcast receives the packet, it responds. Other hosts on the network ignore the broadcast.

◆ An IP address is a Network layer address while a MAC address is a Data Link layer address. Every device on a network must have a MAC address, which is hard-coded into the device's network interface. If a host needs to communicate on a TCP/IP network, it must also have an IP address.

◆ Hosts often keep a cache of ARP results, which enable them to respond more quickly to ARP requests (this works as long as IP addresses don't often change). Bridges depend on ARP to help them direct packets to the correct recipient.

◆ **Telnet** is a terminal emulation program that facilitates connections between hosts on a TCP/IP network. Prior to the World Wide Web, Telnet provided the primary means of connecting to other hosts over the Internet.

◆ You can initiate a Telnet session simply by typing **telnet Y**, where Y is the host name or IP address of the remote host. Many options can be used in conjunction with the Telnet command, including an echo function, flow control, and the selection of full- or half-duplex communication.

◆ Connecting to a host through Telnet requires an authorized log-on ID and password. Telnet is a common way to send commands to a server or network device. Routers, for example, can be controlled and managed remotely using the telnet command.

◆ Telnet relies on TCP; thus, it is a connection-oriented service.

◆ The Telnet service uses port 23 by default.

OBJECTIVES ON THE JOB

Telnet is the primary method of connecting to network devices such as routers. It is quick and efficient, but does not come with a GUI interface. For this reason, if you are charged with managing routers and other devices, you should memorize the Telnet command options and syntax.

PRACTICE TEST QUESTIONS

1. **What type of transmission does ARP use to find a host with a specific IP address?**
   - a. multicast
   - b. unicast
   - c. broadcast
   - d. loopback

   ANSWER

2. **Which of the following devices could not be controlled through the Telnet utility?**
   - a. router
   - b. DOS client
   - c. UNIX server
   - d. modem

   ANSWER

3. **What port does the Telnet utility use by default?**
   - a. 23
   - b. 21
   - c. 20
   - d. 25

   ANSWER

4. **What kind of information will an ARP command return?**
   - a. an IP address
   - b. a socket address
   - c. an IPX address
   - d. a MAC address

   ANSWER

5. **Which two of the following utilities allow you to view the directory contents on a remote host, given the necessary authority?**
   - a. PING
   - b. TRACERT
   - c. NETSTAT
   - d. Telnet
   - e. FTP

   ANSWER

6. **What do network hosts do to improve the speed of ARP responses?**
   - a. hold ARP tables in cache
   - b. keep ARP numbers in their TCP/IP configuration
   - c. reassign MAC addresses if a response is not received quickly enough
   - d. issue multiple broadcasts to ensure prompt responses

   ANSWER

7. **Which of the following is a good use for the Telnet utility?**
   - a. to browse the contents of an online store
   - b. to assess network performance between hosts on the Internet
   - c. to send commands to a router
   - d. to reconfigure a client whose TCP/IP stack has been damaged

   ANSWER

7.1
cont.
Explain how and when to use TCP/IP utilities to test, validate, and troubleshoot IP connectivity

NBTSTAT, TRACERT, AND NETSTAT

UNDERSTANDING THE OBJECTIVE

NBTSTAT is a utility that reveals the NetBIOS names and status of connected devices running NetBIOS over TCP/IP (NBT). NETSTAT is a similar utility, but provides information about all connected TCP/IP hosts, including the connections' port numbers and status. TRACERT is a utility that sends a packet to a specified host and retrieves information on the path the packet took to reach the host.

WHAT YOU **REALLY** NEED TO KNOW

◆ **NBTSTAT** displays information about connected devices running NetBIOS over TCP/IP (NBT). Because it discovers NetBIOS information, NBTSTAT is useful only on Windows-based networks.

◆ NBTSTAT can be used with several parameters to discover, for example, the workgroup and domain to which the NetBIOS machine belongs, MAC addresses, IP addresses, and sessions with connected hosts.

◆ NBTSTAT is most commonly used with the following syntax to determine the NetBIOS name of a machine: **NBTSTAT —a X** (where X is the machine's IP address).

◆ **TRACERT** (or TRACEROUTE on UNIX systems) is a TCP/IP utility that traces the path of a packet from the originating host to another host. In its simplest form, it displays the number of router hops the packet traverses, those routers' addresses, and how long the packet took to go from one router to the next.

◆ TRACERT is most useful for determining where network bottlenecks are occurring. It also indicates whether a host is unreachable.

◆ The most commonly used expression of the TRACERT command is **tracert Y**, where Y is the IP address or host name of a system.

◆ **NETSTAT** is a utility that displays specifics about active inbound and outbound TCP/IP connections on a host. When used in its most basic form, NETSTAT displays the address (or host name) of connected systems, and the connected port, the type of Transport layer protocol in use, and the connection status.

◆ NETSTAT can be used with numerous parameters that supply more information about a host's connections, including statistics for network interfaces and routing tables for active connections.

◆ NETSTAT helps to determine how and where a host is connected. It can also show whether unauthorized connections are active, aiding in the discovery of hack attempts.

OBJECTIVES ON THE JOB

NBTSTAT, NETSTAT, and TRACERT are important utilities included with the TCP/IP software provided with every modern operating system. Although many software developers have created updated versions of these utilities, they are so easy to use that many network administrators don't bother with newer, modified versions.

PRACTICE TEST QUESTIONS

1. Which two of the following can reveal the time it takes a packet to reach a host?
   - a. Telnet
   - b. PING
   - c. TRACERT
   - d. NETSTAT
   - e. NBTSTAT

   ANSWER

2. Which of the following can reveal hackers connected to a TCP/IP host?
   - a. PING
   - b. Telnet
   - c. TRACERT
   - d. NETSTAT

   ANSWER

3. Which of the following can reveal the number of router hops a packet has taken on its way to a remote host?
   - a. NETSTAT
   - b. PING
   - c. TRACERT
   - d. Telnet

   ANSWER

4. If you are working on the help desk when a user calls and complains about slow connection times to a particular Web site, what utility would you recommend to locate the performance problem?
   - a. SNMP
   - b. NETSTAT
   - c. NBTSTAT
   - d. TRACERT

   ANSWER

5. What parameter should be used with the NBTSTAT command when attempting to determine the NetBIOS name of a machine whose IP address you know?
   - a. -a
   - b. -s
   - c. -i
   - d. -l

   ANSWER

6. If you are logged on to the Internet and have retrieved the *www.yahoo.com* Web site, then want to determine what port on your machine is being used to connect to the Web site, what utility should you use?
   - a. NBTSTAT
   - b. NETSTAT
   - c. Telnet
   - d. TRACERT

   ANSWER

7. Which two of the following utilities can easily show whether an IP gateway to the Internet is down?
   - a. TRACERT
   - b. PING
   - c. NETSTAT
   - d. NBTSTAT
   - e. SMTP

   ANSWER

OBJECTIVES

7.1
cont. Explain how and when to use TCP/IP utilities to test, validate, and troubleshoot IP connectivity

IPCONFIG/WINIPCFG

UNDERSTANDING THE OBJECTIVE

When run from the MS DOS prompt on a Windows NT machine, IPCONFIG displays the IP address, subnet mask, and default gateway address. When run from the MS DOS prompt on a Windows 9x machine, WINIPCFG displays the workstation's MAC address, IP address, subnet mask, and default gateway in the IP Configuration dialog box.

WHAT YOU **REALLY** NEED TO KNOW

◆ **IPCONFIG** is a utility that comes with the Windows NT operating system. When run from a machine's MS DOS prompt, it displays the TCP/IP configuration information.

◆ In its simplest form, IPCONFIG displays only the IP address, subnet mask, and default gateway for each adapter bound to TCP/IP.

◆ To display all the current TCP/IP configuration values, including the IP address, subnet mask, default gateway, and WINS and DNS configuration, use the following command: `ipconfig /all`.

◆ `ipconfig /?` displays a help message describing use of the IPCONFIG utility.

◆ On systems that use DHCP, you can use the /release or /renew options with IPCONFIG to release the IP address of a network adapter.

◆ **WINIPCFG** utility, when run from the MS DOS prompt, displays TCP/IP settings on Windows 9x workstations.

◆ In its simplest form, WINIPCFG displays the workstation's MAC address, IP address, subnet mask, and default gateway in the IP Configuration dialog box.

◆ WINIPCFG can be used with many different switches to reveal more information about a workstation's TCP/IP settings.

◆ The `winipcfg /?` displays a help message describing the use of the WINIPCFG utility.

◆ For more information about TCP/IP settings on a Windows 9x workstation, click the `More Info` button in the lower-right corner of the IP Configuration dialog box. Other settings you can view include DHCP server IP address, node type, and NetBIOS ID.

◆ On systems that use DHCP, you can use the /release or /renew options with WINIPCFG to release the IP address of a network adapter.

◆ One caveat to using WINIPCFG is that if a user is connected to a network through dial-up networking using PPP, the DHCP lease dates will be incorrect.

OBJECTIVES ON THE JOB

IPCONFIG and WINIPCFG should be familiar to network technicians and even end users. Often, a help desk analyst will ask a user to type one of these commands (whichever is appropriate for their operating system) to determine basic TCP/IP information when a user is having connectivity problems. If a network uses DHCP, IPCONFIG and WINIPCFG are the methods through which the DHCP leases are released or renewed.

PRACTICE TEST QUESTIONS

1. Which two of the following can be displayed by typing `ipconfig` at the MS DOS prompt of a Windows NT 4.0 workstation?

    a. subnet mask

    b. NIC MAC address

    c. DHCP server address

    d. default gateway address

    ANSWER

2. Which command will display the DHCP server address for a Windows 98 workstation?

    a. `ipconfig /all`

    b. `ipconfig /?`

    c. `winipcfg /all`

    d. `winipcfg`

    ANSWER

3. A user calls and complains of receiving the following error message after trying unsuccessfully to log into the network: "This address in use by station AC:05:20:41:CC:2D." Once you find the Windows NT workstation with this MAC address, what do you do?

    a. Type `ipconfig /release` at the MS DOS prompt.

    b. Type `ipconfig /all` at the MS DOS prompt.

    c. Type `winipcfg /renew` at the MS DOS prompt.

    d. Type `winipcfg /all` at the MS DOS prompt.

    ANSWER

4. What command would you use to discover the NetBIOS ID of a Windows 98 workstation?

    a. `ipconfig /all`

    b. `winipcfg /all`

    c. `ipconfig /NB`

    d. `winipcfg /NB`

    ANSWER

5. How can you determine if a Windows 95 workstation is using DHCP?

    a. Use the winipcfg command at the MS DOS prompt.

    b. Choose Control Panel – Network – TCP/IP Properties, DHCP Settings tab.

    c. Choose Control Panel – Network – TCP/IP Properties, IP Address tab.

    d. Use the ipconfig /all command at the MS DOS prompt.

    ANSWER

6. What is the fastest way to view the IP address of a Windows NT workstation?

    a. Type `winipcfg` at the MS DOS prompt.

    b. Type `ping` 127.0.0.1 at the MS DOS prompt.

    c. Type `ipconfig` at the MS DOS prompt.

    d. Type `winipcfg /all` at the MS DOS prompt.

    ANSWER

7. If a Windows NT server has two NICs bound to the TCP/IP protocol, how many different subnet masks will be displayed when you type the `ipconfig /all` command?

    a. one

    b. two

    c. three

    d. none

    ANSWER

FTP

UNDERSTANDING THE OBJECTIVE

FTP is a well-known and frequently used protocol to transfer files between FTP hosts. It provides a simple way for users to download software and software patches from the Web. FTP can also assist in repairing damaged files or directory structures on remote hosts, modifying files, or determining whether hosts are responding. As with other TCP/IP utilities, FTP can be used from any node on the network to any other node, as long as both are running the TCP/IP protocol and the user has authorized access to connect.

WHAT YOU **REALLY** NEED TO KNOW

- ◆ **File Transfer Protocol (FTP)** is an Application layer protocol in the TCP/IP suite that enables a client and server to directly exchange data through a series of commands. FTP is often used to upload and download files over the Internet.

- ◆ Although FTP is a simple protocol, you can use it with many commands to control the way it sends and receives data.

- ◆ When the GUI interface to a host is inoperable, FTP can be used to send data to the host, make new files or directories, and retrieve information about the host's file structure. For example, FTP can help replace a damaged host file on a UNIX server so it can once again handle DNS queries.

- ◆ Although many FTP sites are anonymous, meaning they do not require a secure log-on, if FTP is being used for troubleshooting or file structure correction on a host, a secure connection should be required.

- ◆ FTP can also indicate whether a host is responding. If a user attempts to open an FTP channel with a malfunctioning system, the following error message appears: `unknown host Y`, where Y is the address or host name of the system.

- ◆ Following are some useful and common FTP commands: `open` attempts to create a connection with a host; `?` displays the list of commands available to the FTP utility; `ls` or `dir` lists the directories on the connected host; `cd` allows the connected user to change directories; `put` allows the user to copy files to the host while `get` allows the user to download files from the host; `close` closes the FTP connection.

- ◆ The FTP utility responds to commands with codes plus text, including the following: 125 - the connection has been established and a transfer of data can begin; 425 - FTP couldn't open the connection; 500 - the command was unrecognized (possibly a syntax error).

OBJECTIVES ON THE JOB

FTP is used most often when downloading software from the Internet. However, it can also be used within LANs and WANs to aid in troubleshooting. Using FTP, a network administrator can connect to a system with damaged files and copy new files or directories to that server. The response to the FTP commands can also provide clues to the problem with the server. Unlike PING and TRACERT, however, FTP does not provide much information about network problems. In fact, if a problem exists on the network between the local host and the remote host, FTP cannot establish a connection.

PRACTICE TEST QUESTIONS

1. **What command is used to initiate an FTP connection with a TCP/IP host?**
   a. login
   b. open
   c. connect
   d. mkcon

   ANSWER

2. **Which two of the following can be accomplished using the FTP utility?**
   a. Determine how many router packets have passed on their way to the host.
   b. Determine whether packets have been damaged on their way to or from the host.
   c. Append existing files on the host with additional data.
   d. Modify the IP address on a host.
   e. Rename files on the host.

   ANSWER

3. **What Transport layer protocol does FTP rely on?**
   a. FDP
   b. TCP
   c. UDP
   d. ARP

   ANSWER

4. **Which of the following commands, when used with the FTP utility, shows the contents of a directory?**
   a. mkdir
   b. dircon
   c. list
   d. ls

   ANSWER

5. **If the code 125 appears in response to a user's attempt to connect to a remote host, what has happened?**
   a. The user typed the command incorrectly.
   b. The host is not available.
   c. The network is experiencing excessive packet loss.
   d. The connection has been established.

   ANSWER

6. **Which of the following TCP/IP utilities is the best choice to use first to determine whether a router is down?**
   a. FTP
   b. SMTP
   c. PING
   d. HTTP
   e. TRACERT

   ANSWER

7. **What FTP command is used to terminate a connection with a host?**
   a. close
   b. end
   c. logout
   d. endcon

   ANSWER

7.1
cont. Explain how and when to use TCP/IP utilities to test, validate, and troubleshoot IP connectivity

PING

UNDERSTANDING THE OBJECTIVE

The PING command is one of the most commonly used troubleshooting techniques. PING sends at least one packet to the specified host and waits for a response. If there is no response, you can assume that the device or its TCP/IP stack is not functioning properly. If there is a response, information about the packets' return, such as the time it took them to reach the host, helps in discovering network performance problems.

WHAT YOU **REALLY** NEED TO KNOW

◆ **Packet Internet Groper (PING)** is a TCP/IP utility that sends a single packet to a specified address and waits for a response.

◆ PING is a powerful troubleshooting tool. It can help determine whether a network node is responding and at what point a connection is being lost or slowed down.

◆ PING assigns a sequence number and time stamp on the packets it sends. Thus, if the response from the device is positive, PING can also detect how long the packets took to return and whether any were damaged in transmission. This can be helpful in troubleshooting network performance problems.

◆ PING is often the first troubleshooting tool used when a client cannot communicate with a server or vice versa.

◆ The syntax of a simple PING command is `ping X`, where X is the IP address or host name of the device. If the host responds, the output contains the following message: `reply from X: bytes=32 time=100 ms TTL=252`, where X is the IP address or host name. The other numbers may vary.

◆ One of the first PING commands to try is `ping 127.0.0.1`. This IP address is reserved for the loopback address. Use this command to attempt to contact your own device's TCP/IP stack. If this command results in a negative response, chances are your TCP/IP protocol is either not installed or improperly installed.

◆ If the loopback PING test results in a positive response, the next devices to ping include the default IP gateway, the DNS server, or other critical devices on the network. Pinging different devices can uncover a network bottleneck.

◆ PING can be used with different options. For example, the `−f` parameter stands for "flood." Use it to send packets as fast as the receiving host can handle them, at least 100 per second, which can be useful for "stress testing" a system.

OBJECTIVES ON THE JOB

PING is perhaps the most useful and frequently used utility in the network technician's troubleshooting repertoire. In a situation where a client cannot access a server, PING can help determine where the problem is occurring. In most cases, sufficient information about a network bottleneck can be obtained from the simple PING command. However, in some cases, using one of the many PING parameters provides a necessary troubleshooting clue.

PRACTICE TEST QUESTIONS

1. **What Application layer TCP/IP protocol does PING use to request responses from devices?**
   a. SNMP
   b. SMTP
   c. ICMP
   d. RARP

ANSWER

2. **Which of the following is the loopback address?**
   a. 100.100.100.100
   b. 01.01.01.01
   c. 122.0.0.7
   d. 127.0.0.1

ANSWER

3. **What does TTL stand for?**
   a. time to live
   b. time to link
   c. transfer time load
   d. transfer time lost

ANSWER

4. **Which two of the following can a PING test indicate?**
   a. what type of device is being contacted
   b. whether a packet has been damaged in transit
   c. how a packet was damaged in transit
   d. how many routers a packet has to traverse on its way to a host
   e. how long it takes for a packet to reach a host

ANSWER

5. **Which of the following is cause for concern if detected from the response to a PING command?**
   a. fluctuating TTL values
   b. excessive damaged packets
   c. some dropped packets
   d. a different host name than that listed in the original PING command

ANSWER

6. **If a client on a private LAN cannot reach the www.microsoft.com Web page and the client's loopback PING test reflects a positive result, plus the client can reach *www.netscape.com*, what should logically be pinged next?**
   a. the LAN's gateway router
   b. the core Internet gateway
   c. the ISP's DNS server
   d. *www.microsoft.com*

ANSWER

7. **What Transport layer protocol does PING rely on?**
   a. TCP
   b. UDP
   c. ARP
   d. FTP

ANSWER

DISTINCTION BETWEEN PPP AND SLIP

UNDERSTANDING THE OBJECTIVE

PPP and SLIP are two communications protocols that enable hosts to exchange data without using a NIC. Typically, PPP or SLIP is used in the context of a dial-in user connecting to a remote access server. PPP is preferred over SLIP because it can accept both synchronous and asynchronous data streams, and is easier for clients to configure. Choose whether to use PPP or SLIP for a dial-up connection in the client's dial-up networking properties.

WHAT YOU **REALLY** NEED TO KNOW

◆ **Serial line Internet Protocol (SLIP)** and **Point-to-point Protocol (PPP)** are communications protocols that enable a workstation to connect to a server using a serial connection (in the case of dial-up networking, "serial connection" refers to a modem). Once connected via SLIP or PPP, a remote workstation can act as a client on the local LAN, with its modem and serial port serving the purpose of a NIC.

◆ Such protocols are necessary to transport Network layer traffic over serial interfaces, which belong to the Data Link layer of the OSI model. Both SLIP and PPP encapsulate higher-layer networking protocols in their lower-layer data frames.

◆ SLIP is a version of the protocol that can only carry IP packets, while PPP can carry many different types of Network layer packets, such as IPX or AppleTalk.

◆ Another difference between SLIP and PPP is that SLIP can only support asynchronous data transmission at the Physical layer, while PPP can support both asynchronous and synchronous transmission.

◆ **Asynchronous** refers to a communications method in which data being transmitted and received by nodes do not have to conform to any timing scheme. In asynchronous communications, a node can transmit at any time and the destination node has to accept the transmission as it comes.

◆ **Synchronous** refers to a communications method in which data being transmitted and received by nodes must conform to a timing scheme.

◆ PPP is the more popular communications protocol for dial-up connections to the Internet, primarily because it does not require as much configuration on the client as SLIP. When using the SLIP protocol, you typically have to specify the IP address for your client and server in your dial-up networking profile. But PPP can automatically obtain this information as it connects to the server. Because it is more difficult to configure, SLIP is rarely used on modern networks.

OBJECTIVES ON THE JOB

Although PPP and SLIP can be used for many types of communication, they are most often employed to connect dial-up workstations to a server, as in the case of an ISP subscriber logging on to the ISP's IP network. In this context, a network technician must understand how to select PPP or SLIP as the preferred type of connection in a client's dial-up networking configuration. On the server side, a network administrator might have to configure a server to accept SLIP or PPP connections, as when a company wants to allow its employees to dial into its network from home. Most companies use PPP rather than SLIP because it is more flexible and easier to configure.

PRACTICE TEST QUESTIONS

1. **What do the letters "SL" stand for in SLIP?**
   a. subnet line
   b. serial line
   c. sublayer link
   d. subnet layer

   ANSWER

2. **Which of the following can accept synchronous data transmission?**
   a. SLIP
   b. PPP
   c. DLC
   d. IP

   ANSWER

3. **Which of the following can support IPX transmission?**
   a. PPP
   b. SLIP
   c. DLC
   d. TCP

   ANSWER

4. **By what mechanism do SLIP and PPP enable Network layer data transmission over a serial interface?**
   a. segmentation
   b. padding
   c. flow control
   d. encapsulation

   ANSWER

5. **On a Windows 9x workstation, what options would you choose to select PPP as the remote networking communication protocol?**
   a. Control Panel – Modems – General
   b. Control Panel – Network Properties – Adapter
   c. Dial-Up Networking – Connection Properties – Server Type
   d. Control Panel – System Properties – Device Manager

   ANSWER

6. **Which of the following must you specify in the client software to connect to a server using SLIP?**
   a. the server's IP address
   b. the DHCP server address
   c. the network adapter type
   d. the network transmission speed

   ANSWER

7. **Which of the following is the most popular method of enabling network communications over dial-up links?**
   a. SLIP
   b. IPSEC
   c. PPP
   d. PPP2

   ANSWER

PURPOSE AND FUNCTION OF PPTP AND THE CONDITIONS UNDER WHICH IT IS USEFUL

UNDERSTANDING THE OBJECTIVE

PPTP is a method of connecting to a server, similar to PPP, that Microsoft devised in 1996. PPTP expands on PPP to support more sophisticated encapsulation, authentication, and encryption. PPTP, which runs on a Windows NT server, can enable a remote workstation to dial into an ISP and through the public network gain access to a private network over the Internet. PPTP is gradually being replaced by L2TP, a more standard and feature-rich protocol.

WHAT YOU **REALLY** NEED TO KNOW

- ◆ **Point-to-Point Tunneling Protocol (PPTP)** expands on PPP by encapsulating it, so that any type of PPP data can traverse the Internet masked as pure IP transmissions.
- ◆ PPTP supports the encryption, authentication, and LAN access services provided by RASs (remote access servers). But instead of users dialing in directly to an access server, they can dial into their ISP using PPTP and gain access to their corporate LAN over the Internet.
- ◆ The process of encapsulating one protocol to make it appear as another type of protocol is known as **tunneling**. Tunneling makes a protocol fit a type of network that it wouldn't normally fit.
- ◆ PPTP is available with Windows NT Server 4.0 and Windows NT Workstation 4.0 as part of RASs. You can purchase an upgrade from Microsoft to enable PPTP to work with the Windows 95 dial-up networking client. PPTP support is included in the Windows 98 operating system.
- ◆ **Layer 2 Forwarding (L2F)** is similar to PPTP. It is a Layer 2 protocol that provides tunneling for other protocols and can work PPP.
- ◆ The only differences between PPTP and L2F are the type of encryption each supports and the fact that while PPTP was developed by Microsoft, L2F was developed by Cisco Systems.
- ◆ One disadvantage of L2F compared to PPTP is that it requires special hardware on the host system, whereas PPTP works with any Windows NT server. On the other hand, L2F can encapsulate protocols to fit more than the IP format, unlike PPTP.
- ◆ Both PPTP and L2F, however, will gradually be replaced by a third type of tunneling protocol called **Layer 2 Tunneling Protocol (L2TP)**. L2TP was developed by a number of industry consortia.

OBJECTIVES ON THE JOB

If your organization allows its users to send secure data over the Internet, you should understand PPTP and the more recent protocols similar to PPTP, including L2TP. These form the basis for creating virtual private networks (VPNs) over the Internet.

PRACTICE TEST QUESTIONS

1. Which two of the following can encapsulate multiple types of Network layer protocols?
   - a. PPTP
   - b. SLIP
   - c. L2F
   - d. PPP
   - e. UDP

   ANSWER

2. Which two of the following can provide security for transmissions across the Internet?
   - a. PPP
   - b. TCP
   - c. PPTP
   - d. SLIP
   - e. L2TP

   ANSWER

3. What type of operating system can be used to supply a PPTP server?
   - a. Banyan VINES
   - b. Novell NetWare 3.12 or higher
   - c. Windows NT Server 4.0 or higher
   - d. Novell NetWare 4.11 or higher

   ANSWER

4. Which of the following is a disadvantage of L2F compared to PPTP?
   - a. L2F requires special hardware while PPTP does not.
   - b. L2F is much more difficult to configure.
   - c. L2F is only supported in the UNIX environment.
   - d. L2F servers are limited to eight simultaneous connections.

   ANSWER

5. What is one significant advantage of using VPNs?
   - a. They are less expensive than dedicated lines.
   - b. They are easier to configure than other types of WANs.
   - c. They can reach more remote locations than other types of WANs.
   - d. They can run multiple Network layer protocols.

   ANSWER

6. What is one significant concern about using VPNs?
   - a. Once they are established, they are difficult to expand.
   - b. Since they use public transmission facilities, data must be carefully secured.
   - c. They are dependent on outside telecommunications carriers who may be unreliable.
   - d. They cannot transmit connectionless protocols.

   ANSWER

7. What does "L2" in L2F stand for?
   - a. link to
   - b. layer 2
   - c. lease to
   - d. logical link

   ANSWER

THE ATTRIBUTES, ADVANTAGES, AND DISADVANTAGES OF ISDN

UNDERSTANDING THE OBJECTIVE

ISDN was developed in the mid–1980s to send digital data over public transmission lines. ISDN can be a dial-up connection or dedicated solution. It has been a popular choice for individuals and small businesses who want a faster and more secure connection than PSTN can offer.

WHAT YOU **REALLY** NEED TO KNOW

- ◆ **Integrated Services Digital Network (ISDN)** is a standard established by the International Telecommunications Union (ITU) for transmitting data over digital lines.
- ◆ ISDN is a circuit-switched technology that uses the telephone carrier's lines and dial-up connections, like PSTN. Unlike PSTN, ISDN travels exclusively over digital connections and can carry data and voice simultaneously.
- ◆ All ISDN connections are based on two types of channels: B channels and D channels.
- ◆ The **B channel** is the bearer channel that uses circuit-switching techniques to carry voice, video, audio, and other types of data over the ISDN connection. A single B channel has a maximum throughput of 56 Kbps. The number of B channels in a single ISDN connection can vary.
- ◆ The **D channel** is the data channel that uses packet switching techniques to carry information about the call, such as session initiation and termination signals, caller identity, call forwarding, and conference calling signals.
- ◆ A single D channel has a maximum throughput of 16 Kbps.
- ◆ North American users commonly use two types of ISDN connections: Basic Rate ISDN (BRI) or Primary Rate ISDN (PRI).
- ◆ **BRI** uses two B channels and one D channel, as summarized with the following notation: 2B+D. The two B channels are treated as separate connections by the network, and can carry voice and data or two data streams simultaneously and separately.
- ◆ Through a process called **bonding**, two 64-Kbps B channels can be combined to achieve an effective throughput of 128 Kbps, the maximum throughput for BRI.
- ◆ **PRI** uses 23 B channels and one 64-Kbps D channel, as in the following notation: 23B+D. PRI is less commonly used by individual subscribers than BRI, but can be used by organizations needing more throughput. The separate B channels in a PRI link can carry voice and/or data independent of each other or bonded together.
- ◆ The maximum potential throughput for a PRI connection is 1.544 Mbps.

OBJECTIVES ON THE JOB

ISDN lines have been a popular choice for small businesses to receive moderately fast connections to the Internet. Due to their ability to transmit voice and data simultaneously, ISDN lines can also eliminate the need to pay for separate phone lines to support faxes, modems, and voice calls at one location.

PRACTICE TEST QUESTIONS

1. **How much throughput is optimally available through BRI?**
   a. 1.455 Mbps
   b. 56 Kbps
   c. 128 Kbps
   d. 768 Kbps

2. **Which of the following is an advantage of ISDN over PSTN?**
   a. It's less expensive.
   b. It provides greater throughput.
   c. It is easier to configure.
   d. It doesn't depend on public transmission lines.

3. **Which of the following is an advantage of DSL over BRI?**
   a. It provides greater throughput.
   b. It's easier to configure.
   c. It doesn't require any special hardware.
   d. It doesn't depend on public transmission lines.

4. **In relation to ISDN services, what does "2B+D" stand for?**
   a. two basic and one denominator
   b. basic, broadband, and digital
   c. two bearer and one data
   d. bearer, broadband, and digital

5. **What is the maximum throughput of one B channel?**
   a. 8 Kbps
   b. 16 Kbps
   c. 64 Kbps
   d. 128 Kbps

6. **What is the Physical layer difference between PSTN and ISDN?**
   a. ISDN uses all digital lines while PSTN may use analog lines.
   b. ISDN can encapsulate IP packets while PSTN cannot.
   c. ISDN uses Ethernet NICs while PSTN uses Token Ring NICs.
   d. ISDN lines can handle no more than 128 Kbps while PSTN lines can handle no more than 56 Kbps.

7. **In which of the following situations might ISDN be the best selection?**
   a. for a small nonprofit organization that needs a connection to the Internet to pick up mail every other day
   b. for a multinational insurance company that expects its salespeople to dial in each night from their hotel rooms
   c. for a large software development company that needs to transmit and receive programs all day and all night
   d. for a small, rural architectural firm that needs to pick up e-mail frequently and send and receive drawings

ANSWER

ANSWER

ANSWER

ANSWER

ANSWER

ANSWER

ANSWER

THE ATTRIBUTES, ADVANTAGES, AND DISADVANTAGES OF PSTN (POTS)

UNDERSTANDING THE OBJECTIVE

The PSTN (or POTS) is the original phone system constructed of copper wire in the early twentieth century. It has since been updated with fiber-optic, wireless, and other media capable of transmitting digital signals, but some of it can still transmit only analog signals. PSTN is most frequently used now for individual dial-up connections to an Internet Service Provider. Its maximum theoretical throughput is 56 Kbps.

WHAT YOU **REALLY** NEED TO KNOW

◆ **PSTN** stands for **Public Switched Telephone Network** and refers to the network of typical telephone lines that service most homes. PSTN may also be called **plain old telephone service (POTS)**.

◆ The PSTN was originally composed of analog lines and developed for voice needs. Now, though, most of the PSTN uses digital transmission through fiber-optic and copper twisted-pair cable, microwave, and satellite connections.

◆ A **dial-up** connection uses a PSTN or other line to access a remote server via modems at both the source and destination. A dial-up connection is only live when a user (or device) chooses to make the connection. In contrast, a **dedicated connection** is always live.

◆ The PSTN has two main disadvantages: it is slower than other types of connections and it cannot ensure the quality of the data transmitted.

◆ Currently PSTN modems advertise a connection speed of 56 Kbps. The 56-Kbps maximum is actually a *theoretical* threshold that assumes the connection between the initiator and the receiver is unfettered. Splitters, fax machines, or other devices that a modem connection traverses between the sender and receiver reduce the throughput.

◆ The number of telecommunication carrier Points of Presence (POPs) through which a PSTN connection travels also reduces throughput.

◆ The PSTN uses **circuit switching**, a means of transmitting data between two nodes with a dedicated point-to-point connection. Circuit switching, and therefore the PSTN, offers only marginal security.

◆ Since it is a public network, the PSTN presents many points at which communications can be intercepted and interpreted on its path from sender to receiver. To secure PSTN transmissions, you must encrypt data before it is sent.

OBJECTIVES ON THE JOB

The typical modern user of a PSTN connection is a home Internet user who needs to send and receive e-mail and occasionally surf the Web. If you work on a help desk for an ISP, for example, you should be very familiar with how PSTN connections are established through dial-up networking on Windows clients. For troubleshooting purposes, you should also understand how fluctuations in carrier traffic affect PSTN connections. In addition, you should be aware of how multiple carrier locations between a client and host can detrimentally affect the connection's throughput and quality.

PRACTICE TEST QUESTIONS

1. Which of the following is the most secure means of transmitting data (without using data encryption)?
   a. satellite
   b. cellular dial-up
   c. PSTN
   d. T1

   ANSWER

2. In the context of the PSTN, what does POP stand for?
   a. post office protocol
   b. point of purchase
   c. point of presence
   d. public over private

   ANSWER

3. Which of the following may use analog lines?
   a. PSTN
   b. ISDN
   c. T1
   d. SONET

   ANSWER

4. Which of the following transmission methods does PSTN use?
   a. circuit switching
   b. packet switching
   c. OSPF routing
   d. BGP routing

   ANSWER

5. What is the maximum theoretical throughput that can currently be obtained over a PSTN connection?
   a. 16 Kbps
   b. 56 Kbps
   c. 128 Kbps
   d. 768 Kbps

   ANSWER

6. Which of the following may decrease the throughput available to a PSTN connection?
   a. modem
   b. static electricity
   c. EMI
   d. splitter

   ANSWER

7. What medium was used to create the original PSTN?
   a. fiber-optic cable
   b. satellite transmissions
   c. copper wire
   d. aluminum wire

   ANSWER

OBJECTIVES

8.2 Specify elements of Dial-Up Networking

THE MODEM CONFIGURATION PARAMETERS THAT MUST BE SET, INCLUDING SERIAL PORT IRQ, I/O ADDRESS, AND MAXIMUM PORT SPEED

UNDERSTANDING THE OBJECTIVE

If a modem is external and connects to a PC through its serial port, the serial (COM) port must have unique and appropriate IRQ, I/O address, and memory address range, just as with a NIC. A modem's maximum port speed can be configured through the operating system, though setting the maximum port speed to 112,000 bps, for example, will not allow the modem to run faster than the threshold of 57,600 bps.

WHAT YOU **REALLY** NEED TO KNOW

- ◆ The word **modem** is derived from its function as a MODulator/DEModulator. A modem converts a computer's digital pulses into analog signals for the PSTN (because not all of the PSTN is necessarily capable of digital transmission), then converts the analog signals back into digital pulses at the receiving computer's end.

- ◆ On modern PCs, modems are typically connected to the machine's system board through an expansion slot. However, if an external modem is used, it uses a standard RS-232 cable to connect to the PC's serial port. Almost all PCs have serial ports and can accept this type of modem.

- ◆ You can specify many settings necessary for successful modem communication on a Windows 9x client, either by choosing Control Panel – System – Device Manager – Modem, or Control Panel – Modems. Click the Properties button on the General tab to change modem characteristics such as the maximum transmission speed.

- ◆ You can change port settings on the Diagnostics tab of the Modems Properties dialog box on a Windows 9x computer. Often the default values assigned when the modem is installed are correct. However, the ISP a user dials might prefer different port settings (including parity, data bits, and stop bits).

- ◆ To use FIFO buffers, a modem must have a 16550 UART compatible chip. The higher the buffer settings, the faster data will be transmitted; however, less data correction will be employed.

- ◆ The IRQ, I/O base address, and memory range for a modem on a modern PC is likely to be assigned by the BIOS. IRQ 4 is commonly assigned to the COM1 or COM3 serial ports, which are used for modem connections.

- ◆ A modem's speed is measured in bits per seconds (older, slower modems measured speed in baud per second). The fastest modem transmission possible with current technology is 56 Kbps.

OBJECTIVES ON THE JOB

As with NICs, modems require a unique IRQ, base I/O address, and memory address range, as well as the proper device drivers and the proper hardware installation. Modem device drivers change from time to time, so you should check the modem manufacturer's Web site to find out whether a driver has been updated.

PRACTICE TEST QUESTIONS

1. What type of chip is needed for a modem to support FIFO buffering?
   a. 3000 UART or better
   b. 10000 UART or better
   c. 16550 UART or better
   d. 56000 UART

   ANSWER

2. Which of the following IRQs is often used for the COM1 port?
   a. 1
   b. 4
   c. 6
   d. 10

   ANSWER

3. What kind of cable is used to connect an external modem to a PC?
   a. RS-32
   b. RJ-45
   c. RS-232
   d. RJ-04

   ANSWER

4. Where does the term "modem" originate?
   a. modulator/demodulator
   b. modicum/demitasse
   c. modify/demodify
   d. moderate/demoderate

   ANSWER

5. How do most modern PCs connect to a modem?
   a. serial port
   b. parallel port
   c. RJ-45 plug
   d. expansion slot

   ANSWER

6. If a user sets her modem's maximum port speed to 115,200 bps, what is the maximum speed at which she will connect to her ISP?
   a. 115,200 bps
   b. 115,200 Kbps
   c. 111,000 bps
   d. 57,600 bps

   ANSWER

7. Who or what determines the proper connection preferences, including data bits and parity bit, for a modem connection?
   a. the server
   b. the modem manufacturer
   c. the client
   d. the modem's device drivers

   ANSWER

REQUIREMENTS FOR A REMOTE CONNECTION

UNDERSTANDING THE OBJECTIVE

Many utilities, software programs, protocols, and hardware combine to establish a remote connection. The modem on the client must be properly installed and configured. For Windows 9x clients, the dial–up networking (DUN) software must be installed; then the DUN software and the TCP/IP protocol must be bound to both TCP/IP and the Client for Microsoft Networks. Beyond that, the access provider determines settings for the dial–up networking connection.

WHAT YOU **REALLY** NEED TO KNOW

◆ The most common type of remote access involves dial-up networking. **Dial-up networking (DUN)** typically refers to a modem connection to a server through the PSTN. It is also the name of the utility that Microsoft provides with its operating systems to achieve this type of connectivity. To use dial-up networking successfully, the modem and the networking client software must be properly installed and configured.

◆ To connect to a remote access server from a Windows 9x workstation, the Client for Microsoft Networks and the TCP/IP protocol must be installed. Also, the dial-up networking utility must be installed and bound to TCP/IP and the Client for Microsoft Networks.

◆ A DUN connection (or profile) needs to be established through Dial-Up Networking – Make a new connection. This option guides the user through steps to identify the new connection.

◆ Settings you can identify through the DUN connection properties include the server type, network protocols that will be transmitted, whether data must be encrypted, IP address, and default gateway.

◆ If incomplete or incorrect information is entered into this configuration, a session can be established, but the client might be unable to send or receive data. If the client is dialing into an ISP's server, the ISP must provide this information.

◆ A **remote access server** is a combination of software and hardware that provides a central access point for multiple users to dial into a LAN or WAN.

◆ Once connected to the remote access server, the LAN treats the direct-dial remote client like any other client on the LAN. The computer dialing into the LAN becomes a **remote node** on the network.

◆ Many different software and hardware combinations can provide remote connectivity. The simplest dial-in server is Windows NT Server's **Remote Access Service (RAS)**.

OBJECTIVES ON THE JOB

Knowing how to establish and troubleshoot a dial–up networking connection is a basic skill related to knowing how to establish and troubleshoot any other connection to the LAN. The key things to verify include a proper Physical layer connection, appropriate protocols and clients and how they are bound to the hardware and dial–up networking software, and address settings.

PRACTICE TEST QUESTIONS

1. Which of the following must be specified by an ISP for its clients to establish DUN connections to its remote access server?
    a. default gateway address
    b. TCP/IP version
    c. maximum modem port speed
    d. modem IRQ

    ANSWER

2. In order for a Windows 9x machine to send and receive data via DUN, to which two of the following should the DUN software be bound?
    a. TCP/IP
    b. IPX/SPX
    c. Client for Novell Networks
    d. Client for Microsoft Networks
    e. network adapter

    ANSWER

3. What option would you choose to create a DUN connection?
    a. Control Panel – Modems – Connections
    b. Control Panel – Modems – General
    c. Dial-Up Networking – Make a new connection
    d. Dial-Up Networking – Properties

    ANSWER

4. What does RAS stand for?
    a. remote authentication service
    b. remote access server
    c. remote accounting service
    d. remote addressing server

    ANSWER

5. What option would you choose to indicate that PPP is being used for a dial-up connection?
    a. Control Panel – Modems – General – Properties
    b. Dial-Up Networking – Connection Properties – Server Type
    c. Control Panel – System – Device Manager
    d. Control Panel – Network – Dial-Up Adapter – Advanced

    ANSWER

6. What transmission media does DUN typically use?
    a. PSTN
    b. ISDN
    c. T1
    d. T3

    ANSWER

7. Which two of the following protocols can be supported through the Windows DUN connection?
    a. SNA
    b. IPX
    c. IP
    d. DLC
    e. AppleTalk

    ANSWER

SELECTION OF A SECURITY MODEL (USER AND SHARE LEVEL)

UNDERSTANDING THE OBJECTIVE

Providing user-level security and share-level security are two different techniques that enable users to access shared resources on a network. Share-level security, which is simpler and less secure, assigns all users certain rights to resources. User-level security, which is more difficult to administer but more secure, assigns users and groups different rights to resources.

WHAT YOU **REALLY** NEED TO KNOW

◆ Security models can be divided into two types: share-level and user-level security.

◆ In **share-level security**, resources such as drives, files, printers, or CD-ROMs that are attached to a workstation or server are assigned passwords. Access to these resources may be read-only or full access (which includes read, erase, modify, and access rights). Either type of access can be assigned a password.

◆ Share-level security is simple to administer, but not very secure.

◆ Share-level security is the method of choice in peer-to-peer networks such as those that depend on the Windows for Workgroups operating system.

◆ In **user-level security**, access to resources is assigned according to users or groups of users. A centralized server authorizes users to access the network and then validates users' permission to access resources.

◆ User-level security, when used correctly, is much more secure than share-level security. Windows NT Server, NetWare, and UNIX all depend on user-level security.

◆ With user-level security, each user has a login ID (or account) and password with which to access the central server.

◆ User-level security also enables a network administrator to set up groups of users. Groups contain users that may require access to the same types of resources.

◆ Administering rights for groups is easier than administering rights for many users.

◆ On workstations that use one of the Windows operating systems, a user can establish share-level or user-level security to enable other networked workstations to access his or her files or printers. To accomplish this, select the File and Print Sharing option on the Configuration tab of the Network Properties dialog box. Then select whether to provide user-level or share-level access to these resources on the Access Control tab of the Network Properties dialog box.

OBJECTIVES ON THE JOB

Most modern networks are based on network operating systems such as Windows NT Server, NetWare, or UNIX, which use the user-level security technique. To work within the user-level security model, you should understand the benefits of groups, how each network operating system assigns groups, and how groups can be used together to fine-tune each users' rights to resources.

PRACTICE TEST QUESTIONS

1. **In which of the following situations is the share-level security model most appropriate?**
   - a. a nonprofit with three workstations running Windows for Workgroups 3.11
   - b. a multinational insurance company with 3,000 workstations running Windows 2000
   - c. a Midwest shipping company with 15 workstations located in 15 different cities running Novell NetWare version 4.11
   - d. local nursery with eight workstations running Windows NT Server version 4.0

   ANSWER

2. **If all the users in Marketing can print to a shared printer, but a user in the Sales department on the same network cannot, what type of security model is probably in use?**
   - a. share level
   - b. user level
   - c. access level
   - d. permissions level

   ANSWER

3. **In the user-level security model, if a user is a member of two different groups, which groups' rights does the user get?**
   - a. the last group that was assigned by the administrator
   - b. the larger group
   - c. it depends on the network operating system
   - d. the smaller group

   ANSWER

4. **On a network running the NetWare operating system, which of the following rights would enable a user to copy a changed version of a file over the existing version of the file?**
   - a. add
   - b. erase
   - c. write
   - d. read

   ANSWER

5. **On a peer-to-peer network that uses Windows 95 workstations, where can a user choose between share-level and user-level access to his CD-ROM drive?**
   - a. Control Panel – CD-ROM
   - b. Control Panel – System – Device Manager – CD-ROM
   - c. Control Panel – Network – Identification
   - d. Control Panel – Network – Access Control

   ANSWER

6. **Which of the following security models provides the most security?**
   - a. share level
   - b. user level
   - c. permissions level
   - d. peer-to-peer network

   ANSWER

7. **If all users on a network using the share-level security model suddenly can't print to their one printer, which of the following is likely causing the problem?**
   - a. The file server has gone down.
   - b. A cable has been cut.
   - c. The hub has gone down.
   - d. The workstation attached to that printer has gone down.

   ANSWER

STANDARD PASSWORD PRACTICES AND PROCEDURES

UNDERSTANDING THE OBJECTIVE

The selection of secure passwords is the simplest and most effective way of preventing unauthorized access to a network. Network administrators should help and require users to choose secure passwords. Secure passwords include those that are more than six characters long, contain both alphabetical and numeric characters, and are not obvious to anyone who knows the user (for example, a birth date, spouse's or child's name, or a favorite sports team).

WHAT YOU **REALLY** NEED TO KNOW

- ◆ Choosing a secure password is one of the easiest and least expensive ways to guard against unauthorized access. A secure password is one that is difficult for anyone else to find out, even if they use password-cracking programs.
- ◆ Users should not use the familiar types of passwords such as their birth date, anniversary, pet's name, child's name, spouse's name, user ID, phone number, address, or any words or numbers that others might associate with them.
- ◆ Users should not use any word that can be found in a dictionary. Malicious intruders can use programs that try a combination of a user ID and every word in a dictionary to gain access to the network.
- ◆ A secure password should be longer than six characters; the longer the better. It should also contain a combination of letters and numbers. If allowed, special characters such as exclamation marks or hyphens should be added for further security. Most NOSs let a network administrator specify a required minimum password length.
- ◆ A password should never be written down, nor displayed in a place where others can find it, such as under the keyboard or on the monitor.
- ◆ A password should be changed frequently, at least every 90 days. Network administrators should establish controls through the network operating system to force users to change their passwords every 90 days. If a user has access to sensitive data, she should change her password more frequently.
- ◆ Password guidelines should be clearly communicated to everyone in an organization through the security policy. Although users may grumble about having to use a combination of letters and numbers and having to change their passwords frequently, the organization's sensitive data will be safer because of this practice.
- ◆ Network administrators, or a special security team, should periodically review passwords and password policies.

OBJECTIVES ON THE JOB

The reason for secure passwords and the characteristics of secure passwords should be explained to all members of an organization. Network administrators should enforce the use of secure passwords through requirements that can be specified in the NOS. These requirements include a minimum password length and a maximum password use period.

PRACTICE TEST QUESTIONS

1. Which of the following is the most secure password?
    a. castle
    b. ca502tLm09
    c. packers
    d. 123456789

ANSWER

2. Why isn't it a good idea to use a word found in the dictionary for your password?
    a. because a number is easier for you to remember
    b. because malicious intruders may use a password-cracking program that can detect words from the dictionary
    c. because words from the dictionary are too short
    d. because words from the dictionary do not contain numbers

ANSWER

3. Which of the following network operating system restrictions is most likely to stop an intruder who is attempting to discover someone's password?
    a. number of unsuccessful login attempts
    b. time of day
    c. total time logged in
    d. source address

ANSWER

4. Which of the following would not typically be used for authenticating to a system?
    a. IP address
    b. user ID
    c. password
    d. last name

ANSWER

5. Which of the following options should be set in the network operating system to make users' passwords more secure?
    a. login time of day restrictions
    b. maximum password length restriction
    c. minimum password length restriction
    d. maximum number of aliases restriction

ANSWER

6. How often should network passwords be changed?
    a. at least every 90 days
    b. at least every 180 days
    c. at least every year
    d. at least every other time a user logs in

ANSWER

7. Which of the following types of users should pay the most careful attention to the security of his or her network password?
    a. a help desk operator who has access to the history of trouble tickets on the network
    b. a receptionist who has access to the CFO's calendar
    c. a network technician who has access to back up all data contained on servers
    d. a salesperson who has access to his sales forecast spreadsheets

ANSWER

NEED TO EMPLOY DATA ENCRYPTION TO PROTECT NETWORK DATA

UNDERSTANDING THE OBJECTIVE

Data encryption uses an algorithm to scramble data into a format that can only be unscrambled by the same encryption program. Encryption schemes vary in security, ease of use, suitability to different tasks, cost, and maintainability. Many types of encryption depend on a key, or a random string of characters that is woven into the data to make it harder to unscramble. PGP, an encryption scheme for e-mail messages, depends on two types of keys.

WHAT YOU **REALLY** NEED TO KNOW

- ◆ **Encryption** is the use of an algorithm to scramble data into a format that can only be read by reversing the algorithm, or decrypting the data, to keep it private. You can use many forms of encryption, though some are more secure than others. Even as new forms of encryption are developed, new ways of cracking their codes are developed, too.

- ◆ The most popular kind of encryption algorithm weaves a **key** (a random string of characters) into the original data's bits, sometimes several times in different sequences, to generate a unique data block. The longer the key, the less easily the encrypted data can be decrypted by an unauthorized system. For example, a 512-bit key is considered secure, whereas a 16-bit key could be cracked in no time.

- ◆ **Pretty Good Privacy (PGP)** is a key-based encryption and digital signature system for e-mail that uses a two-step verification process. The PGP user generates two keys, a public and private key, to assure the recipient that the message is authentic and unaltered.

- ◆ A **digital certificate** is a password-protected and encrypted file that holds an individual's identification information, including a public key and a private key. The public key verifies the sender's digital signature while the private key allows the individual to log on to a third-party authority who administers digital certificates.

- ◆ **Secure Sockets Layer (SSL)** is a method of encrypting Web pages (or HTTP transmissions) en route on the Internet. If you trade stocks or purchase goods on the Web, chances are you are using SSL to transmit your order information. SSL is supported by the most recent versions of Netscape Navigator and Internet Explorer.

- ◆ **IP Security Protocol (IPSec)** defines encryption, authentication, and key management for the upcoming IPV6. It operates at the Network layer (Layer 3) of the OSI model, adding security information to the header of all IP packets.

OBJECTIVES ON THE JOB

The definition of sensitive data may differ from one organization to the next, but when in doubt, it is wise to encrypt data, especially if it travels over the Internet. Some encryption methods, such as digital certificates, require the purchase and setup of additional software and hardware.

PRACTICE TEST QUESTIONS

1. In which of the following situations is encryption most necessary?
   a. A Japanese plastics manufacturer is sending its patent application to a patent lawyer in the U.S.
   b. A teacher is registering for a continuing education class online.
   c. A student is viewing open positions listed on a company's Web site.
   d. A graphic designer is sending a slide template to his client.

   ANSWER

2. If you are sending an e-mail message to a recruiter indicating that you're interested in applying for a position, what type of encryption is the most appropriate?
   a. digital certificate
   b. PGP
   c. IPSec
   d. SSL

   ANSWER

3. What is the name for the process of unscrambling encrypted information at the receiving end?
   a. cryptography
   b. encoding
   c. encrypting
   d. decrypting

   ANSWER

4. What does encryption use to scramble data?
   a. permissions restrictions
   b. algorithms
   c. derivatives
   d. compression

   ANSWER

5. Which of the following keys will provide the greatest security?
   a. 16-bit
   b. 56-bit
   c. 112-bit
   d. 512-bit

   ANSWER

6. Which of the following types of encryption requires a third-party authority to verify the authenticity of transmissions that use it?
   a. PGP
   b. DES
   c. SSL
   d. digital certificates

   ANSWER

7. If you are viewing your bank account online, what type of encryption are you probably using?
   a. PGP
   b. DES
   c. SSL
   d. digital certificates

   ANSWER

USE OF A FIREWALL

UNDERSTANDING THE OBJECTIVE

Firewalls are combinations of hardware and software that operate at the Network and Transport layers of the OSI model to filter traffic coming in and going out of a network. They are most often types of routers, though they can also work on PCs.

WHAT YOU **REALLY** NEED TO KNOW

◆ A **firewall** is a specialized device (typically a router, but possibly only a PC running special software) that selectively filters or blocks traffic between networks.

◆ A firewall typically involves a combination of hardware and software (for example, the router's operating system and configuration). It can be placed between two interconnected private networks or between a private network and a public network.

◆ The term "firewall" is derived from the physical "wall" installed in automobiles to help prevent engine fires from spreading to the passenger area.

◆ The simplest and most common form of a firewall is a **packet filtering firewall**, which is a router that operates at the Network and Transport layers of the OSI model, examining the header of every packet of data that it receives to determine whether that type of packet is authorized to continue to its destination. Packet filtering firewalls are also called **screening firewalls**.

◆ Network administrators must customized a packet filtering firewall to make it effective. They must configure the firewall to accept or deny certain types of traffic. Some of the criteria a firewall can use to accept or deny data include: source and destination IP addresses; source and destination ports (such as ports that supply TCP/UDP connections, FTP, Telnet, SNMP, and RealAudio); TCP, UDP, or ICMP protocol; whether a packet is the first packet in a new data stream or a subsequent packet; whether the packet is inbound or outbound to or from a private network; whether the packet came from or is destined for an application on your private network.

◆ Because firewalls must be tailored to your network's needs, you cannot simply purchase a firewall and install it between your private LAN and the Internet and expect it to offer much security.

◆ Packet filtering routers cannot distinguish which user is trying to get through the firewall and determine whether that user is authorized to do so.

OBJECTIVES ON THE JOB

To properly configure a firewall, you must first consider what type of traffic you want to filter, and then implement your filters. It can take weeks to configure the firewall so that it is not so strict that it prevents authorized users from transmitting and receiving necessary data, and not so lenient that you risk security breaches. Also plan to create exceptions to the rules.

PRACTICE TEST QUESTIONS

1. **On which two of the following devices could a firewall run?**
   a. server
   b. printer
   c. hub
   d. router
   e. switch

2. **At what layers of the OSI model do firewalls operate?**
   a. Application and Session
   b. Data Link and Physical
   c. Transport and Network
   d. Presentation and Session

3. **Which two of the following criteria could be used to filter traffic on a firewall?**
   a. IP address
   b. login ID
   c. password
   d. operating system type
   e. destination port

4. **Which of the following types of networks necessarily uses more than one firewall?**
   a. WAN
   b. VPN
   c. LAN
   d. MAN

5. **Which of the following protocols can be interpreted by a firewall?**
   a. SNA
   b. AppleTalk
   c. TCP/IP
   d. NetBEUI

6. **Before a firewall can effectively filter unwanted traffic, it must be:**
   a. placed between a private and public network
   b. configured according to an organization's security needs
   c. combined with a proxy server
   d. attached to switch on the internal LAN

7. **A type of firewall that masks the IP addresses of internal devices by replacing them with its own is called a:**
   a. gateway
   b. proxy
   c. packet filtering firewall
   d. screening firewall

ANSWER

ANSWER

ANSWER

ANSWER

ANSWER

ANSWER

ANSWER

This domain covers good networking practices and the application of fundamental networking knowledge, such as how to troubleshoot a connectivity problem. This domain is largely scenario-based and is therefore less objective than Domain I. Test questions from this domain can resemble story problems and have more than one correct answer.

Below are percentages of the domain and each objective reflected in the exam questions. The objectives are a percentage of the total exam, not of the domain.

Domain	Percentage of the Net+ Exam Content
II. Knowledge of Networking Practices	23% total
1. Implementing the Installation of the Network	6%
2. Maintaining and Supporting the Network	6%
3. Troubleshooting the Network	11%

DEMONSTRATE AWARENESS THAT ADMINISTRATIVE AND TEST ACCOUNTS, PASSWORDS, IP ADDRESSES, IP CONFIGURATIONS, RELEVANT SOPS, ETC, MUST BE OBTAINED PRIOR TO NETWORK IMPLEMENTATION

UNDERSTANDING THE OBJECTIVE

Many steps are involved in preparing to install a network, let alone performing the actual network installation. Once project sponsors have approved the network installation, and you have identified the project scope, evaluated your choices for operating systems, hardware, and architecture, and composed an implementation team, you must identify all the elements of the network that will be part of the implementation.

WHAT YOU **REALLY** NEED TO KNOW

◆ Administrative accounts have unrestrained privileges on the network. Such accounts can create, modify, erase, and determine access rights for resources on the network.

◆ Administrative accounts are typically used to accomplish the initial installation of the network, as well as subsequent changes. For security reasons, very few users should know the administrative account name and password, and the administrative account's password should be changed frequently.

◆ Test accounts are used during and after the network installation to ensure that typical users can access and use all the resources they need. Test accounts should have the same privileges that an average user can have. In cases where different types of users have different privileges, multiple test accounts are necessary.

◆ Before installing a network, IP addresses should be obtained from the Internet authority, InterNIC (allow at least six weeks for this process). An addressing scheme, or strategy for assigning IP addresses to devices on the network, should also be determined prior to installation. In cases where a proxy is used between private and public segments of the network, the IP addressing scheme can be logically determined according to location, department, or other reasonable division.

◆ **Standard Operating Procedures (SOPs)** are guidelines that establish standards for how to accomplish something. In networking, write SOPs before installing the network. SOPs should be written and revised by a team.

◆ SOPs can be established for adding a new workstation to the network, making changes to a server's configuration, making cables, or recording the specifics about a call to the help desk.

◆ Once the network is in place, you should document its current state, including physical and logical topology; protocols, applications, and operating systems in use; number; and type and location of devices. Keep this documentation in a centrally accessible location.

OBJECTIVES ON THE JOB

Planning for a network installation is much wiser and more efficient than having to backtrack and reinstall or reconfigure part of the network. Consider that it may take you over two hours to install and configure a network operating system.

PRACTICE TEST QUESTIONS

1. **If a network administrator decides to use DHCP on her network, at what point should she configure the DHCP server?**
    a. after all the servers and clients are configured and connected to the network
    b. after all the servers are configured and connected to the network
    c. after the NOS is installed on the DHCP server and before clients are connected
    d. before the NOS is installed on the DHCP server and before clients are connected

    ANSWER

2. **Which of the following tasks should definitely have a standard operating procedure?**
    a. making nightly tape backups
    b. copying files to the server
    c. storing CDs in a CD tower
    d. handling virus-infected disks

    ANSWER

3. **What type of device is necessary if a network administrator decides to assign IP addresses according to the following scheme: 10.10.1.x for the first-floor offices, 10.10.2.x for the second-floor offices, and 10.10.3.x for the third-floor offices?**
    a. DHCP server
    b. WINS server
    c. proxy server
    d. DNS server

    ANSWER

4. **What doesn't have to be determined prior to installing an NOS on a server?**
    a. media type
    b. server name
    c. protocols used by the network
    d. server IP address

    ANSWER

5. **If a network administrator creates five different user groups, and two of the groups have identical privileges, how many test accounts should she create?**
    a. at least one
    b. at least four
    c. at least five
    d. at least six

    ANSWER

6. **What kind of user should modify the TCP/IP configuration on a file server?**
    a. administrative
    b. test
    c. guest
    d. authoritative

    ANSWER

7. **Who should write and maintain standard operating procedures?**
    a. the LAN administrator
    b. help desk analysts
    c. the chief information officer
    d. a team of LAN administrators, technicians, and others

    ANSWER

EXPLAIN IMPACT OF ENVIRONMENTAL FACTORS ON COMPUTER NETWORKS. GIVEN A NETWORK INSTALLATION SCENARIO, IDENTIFY UNEXPECTED OR ATYPICAL CONDITIONS THAT COULD EITHER CAUSE PROBLEMS FOR THE NETWORK OR SIGNIFY THAT A PROBLEM CONDITION ALREADY EXISTS, INCLUDING ROOM CONDITIONS (E.G., HUMIDITY, HEAT, ETC.), PLACEMENT OF BUILDING CONTENTS AND PERSONAL EFFECTS (E.G., SPACE HEATERS, TVS, RADIOS, ETC.), COMPUTER EQUIPMENT, AND ERROR MESSAGES

UNDERSTANDING THE OBJECTIVE

Environmental threats to a network include EMI, RFI, moisture, heat, dust, and physical security breaches.

WHAT YOU **REALLY** NEED TO KNOW

◆ Copper cabling such as UTP, STP, and coaxial are susceptible to noise (interference), which can alter the signal carried by the cable.

◆ Two types of noise can affect data transmission: **Electromagnetic Interference (EMI)** or **Radio Frequency Interference (RFI)**; both are waves that emanate from electrical devices or cables carrying electricity. Motors, power lines, televisions, copiers, fluorescent lights, and other sources of electrical activity can cause both EMI and RFI. RFI may also be caused by strong broadcast signals from radio or TV towers.

◆ To limit noise's impact on your network, install cabling away from powerful electromagnetic forces. Choose transmission media that limits the noise affecting the signal.

◆ Cabling can attain noise immunity through shielding, thickness, or anti-noise algorithms. If shielded cabling still doesn't ward off interference, you might need to use a metal or PVC **conduit,** or pipeline, to contain and further protect the cabling.

◆ Symptoms of EMI or RFI affecting signals can include data loss, data corruption, or intermittent transmission problems.

◆ Keep computer equipment in a closed room with controls that can maintain constant humidity and temperature.

◆ Symptoms of humidity or temperature affecting components can include overheating, data loss, data corruption, and performance degradation. Some components generate error messages when they begin to overheat.

◆ Other environmental threats to networks include dust, smoke, fire, natural disasters, and physical security breaches.

◆ Keep data backups in a location away from your servers.

◆ Physical security breaches can be prevented by using badge access or biometric scanning systems to enter computer rooms, camera monitoring, and restricted doors.

OBJECTIVES ON THE JOB

Because you are probably not in a position to monitor environmental conditions manually, you should invest in a means of automatically gauging temperature, humidity, dust, and smoke, moisture on or under the floor, unauthorized access, and power supply. A monitoring system can alert you (by pager, if desired) before an environmental hazard becomes serious.

PRACTICE TEST QUESTIONS

1. Five workstations in two offices are connected to the same hub in a telecommunications closet away from the workstations. They have intermittent problems connecting to the network. What could cause the problem?
    a. The workstations are overheating.
    b. The cabling to the workstations is not plenum-rated, and is suffering from EMI.
    c. The cabling to the hub or patch panel in the closet is too close to fluorescent lights.
    d. The hub in the closet is too close to the floor and is overheating.

2. Your environmental monitoring system alerts you that excessive particulate in the air, indicating possible smoke, has been detected in the computer room. What do you do?
    a. Call the fire department.
    b. Go into the computer room and find the cause of the smoke or dust.
    c. Turn off the alarm and wait to make sure the first alarm wasn't false.
    d. Turn on the building's alarms and take a fire extinguisher into the computer room.

3. To prepare for a possible natural disaster, what should you do with your daily backup tapes?
    a. Keep them in on the shelf in the computer room.
    b. Keep them in a file drawer beside your desk.
    c. Keep them in a fireproof safe in the office.
    d. Keep them at an offsite location.

4. Which of the following is the most susceptible to EMI?
    a. fiber-optic cable
    b. coaxial cable
    c. shielded twisted-pair cable
    d. unshielded twisted-pair cable

5. Which of the following will not cause EMI?
    a. hammer
    b. microwave
    c. space heater
    d. television

6. In a new data center in Houston, the environmental controls have not yet been installed, although engineers are installing equipment. As contractors work, they leave the door open to the outside. What environmental threat are you concerned about?
    a. smoke damage
    b. excessive humidity
    c. security breaches
    d. flood damage

7. What does not help prevent physical security breaches?
    a. metal detector
    b. biometric scanning
    c. badge access
    d. closed-circuit cameras

RECOGNIZE VISUALLY, OR BY DESCRIPTION, COMMON PERIPHERAL PORTS, EXTERNAL SCSI (ESPECIALLY DB-25 CONNECTORS)

UNDERSTANDING THE OBJECTIVE

The most common ports used for peripherals are serial and parallel. Serial ports, which connect through a DB-9- or 25-pin interface and follow the RS232 standard, are most frequently used to connect external modems or older mice. Parallel ports, which use a DB-25–pin male connector are most often used to connect printers.

WHAT YOU **REALLY** NEED TO KNOW

- ◆ Parallel cables used for printers can be bidirectional or monodirectional, and use a DB25-pin male connector at the computer end and a 36-pin Centronics connector at the printer end, as illustrated here.

- ◆ Parallel ports are DB-25 female inputs. Most modern PCs have one parallel port.

- ◆ Serial ports, like those used to connect external modems and older external mice, are 9- or 25-pin male, D connectors. Most modern PCs have at least one serial port.

- ◆ **RS232**, which stands for **Recommended Standard-232**, is the standard for serial communications. A serial port is sometimes called an RS232 port.

- ◆ **SCSI** stands for **Small Computer System Interface**, used to connect external devices such as hard disks or CD-ROM drives to computers. SCSI connectors come in many different varieties, depending on their transmission speed and type. A typical SCSI connector is illustrated here.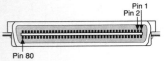

- ◆ The latest SCSI technology is called Ultra3 SCSI and uses a 16-bit bus that supports a data rate of up to 160 Mbps. A newer SCSI technology, Ultra320, which can support up to 320 Mbps, is now emerging.

- ◆ Common network interfaces are BNC or RJ-45 connectors. **BNC**, which stands for **British Naval Connector**, identifies the Ethernet 10Base2 interface, and is illustrated here.

- ◆ **RJ-45**, which stands for **registered jack-45**, identifies the Ethernet 10BaseT and 100BaseT interfaces. An RJ-45 jack, illustrated here, typically contains eight wires (four wire pairs) and looks like a large telephone jack.

- ◆ **RJ-11**, which stands for **registered jack-11**, is the standard interface for phone (or modem) connections, and is illustrated here. An RJ-11 jack contains four or six wires. Prior to the advent of CAT5 cabling, RJ-11 plugs and jacks could be used for LAN communications as well as phone communications.

OBJECTIVES ON THE JOB

You should not only be able to identify an RJ-45 jack, but you should also know how to create one with a punch–down tool, empty jack, and cable. If you are charged with purchasing supplies for the network, you should also be very familiar with the varieties of each different type of cable.

PRACTICE TEST QUESTIONS

1. What kind of connector would you find on a CAT5 patch panel?
   a. DB-25 male
   b. RS-232
   c. RJ-11
   d. RJ-45

   ANSWER

2. What kind of cable would you use to connect an external modem to a PC?
   a. COM3
   b. serial
   c. LPT1
   d. parallel

   ANSWER

3. Which two of the following could connect an Ethernet cable to an Ethernet NIC?
   a. RS-232
   b. DB-25
   c. RJ-45
   d. SCSI
   e. BNC

   ANSWER

4. Which two of the following are synonymous with an RS232 port?
   a. COM port
   b. RJ-11 port
   c. serial port
   d. LPT port
   e. SCSI port

   ANSWER

5. What type of connector is typically used to plug a parallel cable into a printer?
   a. Centronics
   b. RJ-11
   c. DB-9
   d. DB-25

   ANSWER

6. Which of the following is most likely to be used when connecting an external hard disk to a PC?
   a. DB-25
   b. BNC
   c. Centronics
   d. SCSI

   ANSWER

7. How many pins are contained in the interface used to connect a parallel cable to a PC?
   a. 5
   b. 9
   c. 25
   d. 80

   ANSWER

RECOGNIZE VISUALLY, OR BY DESCRIPTION, COMMON NETWORK COMPONEN-TRY, INCLUDING PRINT SERVERS, PERIPHERALS, AND HUBS

UNDERSTANDING THE OBJECTIVE

Print servers can run on file servers, or they can exist as separate, standalone devices attached to the network. Other peripherals on a network can include shared modems, CD towers, terminals, fax machines, and tape backup devices. Most peripherals depend on a server to be shared.

WHAT YOU **REALLY** NEED TO KNOW

- ◆ A **print server** is a combination of hardware and software that controls printer configuration, availability, job queuing, identification, and privileges. Most network operating systems supply software to run print servers on the central file server. Alternatively, print servers can be separate devices dedicated to managing printers.

- ◆ A standalone print server typically contains a power cord, power switch, at least one parallel port, and at least one network port. It can also contain one or more serial ports.

- ◆ A print server can connect printers that do not contain internal NICs to the network. The parallel and/or serial port on the print server connects to the printer.

- ◆ Print servers can be found in Ethernet or Token Ring compatible models. In both models, modern print servers can adapt automatically to multiple transmission speeds.

- ◆ Popular print server manufacturers include Hewlett-Packard and Intel.

- ◆ Network peripherals include CD towers (drives that hold multiple CDs, printers, fax machines, terminals, tape backup devices, and modems. Peripherals are typically attached to a server so that multiple network users can share them.

- ◆ A **hub** is a multiport repeater containing one port that connects to a network's backbone (a **backbone port)** and from 4 to 48 ports that connect to a group of workstations (or a patch panel).

- ◆ Modern, sophisticated hubs contain lights at each port to indicate whether traffic is being transmitted through that port. All hubs contain ventilation fans to prevent the equipment from overheating.

- ◆ Most hubs also contain an **uplink port**, the receptacle connecting one hub to another hub in a daisy-chain or hierarchical fashion. An uplink port looks like any other port, but it should only be used to interconnect hubs.

- ◆ An Ethernet hub can contain 10BaseT or 100BaseT ports, or both. A token ring hub, which can contain 4-Mbps or 16-Mbps ports (or both), is called a **Multistation Access Unit**, or **MAU**.

OBJECTIVES ON THE JOB

Each peripheral can have different configuration requirements and almost certainly come from different vendors. Because you cannot memorize the idiosyncrasies of every piece of equipment, you should have an organized system for storing the manufacturer's documentation as well as information about how the device was installed and originally configured.

PRACTICE TEST QUESTIONS

1. You are the network administrator for an elementary school. The social studies teachers have two older H-P 5M printers that they want you to connect to the network. However, these printers do not contain NICs. What do you do?
   - a. Purchase print servers to install in each of the printers.
   - b. Connect the printers to a standalone print server.
   - c. Explain to the teachers that it is impossible to connect the printers to the network.
   - d. Configure the printers to connect to the network in the network operating system.

   ANSWER

2. You discover that a number of workstations connecting to the same hub are experiencing data transmission problems over the network. When you check the hub, it feels extremely hot and makes a loud buzzing noise. What might be the problem?
   - a. The hub's uplink port is faulty.
   - b. The hub's backbone port is faulty.
   - c. The hub's power supply is faulty.
   - d. The hub's ventilation fan is faulty.

   ANSWER

3. Which of the following manufacturers is a popular supplier of standalone print servers?
   - a. Microsoft
   - b. Cisco
   - c. Novell
   - d. Hewlett-Packard

   ANSWER

4. When a hub's port is faulty, what does its LED probably look like?
   - a. blinking green
   - b. solid green
   - c. solid amber
   - d. It will not be lit.

   ANSWER

5. What component of a hub connects it in series with other hubs?
   - a. backbone port
   - b. patch panel port
   - c. uplink port
   - d. COM port

   ANSWER

6. If you purchase a hub that contains in its description "10/100 autosensing," what kind of transmission will it support?
   - a. Some of its ports will support 10BaseT while other ports will support 100BaseT.
   - b. All of its ports will support both 10BaseT and 100BaseT.
   - c. Some of its ports will support 10Base2, 10Base5, or 10BaseT while other ports will support 100BaseT or 100VG-AnyLAN.
   - d. All of its ports will support 10Base2, 10Base5, 10BaseT, 100BaseT, and 100VG-AnyLAN.

   ANSWER

7. How can a fax machine be shared across a network?
   - a. It must have its own NIC.
   - b. It must be attached to a server.
   - c. It must be attached to a router.
   - d. It cannot be shared on a network.

   ANSWER

RECOGNIZE VISUALLY, OR BY DESCRIPTION, COMMON NETWORK COMPONENTRY, INCLUDING ROUTERS, BROUTERS, AND BRIDGES

UNDERSTANDING THE OBJECTIVE

Routers, brouters, and sophisticated bridges contain similar elements: internal processors, memory, multiple network ports, power supplies, ventilation fans, link LEDs, and management console interfaces. Their differences lie in their functionality and what type and how many network ports they accommodate.

WHAT YOU **REALLY** NEED TO KNOW

- ◆ A **router** is a multiport device that can connect dissimilar LANs and WANs running at different transmission speeds and using a variety of protocols.
- ◆ A typical router has an internal processor, its own memory and power supply, input and output jacks for different types of network connectors (depending on the network type), at least one NIC to connect it to the network backbone, at least one fan to prevent overheating, and usually a management console interface. In addition, routers typically have LEDs by each port to indicate their status.
- ◆ High powered, multiprotocol routers can have several slot bays to accommodate multiple network interfaces (RJ-45, BNC, FDDI, etc.). A router with multiple slots that can hold different interface cards or other devices is called a **modular router**.
- ◆ A **brouter** is a router with the characteristics of a bridge. The advantage of crossing a router with a bridge is that you can forward nonroutable protocols, such as NetBEUI, and connect multiple network types through one device.
- ◆ Like a router, a brouter has an internal processor, its own memory and power supply, input and output jacks for different types of network connectors, at least one NIC to connect it to the network backbone, at least one fan to prevent overheating, and usually a management console interface.
- ◆ A **bridge** is a device that analyzes incoming frames and makes decisions on how to direct them to their destination. Bridges read the destination (MAC) address information and decide whether to forward (retransmit) the packet to another segment or, if it belongs to the same segment as the source address, filter (discard) it.
- ◆ Simple bridges resemble hubs, with only a few ports (one for each connected LAN segment), a power supply, ventilation fan, management console interface, and link LEDs. More sophisticated bridges look similar to routers, with multiple ports that can accommodate many different network connections.

OBJECTIVES ON THE JOB

Any competent network administrator should be able to distinguish between a hub and a router in a single glance. However, as more networking devices acquire the characteristics of others (bridges and routers, switches and routers), it becomes increasingly difficult to tell them apart by sight. Use the vendor's documentation for specific information on a device's components, paying close attention when installing the device.

PRACTICE TEST QUESTIONS

1. **Which two of the following could contain a network input for FDDI, another network input for 100BaseT, and yet another for token ring?**
   a. bridge
   b. router
   c. hub
   d. brouter
   e. UPS

ANSWER

2. **Which of the following devices does not pay attention to the protocol type of the data it handles?**
   a. brouter
   b. bridge
   c. router
   d. server

ANSWER

3. **Which two of the following devices can forward NetBEUI packets?**
   a. bridge
   b. modular router
   c. brouter
   d. core router
   e. firewall

ANSWER

4. **If a router's backbone port is operating correctly on a live network, what will its LED look like?**
   a. solid green
   b. blinking green
   c. solid amber
   d. It won't be lit.

ANSWER

5. **At what layers of the OSI model do brouters operate?**
   a. layers 1 and 2
   b. layers 2 and 3
   c. layers 3 and 4
   d. layers 1 and 3

ANSWER

6. **What technique do manufacturers use in high-end routers to ensure that a faulty component does not bring the network down?**
   a. the ability to hot-swap parts without powering the device down
   b. lifetime warranties on all parts
   c. redundant, hot-standby components
   d. load balancing

ANSWER

7. **Which of the following components is optional on a bridge?**
   a. ventilation fan
   b. power source
   c. internal processor
   d. Ring Out port

ANSWER

RECOGNIZE VISUALLY, OR BY DESCRIPTION, COMMON NETWORK COMPONENTRY, INCLUDING PATCH PANELS AND UPSs

UNDERSTANDING THE OBJECTIVE

Patch panels are wall- or rack-mounted rows of data receptors used in telecommunications rooms to connect the punch-down block to connectivity devices such as hubs. A punch-down block is a panel of data receptors that accepts connections from nodes such as workstations. The aim of using punch-down blocks and patch panels is to organize wiring and to troubleshoot connections.

WHAT YOU **REALLY** NEED TO KNOW

◆ A **patch panel** is a wall- or rack-mounted panel of data receptors into which cross-connected patch cables from the punch-down block are inserted. The data receptors can be RJ-45, BNC, token ring, or FDDI, depending on the type of network. Devices such as hubs or routers are typically connected to the patch panel via patch cables.

◆ A **punch-down block** is a panel of data receptors into which horizontal cabling from the workstations are inserted. Both patch panels and punch-down blocks are found in the telecommunications room in a structured cabling environment.

◆ An **Uninterruptible Power Source (UPS)** is a battery-operated power source directly attached to one or more devices and to a power supply (such as a wall outlet), which prevents undesired features of the wall outlet's A/C power from harming the device or interrupting its services.

◆ UPSs vary widely in the type of power aberrations they can rectify, the length of time for which they can provide power, and the number of devices they can support. UPSs also vary widely in price.

◆ Some UPSs are simply designed to keep your PC running long enough for you to properly shut it down in case of a blackout. Other UPSs perform sophisticated operations such as line conditioning, power supply monitoring, and error notification.

◆ UPSs fall into two categories: standby and online. A **standby UPS** is a power supply that provides continuous voltage to a device by switching instantaneously to the battery when it detects a loss of power from the wall outlet. When the power is restored, the standby UPS switches the device back to using A/C power again.

◆ An **online UPS** is a power supply that uses the A/C power from the wall outlet to continuously charge its battery, while providing power to a network device through its battery. In other words, a server connected to an online UPS is always relying on the UPS battery for its electricity.

OBJECTIVES ON THE JOB

No matter what position you have in the networking department of an organization, you need to recognize and understand how to use patch panels and punch-down blocks. They are very simply means of organizing cables. Be sure to document, at the connector end, the corresponding device for each patch panel or port, to make maintenance and troubleshooting easy.

PRACTICE TEST QUESTIONS

1. **What organization set the standard for structured cabling that includes patch panels?**
   - a. IEEE
   - b. IETF
   - c. TIA/EIA
   - d. ISO

   ANSWER

2. **On an Ethernet 10/100 network, what kind of receptacles does the patch panels contain?**
   - a. BNC
   - b. FDDI
   - c. RJ-11
   - d. RJ-45

   ANSWER

3. **In the structured cabling scheme, into what do patch cables from workstation data jacks connect?**
   - a. patch panel
   - b. hub
   - c. punch-down block
   - d. cross-connect

   ANSWER

4. **What kind of UPS is always supplying power to the devices that connect to it?**
   - a. standby
   - b. generator
   - c. A/C
   - d. online

   ANSWER

5. **How long does an online UPS take to switch its attached devices to battery power?**
   - a. 15 seconds
   - b. 10 seconds
   - c. 5 seconds
   - d. no time

   ANSWER

6. **In a structured cabling scheme, a patch panel from a hub would connect to what?**
   - a. punch-down block
   - b. cross-connect
   - c. wall jack
   - d. patch panel

   ANSWER

7. **Over time, what might electrical line noise do to your system?**
   - a. wear down the power supply
   - b. damage the internal circuit boards
   - c. increase network transmission error rates
   - d. increase its susceptibility to viruses

   ANSWER

RECOGNIZE VISUALLY, OR BY DESCRIPTION, COMMON NETWORK COMPONENTRY, INCLUDING NICS AND TOKEN RING MEDIA FILTERS

UNDERSTANDING THE OBJECTIVE

NICs enable devices to transmit and receive data to and from the network. Every device on the network must contain some type of NIC (or transceiver). Common workstation NICs consist of a circuit board, a means of connecting to the system board, and a receptacle for a network connector such as an RJ-45 plug. More sophisticated NICs can have multiple receptacles, on-board processors, and traffic management capabilities.

WHAT YOU **REALLY** NEED TO KNOW

- ◆ **Network Interface Cards (NICs)** are connectivity devices that enable a workstation, server, printer, or other node to receive and transmit data over the network media. NICs are also sometimes called **network adapters**.
- ◆ All network cards have their own circuitry, a system board interface, and at least one receptacle for a connection to the network. They may be external or internal to a device.
- ◆ NICs belong to the Physical layer of the OSI model because they transmit data signals but do not (in general) analyze the data from higher layers.
- ◆ NICs come in a variety of types depending on network transport system (Ethernet vs. token ring), network transmission speed (e.g., 10 Mbps vs. 100 Mbps), connector interfaces (e.g., BNC vs. RJ-45), type of system board (e.g., PCI or ISA) or device (e.g., workstation or printer) they suit, and of course, manufacturer.
- ◆ For laptop computers, **Personal Computer Memory Card International Association (PCMCIA)** slots or in older models, parallel ports, can connect NICs. You also hear PCMCIA NICs called "credit card adapters" because they are approximately the same size as a credit card.
- ◆ NICs can be designed for wireless transmission. Typically, a wireless NIC uses an antenna to exchange signals with a base station transceiver or other wireless NIC adapters. This type of connectivity suits environments where cabling cannot be installed or for clients who need to move about while staying connected to the network.
- ◆ **Token ring media filters** are small devices that allow token ring NICs to use UTP or STP cabling. A token ring media filter consists of a DB9-pin connector on one end (that plugs into the token ring NIC) with an RJ-45 receptacle on the other end to accept STP or UTP cables.
- ◆ Token ring media filters can be designed to work with 4-Mbps or 16-Mbps token ring networks.

OBJECTIVES ON THE JOB

It's a good idea to use the same NIC vendor, if not the same make and model, for all devices on a network. This makes support and maintenance easier. Since token ring networks are becoming rare, and further, since modern token ring NICs include RJ-45 receptacles, it is unlikely that you will need to use token ring media filters unless you are working on an older network.

PRACTICE TEST QUESTIONS

1. Which of the following do all NICs have in common?
    a. antenna
    b. RJ-11 receptacle
    c. RJ-45 receptacle
    d. a means for connecting to the system board

    ANSWER

2. What type of NIC is best suited for inventory control personnel who must quickly travel through a large warehouse entering data into their networked workstation?
    a. PCMCIA
    b. parallel port
    c. ISA
    d. wireless

    ANSWER

3. Which two of the following features that can be found on a sophisticated NIC (such as one found in a server) improves performance of the NIC?
    a. diagnostic LEDs
    b. Direct Memory Access (DMA)
    c. SNMP capabilities
    d. power management capabilities
    e. on-board CPU

    ANSWER

4. A token ring media filter uses what kind of connector at the computer's NIC?
    a. DB-25
    b. DB-9
    c. RJ-45
    d. RJ-11

    ANSWER

5. If a token ring media filter is capable of autosensing, what two transmission speeds can it automatically adjust to?
    a. 1 Mbps and 4 Mbps
    b. 10 Mbps and 100 Mbps
    c. 4 Mbps and 16 Mbps
    d. 100 Mbps and 1 Gbps

    ANSWER

6. What type of NIC is most often found in a modern laptop computer?
    a. PCMCIA
    b. parallel port
    c. ISA
    d. PCI

    ANSWER

7. In a modern desktop workstation, which two of the following buses might a NIC use?
    a. PCI
    b. EIGRP
    c. ISA
    d. ESA
    e. PCMCIA

    ANSWER

GIVEN AN INSTALLATION SCENARIO, DEMONSTRATE AWARENESS OF THE FOL-LOWING COMPATIBILITY AND CABLING ISSUES: CONSEQUENCES OF TRYING TO INSTALL AN ANALOG MODEM IN A DIGITAL JACK, USES OF RJ-45 CONNECTORS MAY DIFFER GREATLY DEPENDING UPON CABLING, AND PATCH CABLES CON-TRIBUTE TO THE OVERALL LENGTH OF THE CABLE SEGMENT

UNDERSTANDING THE OBJECTIVE

Inserting an analog modem line into a digital phone jack can damage the internal circuitry of the modem. A digital jack carries more current than an analog modem can handle. RJ-45 plugs can be used on a variety of LAN and cabling types. The most common use for an RJ-45 plug is on a UTP cable for a 10BaseT or 100BaseT Ethernet network.

WHAT YOU **REALLY** NEED TO KNOW

◆ Modems are analog devices, designed to connect to analog telephone lines like those found in most homes. However, telephones installed in many businesses and hotels are PBX phones, many of which are digital. Although the jacks for digital phones are identical to analog jacks, they may carry too much current for analog modems to handle (>125mA). This excessive current can ruin the modem's circuitry.

◆ A device called a **line tester** can be used to determine if a phone jack is safe for an analog modem.

◆ The RJ-45 plug can be used for multiple types of LANs with either STP or UTP wiring. Different RJ-45 plugs contain different combinations of **pinouts,** or wire pair terminations.

◆ The most common use of an RJ-45 plug is on a UTP wire for 10BaseT or 100BaseT Ethernet LANs. In this instance, the RJ-45 pinouts follow the TIA/EIA T568A specification as specified below.

Pin Number	Use	Color
1	Transmit +	White and green
2	Transmit -	Green
3	Receive +	White and orange
4	Not used	Blue
5	Not used	White and blue
6	Receive -	Orange
7	Not used	White and brown
8	Not used	Brown

◆ ATM, Token Ring, 100VG-AnyLAN, 100BaseT4, and 100BaseT8 LANs all use different config-urations in RJ-45 plugs.

◆ In the TIA/EIA structured cabling scheme, the maximum allowable distance for horizontal wiring (the wiring between a workstation and the punch-down block) in a 10BaseT or 100BaseT Ethernet network is 100 meters. This includes 90 meters to connect a data jack on the wall to the telecommunications closet plus a maximum of 10 meters to connect a workstation to the data jack on the wall.

OBJECTIVES ON THE JOB

Excessive segment lengths (which often result from users trying to add more distance between their workstation and the wall jack) can cause many network transmission problems. When installing and troubleshooting devices, you should bear this in mind.

PRACTICE TEST QUESTIONS

1. **In the TIA/EIA 538A standard for typical Ethernet 10/100BaseT cabling, which pins are not used to either transmit or receive data?**
   - a. 4 and 5, 7 and 8
   - b. 1 and 2, 7 and 8
   - c. 3 and 6, 4 and 5
   - d. 1 and 2, 4 and 5

   ANSWER

2. **What is the consequence of inserting an analog modem line into a digital phone jack?**
   - a. The modem will be unable to dial a carrier.
   - b. The modem will not recognize a dial tone.
   - c. The modem's circuitry may be damaged.
   - d. The modem will receive garbled data.

   ANSWER

3. **Which of the following types of networks doesn't use an RJ-45 plug?**
   - a. 100VG-AnyLAN
   - b. 10BaseT
   - c. 100BaseT4
   - d. 10Base2

   ANSWER

4. **In the TIA/EIA structured cabling standards, what is the maximum distance allowed between a workstation and its wall jack on a 10BaseT network?**
   - a. 1 meter
   - b. 10 meters
   - c. 90 meters
   - d. 100 meters

   ANSWER

5. **What type of device can determine whether a phone jack is safe to use with an analog modem?**
   - a. cable tester
   - b. cable checker
   - c. line tester
   - d. tone locator

   ANSWER

6. **What type of tool is used to insert wires into the pins of RJ-45 jacks?**
   - a. patch tool
   - b. punch-down tool
   - c. hole punch
   - d. crimper

   ANSWER

7. **What characteristic of a digital phone jack makes it incompatible with analog modems?**
   - a. its excessive current
   - b. its reversed pinouts
   - c. its star-ring topology
   - d. its high data transmission rate

   ANSWER

IDENTIFY THE KINDS OF TEST DOCUMENTATION THAT ARE USUALLY AVAILABLE REGARDING A VENDOR'S PATCHES, FIXES, UPGRADES, ETC.

UNDERSTANDING THE OBJECTIVE

A patch is software that replaces a piece of the program's original code to fix a bug or add functionality. Patches are typically released free to registered software users. Upgrades typically replace a software program to fix minor flaws and add functionality. Upgrades are sometimes free to registered users of a program.

WHAT YOU **REALLY** NEED TO KNOW

- ◆ A **patch** is an enhancement to a piece of a software program. A patch differs from a revision or software upgrade because it only changes part of the software, leaving most of the code untouched. Patches are often distributed at no charge by software vendors to fix a bug in their code, or to add slightly more functionality.

- ◆ A patch should come with installation instructions and a description of its purpose, at the very least, in the form of a text file. Most patches can be downloaded from the Web along with their instructions.

- ◆ An **upgrade** is a major change to the existing code, which is sometimes offered free from a vendor and might be comprehensive enough to substitute for the original program. An upgrade to a client program replaces the existing client program. In general, upgrades are designed to add functionality and fix minor bugs in the previous version of the software.

- ◆ Although patches and upgrades should be fully tested by the vendor before their release, you cannot predict that they will work flawlessly on your system. While some automatically back up the system before they begin installation, you should not rely on this method. Always make sure you can reverse a software change, in case the change does more harm than good.

- ◆ Perform patches and upgrades during a time when users cannot and will not attempt to use the network. If the change does cause problems, you will need extra time to reverse the process.

- ◆ To stay apprised of patches and upgrades released by your vendors, regularly check the vendor's technical support Web site or subscribe to its mailing list. Manufacturers usually bundle a number of bug fixes into one patch, and if you're a registered user, they alert you when significant patches are released. News about patches from vendors as large as Novell and Microsoft also appear in trade magazines.

OBJECTIVES ON THE JOB

A vendor might alert you when important patches are released. Or you can look for vendor-supplied patches and alerts on a vendor's Web site. Whatever your means of finding patches and upgrades, you should take responsibility for this task and make the necessary changes to your network's software.

PRACTICE TEST QUESTIONS

1. **What does Microsoft call its patches for the Windows NT Server network operating system?**
   a. systematic patches
   b. NOS upgrades
   c. service packs
   d. MS NOS revisions

   ANSWER

2. **What is a good source for reliable information about a newly released patch?**
   a. the software instruction manual
   b. the vendor's software CD
   c. the vendor's Web site
   d. the software's user forum

   ANSWER

3. **Why is it important to apply patches when no one is using the network?**
   a. so users don't interfere with the process of applying the patch
   b. so the patch doesn't adversely affect users on the network
   c. so the patch doesn't erase data files on the server
   d. so the patch installation can use all the network bandwidth

   ANSWER

4. **What is the name for the process of returning to a software's original state after applying a patch and having it fail?**
   a. backpedaling
   b. repatching
   c. unleashing
   d. reversing

   ANSWER

5. **How does an upgrade differ from a patch (choose two)?**
   a. An upgrade is usually free while a patch is usually costly.
   b. An upgrade is more comprehensive than a patch.
   c. An upgrade replaces only part of a program's code while a patch replaces all of it.
   d. An upgrade is usually unsupported by the manufacturer, while a patch is usually issued by the manufacturer.
   e. An upgrade may be offered for a fee while a patch is typically free to registered users.

   ANSWER

6. **Which of the following is cause for a manufacturer to promptly release a new patch?**
   a. A security hole in the software is discovered and exploited.
   b. The software is discovered to not support token ring networks over STP cabling.
   c. The software does not contain sufficient documentation.
   d. A dialog box in the software has the incorrect title.

   ANSWER

7. **What step should you take before applying a network operating system upgrade to ensure that you can return to its original state if problems occur?**
   a. Mirror the server on which you're upgrading the NOS.
   b. Back up the entire server to a tape backup device.
   c. Back up the server's configuration to a floppy disk.
   d. Copy the server's NOS directory to a CD.

   ANSWER

GIVEN A NETWORK MAINTENANCE SCENARIO, DEMONSTRATE AWARENESS OF STANDARD BACKUP PROCEDURES AND BACKUP MEDIA STORAGE PRACTICES

UNDERSTANDING THE OBJECTIVE

A backup is a copy of data on tape or other storage media made in case the original copy of the data is lost, stolen, or damaged. Backups on modern networks are usually accomplished using a tape backup device, which is connected to a server on the network. Backups can also be saved to an online storage company.

WHAT YOU **REALLY** NEED TO KNOW

- A **backup** is a duplicate copy of data or program files for archiving or safekeeping. Without backing up your data, you risk losing everything through a hard disk fault, natural disaster, erasure, or corruption.
- The most popular method for backing up networked systems is tape backup, because this method is simple and relatively economical. Tape backups require a tape drive connected to the network, software to manage and perform backups, and backup media.
- Consider the following questions when choosing a backup method: Does the backup software use data error checking techniques? Is the backup system quick enough to complete before daily operations resume? How much does the solution cost? Is the backup hardware and software compatible with existing network hardware and software? Does the backup system require frequent manual intervention?
- Some companies on the Internet are now offering to back up data over the Internet, or perform **online backups**. Online backups require an Internet connection and proprietary client software.
- You should devise a backup strategy, and document the strategy in a common area. Address at least the following questions: What kind of rotation schedule will backups follow? At what time of day or night will the backups occur? How will the accuracy of backups be verified? Where will backup media be stored? Who will be responsible for ensuring that backups occur? How long will backups be saved?
- A **full backup** backs up all data on all servers, whether the data are new or changed.
- An **incremental backup** backs up only data that has changed since the last backup.
- A **differential backup** backs up only data that has changed since the last backup, and that data is then marked for subsequent backup, whether or not it has changed.
- Most backup schemes use a combination of periodic full backups with daily incremental backups.
- Backup media should be stored off-site to ensure that critical data can be recovered in case of a disaster.

OBJECTIVES ON THE JOB

Most network operating systems ship with software you can use to perform rudimentary backups (to a CD-ROM, for example). However, in a large organization, it is wise to purchase third-party backup utilities, which are more sophisticated, and backup devices, which are faster. Some examples of tape backup software include Computer Associate's ARCserve, Dantz, H-P OpenView's OmniBack, IBM's TSM, and Legato NetWorker.

PRACTICE TEST QUESTIONS

1. In the popular grandfather-father-son backup rotation scheme, how frequently is a full backup made?
   - a. daily
   - b. weekly
   - c. monthly
   - d. annually

   ANSWER

2. Which two of the following are required to perform online backups?
   - a. DAT tapes
   - b. a tape vault
   - c. client software
   - d. a dedicated connection
   - e. an Internet connection

   ANSWER

3. Which of the following best describes an incremental backup?
   - a. It includes all data.
   - b. It includes all data that has changed in the previous week.
   - c. It includes all data that has changed since the last full backup.
   - d. It includes all data that has changed since the previous backup.

   ANSWER

4. What factor must you consider when using online backups that you don't typically have to consider when backing up to a LAN tape drive?
   - a. reliability
   - b. geographical distance
   - c. security
   - d. time to recover

   ANSWER

5. Which two of the following could be used to store backed-up data?
   - a. RAM
   - b. CD-ROM
   - c. DAT tape
   - d. router
   - e. CPU

   ANSWER

6. Which of the following is a major advantage to performing full system backups only once per month?
   - a. Since they take a long time to finish, they would not affect users as much.
   - b. If they only occur once per month, they will be quicker to restore.
   - c. If they are only performed once per month, they should be more reliable.
   - d. Since they are so large, they require manual intervention, and performing them once a month would limit the time spent on backups.

   ANSWER

7. How can the accuracy of backup tapes be verified?
   - a. by attempting to retrieve a file backed up to the tape
   - b. by attempting to send a file on the backup tape to another location on the WAN
   - c. by viewing the backup tape
   - d. by reading the log of the backup utility software and making sure no errors appear

   ANSWER

GIVEN A NETWORK MAINTENANCE SCENARIO, DEMONSTRATE AWARENESS OF THE NEED FOR PERIODIC APPLICATION OF SOFTWARE PATCHES AND OTHER FIXES TO THE NETWORK, THE NEED TO INSTALL ANTI-VIRUS SOFTWARE ON THE SERVER AND THE WORKSTATIONS, AND THE NEED TO FREQUENTLY UPDATE VIRUS SIGNATURES

UNDERSTANDING THE OBJECTIVE

Maintaining a network includes applying new patches or upgrades as they are necessary. You can find patches, upgrades, and their documentation on the vendor's Web site. Virus protection is another key element in maintaining a network. You can purchase a variety of virus–scanning techniques and programs. A good virus–protection program can detect viruses through multiple means, including signature, integrity, and heuristic scanning. When signature scanning is used, the virus signature database must be frequently updated to recognize new viruses.

WHAT YOU **REALLY** NEED TO KNOW

- Vendors release patches and upgrades to software with different frequency. Generally, the more complex the software (such as an operating system), the more patches it will acquire.
- Virus protection involves more than simply installing antivirus software. It requires choosing the most appropriate antivirus program for your environment, monitoring the network, updating the antivirus program, and educating users. In addition, you should draft and enforce an antivirus policy for your organization.
- Suspect a virus on your system if you notice any of the following symptoms: unexplained increases in file sizes; programs launching, running, or exiting more slowly than usual; unusual error messages appearing without probable cause; significant, unexpected loss of system memory.
- Good antivirus programs can detect viruses through signature scanning, integrity checking, and heuristic scanning.
- **Signature scanning** compares a file's content with known virus signatures (unique identifying characteristics in the code) in a signature database.
- A signature database must be frequently updated to detect new viruses as they emerge. Updates can be downloaded from the antivirus software vendor's Web site.
- **Integrity checking** compares current characteristics of files and disks against an archived version of these characteristics to discover any changes. The most common example of integrity checking is using a checksum.
- The type of scanning that attempts to identify viruses by discovering "virus-like" behavior is known as **heuristic scanning**. It is the most fallible and most likely to emit false alarms.
- Virus protection software running on a client's system should be able to receive regular updates and modifications from a centralized network console.

OBJECTIVES ON THE JOB

When installing antivirus software on a network, one of the most important considerations is where to install it. If you install antivirus software on every desktop, you have addressed the most likely point of entry, but ignored the most important files that might be infected—those on the server. If you put antivirus software on the server and make it check every file and transaction, you protect important files but slow your network performance considerably.

PRACTICE TEST QUESTIONS

1. **If your antivirus software uses signature scanning, what must you do to keep its virus-fighting capabilities current?**

    a. Purchase new virus signature scanning software at least every three months.

    b. Reinstall the virus-scanning software at least each month.

    c. Manually edit the signature-scanning file.

    d. Regularly update the antivirus software's signature database.

    ANSWER

2. **Where is a good place to learn about virus software updates?**

    a. the software's instruction manual

    b. the software's readme text file

    c. the vendor's Web site

    d. the vendor's magazine ads

    ANSWER

3. **Which two of the following are most likely to indicate that a virus has infected your workstation?**

    a. Strange messages appear on the screen.

    b. The computer does not shut down when you turn off the power switch.

    c. Programs take unusually long to load.

    d. The computer hangs at the BIOS screen.

    e. The computer's NIC LED flashes green.

    ANSWER

4. **What is the disadvantage to using virus protection on the server?**

    a. If it finds a virus, it will shut down the network.

    b. It may detrimentally affect the server's performance.

    c. It may use up too much RAM on the server.

    d. It may cause network congestion.

    ANSWER

5. **What type of virus checking compares the characteristics of current versions of files with archived versions of the same files?**

    a. heuristic scanning

    b. signature scanning

    c. backup scanning

    d. integrity scanning

    ANSWER

6. **Which type of virus checking is most likely to result in false alarms?**

    a. heuristic scanning

    b. signature scanning

    c. backup scanning

    d. integrity scanning

    ANSWER

7. **If a patch for your network operating system is released, but the bugs it fixes don't affect you, what should you do?**

    a. Apply the patch anyway.

    b. Research the effects of the patch and weigh their importance against the risk of applying it.

    c. Wait for the next patch to be released.

    d. Call the vendor to inquire about the necessity of installing the patch.

    ANSWER

IDENTIFY THE FOLLOWING STEPS AS A SYSTEMATIC APPROACH TO IDENTIFYING THE EXTENT OF A NETWORK PROBLEM, AND, GIVEN A PROBLEM SCENARIO, SELECT THE APPROPRIATE NEXT STEP BASED ON THIS APPROACH: 1. DETERMINE WHETHER THE PROBLEM EXISTS ACROSS THE NETWORK 2. DETERMINE WHETHER THE PROBLEM IS WORKSTATION, WORKGROUP, LAN OR WAN 3. DETERMINE WHETHER THE PROBLEM IS CONSISTENT AND REPLICABLE 4. USE STANDARD TROUBLESHOOTING METHODS

UNDERSTANDING THE OBJECTIVE

Determining the extent of a network problem is one of the first steps in a troubleshooting methodology. Network problems typically affect single users, users that share the same LAN segment, users in a (permissions) group, remote users, or users within one building, if not all users. Determine whether the problem happens all the time, intermittently (unpredictably), or only during certain times of the day or week.

WHAT YOU **REALLY** NEED TO KNOW

- ◆ In troubleshooting network problems, the best approach is to follow a logical, step-by-step method. First determine the scope of the problem—whether the problem affects only a certain groups of users, certain areas of the organization, or only occurs at certain times.
- ◆ Answering the following questions to identify the extent of a network problem:
  - How many users or network segments are affected? One user or workstation? A workgroup? A department? One location within an organization? An entire organization?
  - When did the problem begin? Has the network, server, or workstation *ever* worked properly? Did the symptoms appear in the last hour or day? Have the symptoms appeared intermittently for a long time? Do the symptoms only appear at certain times of the day, week, month, or year?
  - Does it affect only certain network services (such as printing)?
  - Does it affect data or programs or both? If it affects programs, does it affect a local application, one networked application, or multiple networked applications?
- ◆ Usually, network problems are not catastrophic, and you can take time to correctly identify the scope of the problem. One way to achieve this is by asking users specific questions pertaining to scope. For example, suppose a user complains that his mail program isn't picking up e-mail. You should ask when the problem began, whether it affects only him or everyone in his department, and what error message(s) he receives when he attempts to pick up mail.
- ◆ Narrowing down the time or frequency in which a problem occurs can reveal subtle network problems. For example, if many users cannot log on to the server at 8:05 A.M., the server probably needs additional resources to accept so many logins.

OBJECTIVES ON THE JOB

If you limit the scope of a problem to a department or floor of your organization, examine that network segment, its router interface, its cabling, or a server that provides services to those users. If a problem affects all users in all departments and locations, you are dealing with a catastrophic failure and you should look at core devices such as central switches and backbone connections.

PRACTICE TEST QUESTIONS

1. **A user calls and complains that she can't print to the printer down the hall. What question might help determine the extent of the problem?**
    a. What does the error message on your screen say?
    b. What kind of printer is it?
    c. When did the problem begin?
    d. Have you made any changes to your printer configuration today?

ANSWER

2. **Which of the following symptoms might indicate a hub failure?**
    a. All workstations on a segment cannot communicate with other workstations.
    b. All workstations on a segment are intermittently prevented from connecting.
    c. All workstations on a segment lose their IP addresses.
    d. Only one workstation on a segment is unable to log on to the network.

ANSWER

3. **Which symptom might indicate a problem related to group permissions?**
    a. The group users cannot print documents in landscape orientation.
    b. All users in the group are receiving bounced e-mail from the mail server.
    c. None of the users in the group can save files to the T:\DATA directory.
    d. All users in the group are experiencing slow network performance.

ANSWER

4. **Which of the following symptoms might indicate a network problem caused by EMI?**
    a. Several users in an office cannot log onto the network from 8 A.M. to 8:15 A.M.
    b. One user in the basement reports problems saving files to the T:\DATA directory.
    c. One user dialing in from a hotel experiences intermittent disconnects.
    d. Several users on a factory floor experience data transmission problems once the stamping machines start running.

ANSWER

5. **A user calls and complains that since he reinstalled Windows 98, he can't launch his MS Office program. What can you assume about the extent of this problem?**
    a. It probably affects a group of users on the same LAN segment.
    b. It probably affects only one user.
    c. It probably affects a group of users who belong to the same network group.
    d. It probably affects all users first thing in the morning.

ANSWER

6. **Suddenly 15 users from your Columbus, OH office say they can't retrieve files from the server at your Miami headquarters. Which of the following might be causing the problem?**
    a. A core router on the network backbone has failed.
    b. A workgroup hub in the Columbus office has failed.
    c. The tape backup server at the Miami office has failed.
    d. The mail server at the Miami office has failed.

ANSWER

7. **After you upgrade the network operating system on all of a firm's file servers, two employees from Accounting and five employees from Technical Services call to identify problems logging on to the network. What can you assume about the extent of the problem?**
    a. It is probably limited to a network group.
    b. It is probably limited to a few individuals.
    c. It is probably limited to one LAN segment.
    d. It is probably affecting the entire organization.

ANSWER

IDENTIFY THE FOLLOWING STEPS AS A SYSTEMATIC APPROACH TO DETERMINING WHETHER A PROBLEM IS ATTRIBUTABLE TO THE OPERATOR OR THE SYSTEM, AND, GIVEN A PROBLEM SCENARIO, SELECT THE APPROPRIATE NEXT STEP BASED ON THIS APPROACH: 1. IDENTIFY THE EXACT ISSUE 2. RECREATE THE PROBLEM 3. ISOLATE THE CAUSE 4. FORMULATE A CORRECTION 5. IMPLEMENT THE CORRECTION 6. TEST 7. DOCUMENT THE PROBLEM AND THE SOLUTION 8. GIVE FEEDBACK

UNDERSTANDING THE OBJECTIVE

In troubleshooting problems, follow a systematic, step-by-step method as described below.

WHAT YOU **REALLY** NEED TO KNOW

◆ The following steps provide a logical approach to troubleshooting and solving a network problem:

1. Identify the symptoms. Carefully document what you learn from people or systems that alerted you to the problem and keep that documentation handy. Many organizations use help desk software that enables them to save all the details of a situation in a database, which enables better recordkeeping, easy retrieval, and future correlation of that event with other events.
2. Verify user competency.
3. Identify the scope of the problem (whether universal, or geographically, demographically, or chronologically limited).
4. Reproduce the problem, or ensure that it is reliably reproducible. Try the same operation with a test account and with an administrative account, and then see if the results differ.
5. Verify the physical integrity of the network connection (such as cable connections, NIC installations, or power to devices), starting at the affected node(s) and moving outward toward the backbone.
6. Verify the logical integrity of the network connection (such as addressing, protocol bindings, software installations, and so on).
7. Consider recent changes to the network or to the workstation and how those changes might have caused something to stop working.
8. Implement a solution.
9. Test the solution as both a typical user and as an administrator.
10. Supply feedback to the user(s) affected by the problem.
11. Document the solution in a place where all network personnel can find it. In the case of a problem originally recorded in a help desk database, the solution should also be recorded there.

◆ Experience in your network environment might prompt you to follow the steps in a different order or to skip steps.

OBJECTIVES ON THE JOB

In addition to the organized method of troubleshooting described above, a general rule for troubleshooting is "Pay attention to the obvious!" While some questions sound too simple to bother asking, don't discount them. If a problem is caused by an obvious error, such as a cable being disconnected, you can save yourself a lot of time by checking cable connections first.

PRACTICE TEST QUESTIONS

1. **You receive a call from a user who says the network won't accept her password. How can you determine whether this problem is due to user error or client software?**
   a. Ask her to reboot and try again.
   b. Ask her to change her password.
   c. Ask her for her password; then try logging in under her user ID from your workstation.
   d. Ask her when the problem began.

   ANSWER

2. **Which two facts should always be recorded in the documentation of a network problem?**
   a. when the problem occurred
   b. the user's password
   c. the list of network groups to which the user belongs
   d. the user's IP address
   e. how the problem was resolved

   ANSWER

3. **After you discover a faulty memory chip on a server, what should you do about it?**
   a. Call the server manufacturer for a replacement.
   b. Purchase a new chip from a local computer reseller and replace the faulty chip.
   c. Remove the faulty chip and let the server run on the remaining memory.
   d. Attempt to repair the faulty chip according to the instruction manual.

   ANSWER

4. **If a user can't log on to the network, and you have verified that she is using the right password, that her protocols are correctly installed and bound to the NIC, and that the client software is correctly installed and configured, what should you check next?**
   a. the connection between the hub and the file server
   b. the connection between the workstation's NIC and the wall jack
   c. the connection between the patch panel and the hub
   d. the connection between the hub and the router

   ANSWER

5. **You have just helped a user by logging on to his workstation as administrator, and then changing the permissions on his user ID. After you leave, what do you realize you forgot to do?**
   a. Record the solution in the help desk software.
   b. Log out as administrator, log in as the user, and test the solution.
   c. Similarly change permissions for all other users who share his office.
   d. Check to make sure the user is using the correct password.

   ANSWER

6. **You solved a user's problem by modifying his client's ODBC driver properties. When he asks you to explain why it wasn't working before, how do you respond?**
   a. Tell him that he was missing a driver.
   b. Tell him that he wasn't logging on correctly.
   c. Tell him that it didn't matter because it's fixed now.
   d. Tell him that you had to modify a parameter in his database connection.

   ANSWER

7. **While troubleshooting a campus network performance problem, you discover that the Music Hall's wiring consists of largely CAT3 cables. What do you do?**
   a. Tell users that because of the inferior wiring they can expect poor network performance.
   b. Verify the extent of the problem, notify your colleagues that this building contains older wiring, and schedule a time to upgrade it.
   c. Modify all client software to only run at lower transmission rates.
   d. Check the hubs in the building to make sure they are compatible.

   ANSWER

IDENTIFY THE FOLLOWING STEPS AS A SYSTEMATIC APPROACH TO DETERMINING WHETHER A PROBLEM IS ATTRIBUTABLE TO THE OPERATOR OR THE SYSTEM, AND, GIVEN A PROBLEM SCENARIO, SELECT THE APPROPRIATE NEXT STEP BASED ON THIS APPROACH. 1. HAVE A SECOND OPERATOR PERFORM THE SAME TASK ON AN EQUIVALENT WORKSTATION 2. HAVE A SECOND OPERATOR PERFORM THE SAME TASK ON THE ORIGINAL OPERATOR'S WORKSTATION 3. SEE WHETHER OPERATORS ARE FOLLOWING STANDARD OPERATING PROCEDURE

UNDERSTANDING THE OBJECTIVE

Many network problems are caused by operator errors, and are the simplest problems to diagnose and fix.

WHAT YOU **REALLY** NEED TO KNOW

◆ Because it's natural for people to make mistakes, first make sure that a problem is not caused by human error. This will save time. In fact, a problem caused by human error is usually simple to solve. It's quicker, safer, and easier to assist a user in remapping a network drive, for example, than performing diagnostics on the file server.

◆ The best way to verify that a user is performing network functions correctly is by watching him or her.

◆ If watching the user isn't practical, verify that a user is performing tasks correctly by talking to the user by phone while he or she tries to replicate the error. At every step, calmly ask the user to explain what she sees on the screen and what, exactly, she is doing. After every keystroke or command, ask the user what she sees on the screen. In this methodical manner, you are certain to catch any mistakes she is making. At the same time, if the problem is not caused by human error, you have important clues for further troubleshooting.

◆ If the user can reproduce the problem consistently, ask another operator to attempt to replicate the problem on the same workstation under a test ID. You should also attempt to replicate the problem on that workstation using an ID that has administrative privileges.

◆ If the problem can be consistently replicated on the user's workstation, try to reproduce it on another identical workstation. This test provides information on the extent of the problem.

◆ When trying to replicate a problem on another workstation, make sure that the workstations have identical hardware and software.

◆ If the problem that occurs is covered by a standard operating procedure, refer to the procedure when trying to replicate the problem.

OBJECTIVES ON THE JOB

You have probably experienced a moment when working with computers in which you were certain you were doing everything correctly, but you couldn't access the network, save a file, or pick up your e-mail (and so on). All users experience such problems from time to time. Be patient with users, do not patronize them, and assure them that verification is part of your standard troubleshooting procedure.

PRACTICE TEST QUESTIONS

1. **A user can retrieve files from the network but cannot print to her usual printer. When you attempt to replicate the problem from a nearby workstation using her login ID, you find that you can print to that printer. What can you conclude as a result of this test?**
   a. that the problem is being caused by insufficient print server permissions for her user ID
   b. that the problem lies with her workstation's printer drivers
   c. that the problem lies with her workstation's NIC
   d. that the problem lies with her workstation's protocol bindings

   ANSWER

2. **You are assisting a user who cannot log on to the network. After you successfully log on to the network from your workstation with the user's ID and password, what can you assume?**
   a. that the problem is a result of operator error
   b. that the problem cannot be reproduced
   c. that the problem does not lie on the workstation
   d. that the problem does not lie on the server end

   ANSWER

3. **What is the most common reason for users typing in an incorrect password?**
   a. They wrote it down wrong.
   b. They have Caps Lock on and the password is case sensitive.
   c. They think they have changed the password when they actually haven't.
   d. They don't believe that it matters what password they enter.

   ANSWER

4. **What can testing a problem with a test ID reveal that testing with an administrative ID cannot?**
   a. a problem related to rights
   b. an operator error
   c. a file corruption problem
   d. a network connectivity problem

   ANSWER

5. **A user has a problem logging on to the network. You attempt to replicate the problem both from the user's workstation and from a nearby workstation by logging on as that user. Each time you are successful in logging on. What can you assume about the problem?**
   a. It is related to the user's workstation's NIC.
   b. It is related to the user's client software configuration.
   c. It is related to operator error.
   d. It is related to the user's workgroup hub.

   ANSWER

6. **What should you have in hand when trying to reproduce a difficult-to-diagnose problem?**
   a. the network operating system CDs
   b. the standard operating procedure relating to the problematic operation
   c. the printout of the help database record relating to the problem
   d. the software patch relating to the problematic program

   ANSWER

7. **You try to reproduce a user's inability launch the MS Excel program from the file server on a nearby workstation. Which two of the following could cause misleading results?**
   a. The nearby workstation was not identical to the user's workstation.
   b. The nearby workstation was not on the same LAN segment as the user's workstation.
   c. The user's profile was different on the nearby workstation.
   d. The nearby workstation did not have an icon for MS Excel on its desktop, while the user's workstation did.

   ANSWER

3.4 Troubleshooting the network

GIVEN A NETWORK TROUBLESHOOTING SCENARIO, DEMONSTRATE AWARENESS OF THE NEED TO CHECK FOR PHYSICAL AND LOGICAL INDICATORS OF TROUBLE, INCLUDING: LINK LIGHTS, POWER LIGHTS, ERROR DISPLAYS, ERROR LOGS AND DISPLAYS, PERFORMANCE MONITORS

UNDERSTANDING THE OBJECTIVE

Without performing sophisticated diagnostics, you can sometimes tell at a glance whether a hub port is faulty or a server is processing incoming data. On hubs, routers, and NICs of every sort, LEDs indicate whether they are live and accepting/sending transmissions, experiencing excessive errors, or receiving no power.

WHAT YOU **REALLY** NEED TO KNOW

- ◆ Viewing the link LEDs on hub ports, NICs, router ports, and other devices can reveal transmission problems.
- ◆ In general, a steady or blinking green LED indicates that data is being transmitted and/or received. In general, a steady or blinking orange LED indicates that a problem exists, such as excessive errors. If the LED is not lit, either the port, NIC, or device is not in use or not receiving power.
- ◆ The front of a server or workstation often has a blinking green LED to indicate that data is being written to or read from the hard disk. In addition, another LED indicates in solid green whether the machine is receiving power.
- ◆ Many types of software, including network operating systems, maintain error logs to indicate whether errors have been generated through the use or attempted use of the software.
- ◆ While some software programs save error logs as text files, NOSs provide an interface to easily view error logs. In Windows NT Server, you can display this error log by choosing the Event Viewer from the Administrative Tools submenu.
- ◆ Network operating system logs provide information about errors in loading drivers, recognizing hardware, authenticating users, launching applications, performing maintenance operations, and attempted security breaches.
- ◆ Network operating systems also provide simple interfaces to view important network statistics that can aid in troubleshooting, such as percentage of disk space, memory, and CPU in use, user login statistics, drivers currently loaded, server up time, print queue information, and so on.
- ◆ Network operating systems also provide methods of gauging network performance, identifying bottlenecks, showing performance trends, and determining system capacity. In Windows NT Server, this function is provided by the Performance Monitor utility.

OBJECTIVES ON THE JOB

You should read your equipment manuals and understand the meaning of LED lights for your particular models. You should also become familiar with the kinds of tools available to you through the network operating system, such as Windows NT Server's Event Viewer.

1. **While displaying the Windows NT Server Event Viewer, how can you find out more information about one of the listed events?**
   a. Double-click the event.
   b. Right-click the event.
   c. Choose Event – View from the menu.
   d. Choose View – Options – Full from the menu.

   ANSWER

2. **Which of the following statistics could help you diagnose a server performance problem?**
   a. percent of disk space left on the DATA volume
   b. percent of CPU resources utilized
   c. percent of total users currently logged in
   d. ratio of IP traffic to IPX traffic

   ANSWER

3. **You are a network technician for a small chain of grocery stores. A user from a store 20 miles away tells you he keeps trying to log on to the server and can't. He thinks he might have been using the wrong password initially, but now uses his correct password. What do you check in the NOS?**
   a. whether the server has exceeded the maximum number of simultaneous connections
   b. whether the user's permissions have changed according to the Event Viewer
   c. whether the user's account has been locked because he attempted to log in multiple times with an incorrect password
   d. whether the server is accepting data, according to its hard disk LED

   ANSWER

4. **How can a NIC indicate that a workstation's client software is properly connecting to the network?**
   a. Its LED is steady amber.
   b. Its LED is blinking green.
   c. Its LED remains unlit.
   d. Its LED is steady blue.

   ANSWER

5. **If the LED on the front of a router is not lit, what can you assume about the router?**
   a. It is properly transmitting and receiving data.
   b. It has at least one faulty port.
   c. It is waiting for incoming data.
   d. It is not receiving power.

   ANSWER

6. **What tool would you use on a Windows NT Server to discover trends in the amount of CPU utilization on the server over the last week?**
   a. Event Viewer
   b. Performance Monitor
   c. Account Utility
   d. Volumes Utility

   ANSWER

7. **Viewing your server's resource statistics, you notice a sudden 50% decrease in a server's available hard disk resources. What might you suspect is the cause?**
   a. A user has attempted to back up his workstation to the network.
   b. The server's statistics display program has failed.
   c. The server's RAM has failed and it is relying entirely on virtual memory.
   d. The server is caching large requests for data from the Internet.

   ANSWER

GIVEN A NETWORK PROBLEM SCENARIO, INCLUDING SYMPTOMS, DETERMINE THE MOST LIKELY CAUSE OR CAUSES OF THE PROBLEM BASED ON THE AVAILABLE INFORMATION. SELECT THE MOST APPROPRIATE COURSE OF ACTION BASED ON THIS INFERENCE. ISSUES THAT MAY BE COVERED INCLUDE: RECOGNIZING ABNORMAL PHYSICAL CONDITIONS, ISOLATING AND CORRECTING PROBLEMS IN CASES WHERE THERE IS FAULT IN THE PHYSICAL MEDIA (PATCH CABLE), CHECKING THE STATUS OF SERVERS, CHECKING FOR CONFIGURATION PROBLEMS WITH DNS, WINS, HOST FILE, CHECKING FOR VIRUSES, CHECKING THE VALIDITY OF THE ACCOUNT NAME AND PASSWORD, RECHECKING OPERATOR LOGON PROCEDURES, SELECTING AND RUNNING APPROPRIATE DIAGNOSTICS

UNDERSTANDING THE OBJECTIVE

With experience comes the ability to recognize a network problem from only a few symptoms. Until then, you should follow a methodical troubleshooting approach.

WHAT YOU **REALLY** NEED TO KNOW

◆ After you have determined that a problem's symptoms are reproducible, verify the integrity of connections between devices and the hardware used in those connections. Cables should be inserted firmly in ports, NICs, and wall jacks. Make sure NICs are seated firmly in the system board, and connectors, and cables are not damaged.

◆ Physical connectivity problems often appear as a continuous or intermittent inability to connect to the network and perform network-related functions.

◆ Examine the firmware and software configurations, settings, installations, and privileges. Depending on the type of symptoms, you might need to investigate networked applications, the network operating system, or hardware configurations, such as NIC IRQ settings.

◆ Logical connectivity problems are often more difficult to isolate and resolve than physical connectivity problems. Consider error messages, consistency of errors, and recent software changes.

◆ Some software-based causes for not being able to connect to the network include (but are not limited to): resource conflicts with the NIC's configuration, improperly configured NIC, improperly installed or configured client software, or improperly installed or configured network protocols or services.

◆ Viruses should be suspected in diagnosing network problems if the symptoms include very slow application launching, strange error messages on the server or clients, unexplained changes in file sizes, or file corruption.

OBJECTIVES ON THE JOB

One danger in troubleshooting technical problems is jumping to conclusions about the symptoms. Take time to pay attention to the users, system and network behaviors, and error messages. Treat each symptom as unique (but potentially related to others).

PRACTICE TEST QUESTIONS

1. **You are helping upgrade the client software on 200 workstations connecting to a NetWare 5.0 server. Once the workstations reboot after installing the new client, you log on to the network with a test ID to make sure that the upgrade has worked. On one workstation, you cannot log on after the client upgrade. What could be the problem?**
   - a. You forgot to reset the workstation.
   - b. You mistakenly erased the NetBEUI bindings to the NIC.
   - c. You did not ensure that the client's default context was the same as your test ID's.
   - d. You did not accept the license agreement when upgrading the client software.

2. **A user on a Windows 95 workstation says that she can pick up e-mail and surf the Internet, but she can't connect to the Windows NT server that hosts her SQL database. What do you check?**
   - a. default gateway IP address
   - b. WINS server address
   - c. DNS server address
   - d. proxy server address

3. **You spend time troubleshooting a NIC and its configuration on a workstation that cannot connect to the network. The NIC's diagnostics, and configuration are fine. What do you try next?**
   - a. swapping out the patch cable from the NIC to the wall jack for a new patch cable
   - b. swapping out the NIC for a new NIC
   - c. modifying the NIC's full-duplex/half-duplex settings
   - d. modifying the NIC's IRQ

4. **Two users complain that it takes over three minutes to load MS Word from the server, when just yesterday it only took five seconds. What two things do you check?**
   - a. what time the users logged in
   - b. how many other users are attempting to launch this program simultaneously
   - c. percent usage of the CPU resources on the server
   - d. whether the server has contracted a virus

5. **What do you do if a user says that he forgot his password?**
   - a. Look up his password in the network operating system and read it to him.
   - b. Look up his password in his personnel file and read it to him.
   - c. Ask him to verify that he is who he says he is by providing some personal information that you can check against a personnel record before you reset his password.
   - d. Tell him that you will have to re-create his user ID and assign a new password.

6. **A user works in a very messy office where his network cables, power cords, papers and books are lying on the floor. He complains that he's experiencing occasional problems when trying to send and receive data to and from the network. What do you check?**
   - a. whether he has spilled anything on his keyboard
   - b. whether his workstation is pushed too close to the wall
   - c. whether his computer case has collected too much dust
   - d. whether the patch cable between his workstation and the wall jack is damaged

7. **You have upgraded an application that runs from the file server. Since then, some users can run the application, but others cannot. What could be causing the problem?**
   - a. The upgrade modified some of the users' data files.
   - b. The upgrade created new program directories to which some users don't have permission.
   - c. The upgrade changed the way the application caches requests.
   - d. The upgrade applied a limit to the number of simultaneous users in the application.

ANSWER

ANSWER

ANSWER

ANSWER

ANSWER

ANSWER

ANSWER

SPECIFY THE TOOLS THAT ARE COMMONLY USED TO RESOLVE NETWORK EQUIPMENT PROBLEMS. IDENTIFY THE PURPOSE AND FUNCTION OF COMMON NETWORK TOOLS, INCLUDING CROSSOVER CABLE, HARDWARE LOOPBACK, TONE GENERATOR, TONE LOCATOR (FOX AND HOUND)

UNDERSTANDING THE OBJECTIVE

You can use a crossover cable to make sure that two NICs can communicate without attempting to connect to a file server. A loopback plug, which reverses transmit and receive signals to return to their source, is most often used in NIC diagnostics. Cable checkers determine whether a cable will reliably transmit and receive data. Cable testers can also find cable faults, rate the integrity of the cable, and measure attenuation and crosstalk.

WHAT YOU **REALLY** NEED TO KNOW

◆ A **crossover cable** is a type of patch cable in which the transmit and receive wire pairs are reversed in one of the two RJ-45 connectors. It can connect two workstations and check their NIC functionality.

◆ A **loopback plug** is a connector that plugs into a port and crosses over the transmit line to the receive line so that outgoing signals can be redirected back to the computer for testing. It is often used when performing diagnostic tests on a NIC.

◆ A **tone locator** is a tool that uses a tone generator to apply an electrical tone to a wire or wire pair, and then uses a probe to identify the wire in a bundle, at a cross connect, or at a termination point. Tone locators and generators are used in both voice and data diagnostics.

◆ **Cable checkers** determine whether your cabling can provide connectivity. They apply a small voltage to each conductor at one end of the cable, and then check whether that voltage can be detected at the other end.

◆ A **cable tester** performs all the continuity and fault tests that a cable checker performs, but in addition it ensures the cable is not too long, measures distance to a cable fault, measures attenuation, measures crosstalk, measures termination resistance and impedance for Thinnet cabling, issues pass/fail rating for CAT3, CAT5, CAT6, or even CAT7 standards

◆ Never use a cable checker or tester on a live network cable.

◆ A **network monitor** is a software-based tool that monitors traffic on the network from a server or workstation attached to the network. Network monitors typically can interpret up to Layer 3 of the OSI model.

◆ A **network analyzer** is a portable, hardware-based tool that a network manager connects to the network expressly to determine the nature of network problems. Network analyzers can typically interpret data up to Layer 7 of the OSI model.

OBJECTIVES ON THE JOB

Symptoms of cabling problems can be as elusive as occasional lost packets or as obvious as a break in network connectivity. Test cables for faults with cable checkers and cable testers. A tone generator and locator can determine which wire in a bundle is faulty.

PRACTICE TEST QUESTIONS

1. **What is the best way to verify that a NIC has a hardware problem?**
   a. Perform NIC diagnostics with the NIC manufacturer's utilities.
   b. Reinstall the client software on the workstation.
   c. Swap out the NIC for a new NIC.
   d. Modify user account properties on the file server.

   ANSWER

2. **A colleague tells you that he suspects that some of the cables in the new bundle of patch cables he purchased are faulty. What tool can you use to verify this claim?**
   a. network analyzer
   b. cable checker
   c. loopback plug
   d. network monitor

   ANSWER

3. **You are assisting a colleague by applying a cable checker to his workstation's patch cable. What must you do before inserting the cable's plug into the cable checker?**
   a. Turn off his workstation.
   b. Remove his workstation's NIC.
   c. Attach a loopback plug to the opposite end of the cable.
   d. Remove the cable from the wall jack.

   ANSWER

4. **You are trying to figure out where a workstation's cable terminates on the punch-down block in the telecommunications room. What kind of tool can you use to assist you?**
   a. cable tester
   b. cable checker
   c. network analyzer
   d. tone locator

   ANSWER

5. **What can you use to determine whether a cable meets CAT5 standards?**
   a. cable tester
   b. cable checker
   c. network analyzer
   d. tone generator

   ANSWER

6. **You are troubleshooting problems with a Web server. You suspect that UDP-based traffic is getting through while TCP traffic is not. What tool can you use to verify your suspicion?**
   a. cable tester
   b. cable checker
   c. network analyzer
   d. tone generator

   ANSWER

7. **What tool ships with the Microsoft Windows NT Server and can monitor network traffic?**
   a. NetMon
   b. LANalyzer
   c. Sniffer
   d. PerfMon

   ANSWER

10Base2 — An Ethernet adaptation that, according to IEEE 802.3 standards, uses thin coaxial cable and a simple bus topology. 10Base2 is also called Thinnet or Thin Ethernet. Its name derives from the fact that it can transmit data at 10 Mbps (thus the "10Base") and its maximum segment length is 185, or approximately 200, meters (thus the "2"). See *Thinnet*.

10Base5 — The original cabling standard for Ethernet; it uses a bus topology and thick coaxial cable. It is also known as Thicknet or Thick Ethernet. Its name derives from the fact that it can transmit data at 10 Mbps (thus the "10Base") and its maximum segment length is 500 meters (thus the "5"). See *Thicknet*.

10BaseT — An Ethernet version that uses twisted-pair cabling and a star-bus or hierarchical hybrid topology to transmit data at 10 Mbps. Its name derives from the fact that it can transmit data at 10 Mbps (thus the "10Base") and it requires twisted-pair wiring (thus the "T").

100BaseT — An Ethernet version specified in the IEEE 802.3u standard that enables LANs to run a 100 Mbps data transfer rate without requiring significant investment in new infrastructure. 100BaseT uses baseband transmission in a star-bus or hierarchical hybrid topology, like 10BaseT. Also like 10BaseT, the "T" in 100BaseT refers to the fact that it uses twisted-pair cabling.

100BaseTX — A type of 100BaseT technology that achieves its speed by sending the signal 10 times faster and condensing the time between digital pulses and the time a station is required to wait and listen in CSMA/CD. It requires Category 5 unshielded twisted-pair cabling.

100Base-VG AnyLAN — A network transport model that can transmit data at 100 Mbps. Unlike Ethernet, 100Base-VG uses a demand priority access method rather than CSMA/CD. Like 100BaseTX, 100Base-VG uses all four wire pairs in a twisted-pair cable. The "VG" in its name refers to the fact that it can be used for "voice grade" communications (that is, to carry audio or video signals).

Address Resolution Protocol (ARP) — A core protocol in the TCP/IP suite that belongs in the Internet layer. It obtains the MAC (physical) address of a host, or node, and then creates a local database that maps the MAC address to the host's IP (logical) address.

alias — A nickname for a node's host name. Aliases can be specified in a local host file.

Application Programming Interface (API) — A routine (or set of instructions) that allows a program to interact with the operating system. APIs belong to the Application layer of the OSI model.

Application layer — The seventh layer of the OSI model. The Application layer provides interfaces to the software that enable programs to use network services.

asynchronous — A transmission method in which data being transmitted and received by nodes do not have to conform to any timing scheme. In asynchronous communications, a node can transmit at any time and the destination node must accept the transmission as it comes.

availability — How consistently and reliably a file, device, or connection can be accessed by authorized personnel.

B channel — In ISDN, the "bearer" channel, so named because it bears traffic from point to point.

backbone — The cabling that connects each connectivity device, or the different levels of a hierarchy of connectivity devices.

backbone port — A special port on a hub or other connectivity device used to connect the device to the network's backbone.

backup — A copy of data or program files created for archiving or safekeeping purposes.

bandwidth overhead — The burden placed on the underlying network to support a routing protocol.

baseband — A form of transmission in which digital signals are sent through direct current pulses applied to the wire. This direct current requires exclusive use of the wire's capacity, so baseband systems can transmit only one signal, or one channel, at a time. Every device on a baseband system shares a single channel.

bend radius — The radius of the maximum arc into which you can loop a cable before you will cause data transmission errors. Generally, a cable's bend radius is less than four times the diameter of the cable.

binding — The process of assigning one network component to work with another.

Block ID — The first set of six characters that make up the MAC address and that are unique to a particular vendor.

bonding — The process of combining more than one bearer channel of an ISDN line to increase throughput. For example, BRI's two 64 Kbps B channels are bonded to create an effective throughput of 128 Kbps.

braiding — A braided metal shielding used to insulate some types of coaxial cable.

BRI (Basic Rate ISDN) — A variety of ISDN that uses two 64 Kbps bearer channels and one 16 Kbps data channel, as summarized by the following notation: 2B+D. BRI is the most common form of ISDN employed by home users.

bridge — A device that looks like a repeater, in that it has a single input and a single output port. A bridge is different from a repeater in that it can interpret the data it retransmits.

bridge router (brouter) — A router capable of providing Layer 2 bridging functions.

British Naval Connector (BNC) — A device used to connect coaxial cables and NICs on a 10Base2 network. The male connector uses a twist-lock mechanism to hold it into its female jack.

broadband — A form of transmission in which signals are modulated as radio frequency analog pulses that use different frequency ranges. Unlike baseband, broadband technology does not use binary encoding. The use of multiple frequencies enables a broadband system to use several channels and therefore carry much more data than a baseband system.

brouter — See *bridge router*.

bus topology — A topology in which a single cable connects all nodes on a network without intervening connectivity devices.

cable — Wires or other physical media that can carry data or voice signals. Common types of cable include coaxial, twisted pair, and fiber optic.

cable checker — A simple handheld device that determines whether cabling can provide connectivity. To accomplish this task, a cable checker applies a small voltage to each conductor at one end of the cable, and then checks whether that voltage is detectable at the other end. It may also verify that voltage cannot be detected on other conductors in the cable.

cable tester — A handheld device that not only checks for cable continuity, but also ensures that the cable length is not excessive, measures the distance to a cable fault, measures attenuation along a cable, measures near-end crosstalk between wires, measures termination resistance and impedance for Thinnet cabling, issues pass/fail ratings for wiring standards, and stores and prints cable testing results.

Carrier Sense Multiple Access with Collision Detection (CSMA/CD) — Rules for communication used by shared Ethernet networks. In CSMA/CD each node waits its turn before transmitting data, to avoid interfering with other nodes' transmissions.

circuit switching — A type of switching in which a connection is established between two network nodes before they begin transmitting data. Bandwidth is dedicated to this connection and remains available until users terminate the communication between the two nodes.

cladding — The glass shield around the fiber core of a fiber-optic cable. Cladding acts as a mirror, reflecting light back to the core in patterns that vary depending on the transmission mode. This reflection allows fiber to bend around corners without losing the integrity of the light-based signal.

collapsed backbone — A type of enterprise-wide backbone that uses a router or switch as the single central connection point for multiple subnetworks.

command interpreter — A (usually text-based) program that accepts and executes system programs and applications on behalf of users. Often it includes the ability to execute a series of instructions that are stored in a file.

conduit — Pipeline used to contain and protect the cabling. Conduit is usually made from metal.

connectionless — A feature of some protocols that allows the protocol to service a request without requiring a verified session and without guaranteeing delivery of data.

connectionless protocol — A transport-layer protocol that does not require verification of a connection before it begins exchanging data.

connection-oriented — A feature of some protocols that requires the establishment of a connection between communicating nodes before the protocol will transmit data.

connection-oriented protocol — A Transport-layer protocol that requires verification of a connection before it begins exchanging data.

ConsoleOne — A java-based utility used with Novell's NetWare 5.x operating systems to manage network elements.

convergence time — The time it takes for a router to recognize a best path in the event of a change or outage.

core — The central component of a fiber-optic cable that consists of one or several pure glass fibers.

core gateways — Gateways that make up the Internet backbone. Core gateways are operated by the Internet Network Operations Center (INOC).

crossover cable — A cable in which the transmit and receive pins in one of the two connectors are reversed so that the cable can be used to network two devices. Crossover cables may be used in troubleshooting connectivity problems.

D channel — In ISDN, the "data" channel used to carry information about the call, such as session initiation and termination signals, caller identity, call forwarding, and conference calling signals.

Data Link layer — The second layer in the OSI model. The Data Link layer bridges the networking media with the Network layer. Its primary function is to divide the data it receives from the Network layer into frames that can then be transmitted by the Physical layer.

Data Link layer address — See MAC address.

dedicated connection — A channel or circuit designated for specific use by two communicating devices.

dedicated line — A continuously available link that is leased through another carrier. Examples of dedicated lines include ADSL, T1, and T3.

default gateway — The gateway that first interprets a device's outbound requests and last interprets its inbound requests to and from other subnets. In the postal service analogy, the default gateway is similar to a local post office.

Device ID — The second set of six characters that make up a network device's MAC address. The Device ID, which is added at the factory, is based on the device's model and manufacture date.

dial-up — A type of connection that uses modems at the transmitting and receiving ends and PSTN or other lines to access a network.

dial-up networking (DUN) — The process of dialing in to a LAN's access server or to an ISP. Dial-up Networking is also the name of the utility that Microsoft provides with its operating systems to achieve this type of connectivity.

differential backup — A backup method in which only data that have changed since the last backup are copied to a storage medium, and that information is marked for subsequent backup, regardless of whether it has changed.

digital certificate — A password-protected and encrypted file that holds an individual's identification information, including a public key and a private key. The individual's public key is used to verify the sender's digital signature, and the private key allows the individual to log on to a third-party authority who administers digital certificates.

Direct Memory Address (DMA) channel — A channel for direct memory access, typically used to enable peripheral devices to access a device's memory directly, and thus perform tasks more quickly.

disk mirroring — A RAID technique in which data from one disk are automatically copied to another disk as the information is written.

disk striping — A simple implementation of RAID in which data are written in 64 KB blocks equally across all disks in the array.

distributed backbone — A type of enterprise-wide backbone that consists of a number of hubs connected to a series of central hubs or routers in a hierarchy.

domain — A group of users, servers, and other resources that share account and security information through a Windows NT network operating system.

domain controller — A computer on a Microsoft Windows NT network that maintains a master database of all users, resources, and security information.

domain name — The symbolic name that identifies a domain. Usually, a domain name is associated with a company or other type of organization, such as a university or military unit.

Domain Name System (DNS) — A hierarchical way of tracking domain names and their addresses, devised in the mid-1980s. The DNS database does not rely on one file or even one server, but rather is distributed over several key computers across the Internet to prevent catastrophic failure if one or a few computers go down. DNS is a TCP/IP service that belongs to the Application layer of the OSI model.

Dynamic Host Configuration Protocol (DHCP) — An Application layer protocol in the TCP/IP suite that manages the dynamic distribution of IP addresses on a network. Using a DHCP to assign IP addresses can nearly eliminate duplicate-addressing problems.

dynamic routing — Routing that can automatically adjust to changes in the network, including topology, congestion, and outages, to direct data most efficiently between nodes.

electromagnetic interference (EMI) — A type of interference that may be caused by motors, power lines, televisions, copiers, fluorescent lights, or other sources of electrical activity.

encryption — The use of an algorithm to scramble data into a format that can be read only by reversing the algorithm—or decrypting the data—to keep the information private. The most popular kind of encryption algorithm weaves a key into the original data's bits, sometimes several times in different sequences, to generate a unique data block.

erasable programmable read-only memory (EPROM) — Firmware that belongs on a circuit board and that enables its configuration information to be erased and rewritten. You can write to a NIC's EPROM to change the NIC's default transmission speed, for example.

failure — A deviation from a specified level of system performance for a given period of time. A failure occurs when something doesn't work as promised or as planned.

Fast Ethernet — See *100BaseT*.

fault — The malfunction of one component of a system. A fault can result in a failure.

fault tolerance — The capacity for a system to continue performing despite an unexpected hardware or software malfunction.

fiber-optic cable — A form of cable that contains one or several glass fibers in its core. Data are transmitted via pulsing light sent from a laser or light-emitting diode through the central fiber(s). Outside the fiber(s), a layer of glass called cladding acts as a mirror, reflecting light back to the core in patterns that vary depending on the transmission mode. Outside the cladding, a layer of plastic and a braiding of Kevlar protect the inner core. A plastic jacket covers the braiding.

File Transfer Protocol (FTP) — An Application layer TCP/IP protocol that manages file transfers between TCP/IP hosts.

filtering database — A collection of data created and used by a bridge that correlates the MAC addresses of connected workstations with their locations. A filtering database is also known as a forwarding table.

firewall — A specialized device (typically a router, but possibly only a PC running special software) that selectively filters or blocks traffic between networks. A firewall may be strictly hardware-based, or it may involve a combination of hardware and software.

firmware — A combination of hardware and software. The hardware component of firmware is a read-only memory (ROM) chip that stores data established at the factory and possibly changed by configuration programs that can write to ROM.

flow control — A method of gauging the appropriate rate of data transmission based on how fast the recipient can accept data.

forwarding table — See *filtering database*.

full backup — A backup in which all data on all servers are copied to a storage medium, regardless of whether the data are new or changed.

full-duplexing — An enhancement that allows simultaneous two-way transmission between nodes on a network while eliminating collisions. Full-duplexing can potentially double a network's bandwidth.

full-mesh network — A network in which all nodes have more than one connection to the network. Full-mesh networks are the most fault-tolerant type of WAN.

gateway — A combination of networking hardware and software that connects two dissimilar kinds of networks. Gateways perform connectivity, session management, and data translation, so they must operate at multiple layers of the OSI model. See also *proxy server*.

graphical user interface (GUI) — A pictorial representation of computer functions and elements that, in the case of network operating systems, enables administrators to more easily manage files, users, groups, security, printers, and other issues.

half-duplexing — A transmission technique in which data may travel over a connection in both directions, but not simultaneously.

Hardware Compatibility List (HCL) — A list of computer components proven to be compatible with Windows NT Server. The HCL appears on the same CD as your Windows NT Server software and on Microsoft's Web site.

heuristic scanning — A type of virus scanning that attempts to identify viruses by discovering "virus-like" behavior.

host — A computer connected to a network that uses the TCP/IP protocol.

host file — A text file that associates TCP/IP host names with IP addresses. On Windows 95 and Windows NT platforms, the host file is called "lmhosts."

host name — A symbolic name that describes a TCP/IP device.

hub — A multiport repeater containing one port that connects to a network's backbone and multiple ports that connect to a group of workstations. Hubs regenerate digital signals.

hybrid topology — A complex combination of the simple physical topologies.

Hypertext Markup Language (HTML) — The language that defines formatting standards for Web documents.

Hypertext Transport Protocol (HTTP) — The language that Web clients and servers use to communicate. HTTP forms the backbone of the Web.

I/O base address — The first hexidecimal number in a device's Input/Output (I/O) address range. For example, many NICs use the 300-30Fh I/O address range, in which the I/O base address is "300." Another term for "I/O Base Address" is simply, "I/O address."

IEEE (Institute of Electrical and Electronic Engineers) — An international society composed of engineering professionals. Its goals are to promote development and education in the electrical engineering and computer science fields.

incremental backup — A backup in which only data that have changed since the last backup are copied to a storage medium.

integrity — The soundness of a network's files, systems, and connections. To ensure integrity, you must protect your network from anything that might render it unusable, such as corruption, tampering, natural disasters, and viruses.

integrity checking — A method of comparing the current characteristics of files and disks against an archived version of these characteristics to discover any changes. The most common example of integrity checking involves a checksum.

Internet Mail Access Protocol (IMAP) — A mail storage and manipulation protocol that depends on SMTP's transport system and improves upon the shortcomings of POP. The most current version of IMAP is version 4 (IMAP4). IMAP4 can (and eventually will) replace POP without the user having to change e-mail programs. The single biggest advantage IMAP4 has relative to POP is that it allows users to store messages on the mail server, rather than always having to download them to the local machine.

Internet Protocol (IP) — A core protocol in the TCP/IP suite that belongs to the Internet layer of the TCP/IP model and provides information about how and where data should be delivered. IP is the subprotocol that enables TCP/IP to internetwork.

internetwork — To traverse more than one LAN segment and more than one type of network through a router.

Internetwork Packet Exchange/Sequenced Packet Exchange (IPX/SPX) — A protocol originally developed by Xerox, then modified and adopted by Novell in the 1980s for the NetWare network operating system.

IP address — A logical address used in TCP/IP networking. This unique 32-bit number is divided into four groups of octets, or 8-bit bytes, that are separated by periods.

IPCONFIG — A utility in Microsoft's Windows NT Server and Windows NT Workstation operating systems that supplies information about a computer's TCP/IP configuration.

IP datagram — The IP portion of a TCP/IP frame that acts as an envelope for data, holding information necessary for routers to transfer data between subnets.

IP Security Protocol (IPSec) — A Layer 3 protocol that defines encryption, authentication, and key management for the new version of the TCP/IP protocol suite, IPv6. IPSec adds security information to the header of all IP packets.

IRQ (Interrupt Request Line) — The means by which a device can request attention from the CPU. IRQs are identified by numbers from 0 to 15, and many PC devices reserve specific numbers for their use alone.

ISDN (Integrated Services Digital Network) — An international standard, established by the ITU for transmitting data over digital lines. Like PSTN, ISDN uses the telephone carrier's lines and dial-up connections, but it differs from PSTN in that it exclusively uses digital lines and switches.

key — A series of characters used in many encryption schemes to make decrypting the data more difficult.

Layer 2 Forwarding (L2F) — A Layer 2 protocol similar to PPTP that provides tunneling for other protocols and can work with the authentication methods used by PPP. L2F was developed by Cisco Systems and requires special hardware on the host system end. It can encapsulate protocols to fit more than just the IP format, unlike PPTP.

Layer 2 Tunneling Protocol (L2TP) — A Layer 2 tunneling protocol developed by a number of industry consortia. L2TP is an enhanced version of L2F. Like L2F, it supports multiple protocols; unlike L2F, it does not require costly hardware upgrades to implement. L2TP is optimized to work with the next generation of IP (IPv6) and IPSec (the Layer 3 IP encryption protocol).

line tester — A device that can be inserted into a phone jack to detect whether the amount of voltage in the telephone line may be harmful to analog modems.

link LED — A small light near each port on a hub or other connectivity device that turns green when a successful connection has been made and turns red or amber when a connection has not been made.

Linux — A freely distributable implementation of the UNIX system. It was originally developed by Finnish computer scientist Linus Torvalds.

local area network (LAN) — A network of computers and other devices that is confined to a relatively small space, such as one building or even one office.

loopback address — An IP address reserved for communicating from a node to itself (used mostly for testing purposes). The value of the loopback address is always 127.0.0.1.

loopback plug — A connector used for troubleshooting that plugs into a port (for example, a serial or parallel port) and crosses over the transmit line to the receive line, allowing outgoing signals to be redirected back into the computer for testing.

MAC address — A number that uniquely identifies a network node. The manufacturer hard-codes the MAC address on the NIC. This address is composed of the block ID and device ID.

MAC sublayer — The lower sublayer of the Data Link layer of the OSI model. The MAC sublayer indicates the media access method (such as CSMA/CD or token ring).

manual pages — UNIX online documentation. This documentation describes the use of the commands and the programming interface to the UNIX system.

member server (MS) — A server that takes no responsibility for managing accounts or security in a Windows NT domain. An MS is usually devoted to running a particular application, such as MS SQL Server, that requires dedicated processing resources.

memory address range — See *memory range*.

memory range — A hexadecimal number that indicates the area of memory that the NIC and CPU will use for exchanging, or buffering, data. As with IRQs, some memory ranges are reserved for specific devices—most notably, the system board.

mesh network — An enterprise-wide topology in which routers are interconnected with other routers so that at least two pathways connect some or all nodes.

MIB (management information base) — A collection of data used by management programs (which may be part of the network operating system or a third-party program) to analyze network performance and problems.

Microsoft Message Queueing (MSMQ) — An API used in a network environment. MSMQ stores messages sent between nodes in queues, then forwards them to their destination based on when the link to the recipient is available.

mirroring — The process of simultaneously duplicating data on two storage devices.

modem — A device that modulates analog signals into digital signals at the transmitting end for transmission over telephone lines, and demodulates digital signals into analog signals at the receiving end.

modular router — A router with multiple slots that can hold different interface cards or other devices so as to provide flexible, customizable network interoperability.

monitor module — An NLM in Novell's NetWare versions 3.x and higher that provides information about a server, its network connections, resources, and protocols.

multimode fiber — A type of fiber-optic cable that carries several frequencies of light simultaneously over a single fiber or over multiple fibers. It is the type of fiber-optic system typically used by data networks. Multimode fiber is less expensive than single-mode fiber.

multiprocessing — The technique of splitting tasks among multiple processors to expedite the completion of any single instruction.

multiprotocol network — A network that uses more than one protocol.

Multistation Access Unit (MAU) — A device on a token ring network that regenerates signals; equivalent to a hub.

name server — A server that contains a database of TCP/IP host names and their associated IP addresses. A name server supplies a resolver with the requested information. If it cannot resolve the IP address, the query passes to a higher-level name server.

name space — The database of Internet IP addresses and their associated names distributed over DNS name servers worldwide.

nbtstat — A TCP/IP troubleshooting utility that provides information about NetBIOS names and their addresses. If you know the NetBIOS name of a workstation, you can use nbtstat to determine its IP address.

NDS for NT — Novell's integration tool for Windows NT networks. It works with the NetWare 4.x and 5.0 operating systems and Windows NT servers to enable the Windows NT domains to appear as container objects in NWAdmin.

NetBEUI (NetBIOS Enhanced User Interface) — Microsoft's adaptation of IBM's NetBIOS protocol. NetBEUI expands on NetBIOS by adding an Application layer component. NetBEUI is a fast and efficient protocol that consumes few network resources, provides excellent error correction, and requires little configuration.

netstat — A TCP/IP troubleshooting utility that displays statistics and the state of current TCP/IP connections. It also displays ports, which can signal whether services are using the correct ports.

NetWare Directory Services (NDS) — A system of managing multiple servers and their resources, including users, volumes, groups, profiles, and printers. The NDS model is similar to the concept of domains in Windows NT, but more comprehensive. In NDS, every networked resource is treated as a separate object with distinct properties.

NetWare loadable modules (NLMs) — Routines that enable the server to run programs and services. Each NLM consumes some of the server's memory and processor resources (at least temporarily). The kernel requires many NLMs to run NetWare's core operating system.

network adapter — A synonym for NIC (network interface card). The device that enables a workstation, server, printer, or other node to connect to the network. Network adapters belong to the Physical layer of the OSI model.

network analyzer — A portable, hardware-based tool that a network manager connects to the network expressly to determine the nature of network problems. Network analyzers can typically interpret data up to Layer 7 of the OSI model.

Network Basic Input Output System (NetBIOS) — A protocol designed by IBM to provide Transport and Session layer services for applications running on small, homogenous networks.

network interface card (NIC) — The device that enables a workstation to connect to the network and communicate with other computers. NICs are manufactured by several different companies and come with a variety of specifications that are tailored to the workstation's and the network's requirements.

Network layer — The third layer in the OSI model. The Network layer translates network addresses into their physical counterparts and decides how to route data from the sender to the receiver.

network monitor — A software-based tool that continually monitors traffic on the network from a server or workstation attached to the network. Network monitors typically can interpret up to Layer 3 of the OSI model.

network operating system (NOS) — The software that runs on a file server and enables the server to manage data, users, groups, security, applications, and other networking functions. The most popular network operating systems are Microsoft's Windows NT and Novell's NetWare.

NTFS (New Technology File System) — A file system developed by Microsoft expressly for Windows NT Workstation and Windows NT Server. NTFS integrates reliability, compression, the ability to handle massive files, and fast access. Most Windows NT Server partitions employ either FAT or NTFS.

NWAdmin (NetWare Administrator Utility) — A graphical interface that runs from a workstation and enables network administrators to manage Novell NetWare's NDS objects. Through the use of drop-down menus and toolbars, NWAdmin makes viewing, creating, changing, and deleting NetWare objects simple.

octet — One of the four 8-bit bytes that are separated by periods and together make up an IP address.

online backup — A technique in which data are backed up to a central location over the Internet.

online UPS — A power supply that uses the A/C power from the wall outlet to continuously charge its battery, while providing power to a network device through its battery.

Open Systems Interconnection (OSI) model — A model for understanding and developing computer-to-computer communication developed in the 1980s by ISO. It divides networking architecture into seven layers: Physical, Data Link, Network, Transport, Session, Presentation, and Application.

packet-filtering firewall — A router that operates at the Data Link and Transport layers of the OSI model, examining the header of every packet of data that it receives to determine whether that type of packet is authorized to continue to its destination. Packet-filtering firewalls are also called *screening firewalls*.

Packet Internet Groper (PING) — A TCP/IP troubleshooting utility that can verify that TCP/IP is installed, bound to the NIC, configured correctly, and communicating with the network. PING uses ICMP to send echo request and echo reply messages that determine the validity of an IP address.

parallel backbone — The most robust enterprise-wide topology. This variation on the collapsed backbone arrangement consists of more than one connection from the central router or switch to each network segment.

parity — The mechanism used to verify the integrity of data by making the number of bits in a byte sum either an odd or even number.

parity error checking — The process of comparing the parity of data read from a disk with the type of parity used by the system.

partial-mesh network — A network in which some, but not all, nodes are attached to the network via more than one connection.

patch — An upgrade to a part of a software program, often distributed at no charge by software vendors to fix a bug in their code or to add slightly more functionality.

patch cable — A relatively short section (usually between 3 and 50 feet) of twisted-pair cabling with connectors on both ends that connects network devices to data outlets.

patch panel — A wall-mounted panel of data receptors into which cross-connect patch cables from the punch-down block are inserted.

PCMCIA — An interface developed in the early 1990s by the Personal Computer Memory Card International Association to provide a standard interface for connecting any type of device to a portable computer. PCMCIA slots may hold modem cards, network interface cards, external hard disk cards, or CD-ROM cards.

peer-to-peer networking — A networking scheme in which no computer has more or less authority than another, and all computers can share resources with all others.

Physical layer — The lowest, or first, layer of the OSI model. The Physical layer contains the physical networking media, such as cabling and connectors.

Pinouts — The wire terminations in a cable's connector or plug.

plain old telephone service (POTS) — See *Public Switched Telephone Network*.

Plug and Play (PnP) — The characteristic of a computer system that enables it to automatically configure devices (such as NICs) as they are added.

point-to-point — A link that connects only one site to another site.

Point-to-Point Protocol (PPP) — A communications protocol that enables a workstation to connect to a server using a serial connection. PPP can support multiple Network layer protocols, can use both asynchronous and synchronous communications, and does not require much (if any) configuration on the client workstation.

Point-to-Point Tunneling Protocol (PPTP) — A Layer 2 protocol developed by Microsoft that encapsulates PPP so that any type of data can traverse the Internet masked as pure IP transmissions. PPTP supports the encryption, authentication, and LAN access services provided by RAS. Instead of users having to dial directly into an access server, they can dial into their ISP using PPTP and gain access to their corporate LAN over the Internet.

port — The address on a host where an application makes itself available to incoming data.

Post Office Protocol (POP) — A TCP/IP subprotocol that provides centralized storage for e-mail messages. In the postal service analogy, POP is like the post office that holds mail until it can be delivered.

Presentation layer — The sixth layer of the OSI model. The Presentation layer serves as a translator between the application and the network. Here data are formatted in a schema that the network can understand, with the format varying according to the type of network used. The Presentation layer also manages data encryption and decryption, such as the scrambling of system passwords.

Pretty Good Privacy (PGP) — A key-based encryption system for e-mail that uses a two-step verification process.

Primary Rate ISDN (PRI) — A type of ISDN that uses 23 bearer channels and one 64 Kbps data channel as represented by the following notation: 23B+D. PRI is less commonly used by individual subscribers than BRI, but it may be used by businesses and other organizations needing more throughput.

print server — Combinations of software and hardware that manage the job queuing, configuration, and other tasks of networked printers. Print servers may run on file servers, or they may exist as separate, standalone devices attached to the network.

proxy — The characteristic of one device or service acting on behalf of another.

Public Switched Telephone Network (PSTN) — The network of typical telephone lines that has been evolving for 100 years and still services most homes.

punch-down block — A panel of data receptors into which horizontal cabling from the workstations is inserted.

radio frequency interference (RFI) — A kind of interference that may be generated by motors, power lines, televisions, copiers, fluorescent lights, or broadcast signals from radio or TV towers.

RAID Level 0 — An implementation of RAID in which data are written in 64 KB blocks equally across all disks in the array.

RAID Level 1 — An implementation of RAID that provides redundancy through disk mirroring, in which data from one disk are automatically copied to another disk as the information is written.

RAID Level 3 — An implementation of RAID that uses disk striping for data and parity error correction code on a separate parity disk.

RAID Level 5 — The most popular, highly fault-tolerant data storage technique in use today, RAID Level 5 writes data in small blocks across several disks. At the same time, it writes parity error checking information among several disks.

Recommended Standard-232 (RS232) — The standard for serial communications. A serial port is sometimes called an RS232 port.

redundancy — The use of more than one identical component for storing, processing, or transporting data.

Redundant Array of Inexpensive Disks (RAID) — A server redundancy measure that uses shared, multiple physical or logical hard disks to ensure data integrity and availability. Some RAID designs also increase storage capacity and improve performance. See also *disk striping* and *disk mirroring*.

registered jack-11 (RJ-11) — The standard interface for phone (or modem) connections. An RJ-11 jack contains four or six wires (two or three wire pairs).

registered jack-45 (RJ-45) — The standard interface for Ethernet 10BaseT and 100BaseT connections. An RJ-45 jack typically contains eight wires (four wire pairs) and looks like a large telephone jack.

release — The act of terminating a DHCP lease.

remote access server — A combination of software and hardware that provides a central access point for multiple users to dial into a LAN or WAN.

Remote Access Service (RAS) — One of the simplest dial-in servers. This software is included with Windows NT Server. Note that "RAS" is pronounced *razz*.

remote node — A client that has dialed directly into a LAN's remote access server. The LAN treats a remote node like any other client on the LAN, allowing the remote user to perform the same functions he or she could perform while in the office.

repeater — A device on a network that retransmits a signal. Repeaters are used on both analog and digital networks to regenerate signals weakened by attenuation. Some hubs are simply repeaters.

resolver — Any host on the Internet that needs to look up domain name information.

resource record — The element of a DNS database stored on a name server that contains information about TCP/IP host names and their addresses.

ring topology — A network layout in which each node is connected to the two nearest nodes so that the entire network forms a circle. Data are transmitted unidirectionally around the ring. Each workstation accepts and responds to packets addressed to it, then forwards the other packets to the next workstation in the ring.

root — A highly privileged user ID that has all rights to create, delete, modify, move, read, write, or execute files on a system. This term may specifically refer to the administrator on a UNIX-based network.

root server — A DNS server maintained by InterNIC (in North America) that is an authority on how to contact the top-level domains, such as those ending with .com, .edu, .net, .us, and so on. InterNIC maintains 13 root servers around the world.

routable — Protocols that can span more than one LAN segment because they carry Network layer and addressing information that can be interpreted by a router.

route — To direct data between networks based on addressing, patterns of usage, and availability of network segments.

router — A multiport device that can connect dissimilar LANs and WANs running at different transmission speeds and using a variety of protocols. In addition, a router can determine the best path for data transmission and perform advanced management functions. Routers operate at the Network layer (Layer 3) or higher of the OSI model. They are intelligent, protocol-dependent devices.

routing protocols — The means by which routers communicate with each other about network status. Routing protocols determine the best path for data to take between nodes. They are not identical to routable protocols such as TCP/IP or IPX/SPX, although they may piggyback on top of routable protocols.

screening firewall — See *packet-filtering firewall*.

Secure Sockets Layer (SSL) — A method of encrypting Web pages (or HTTP transmissions) as they travel over the Internet.

segment — A part of a LAN that is separated from other parts of the LAN and that shares a fixed amount of traffic capacity.

serial backbone — The simplest kind of backbone, consisting of two or more hubs connected to each other by a single cable.

Serial Line Internet Protocol (SLIP) — A communications protocol that enables a workstation to connect to a server using a serial connection. SLIP can support only asynchronous communications and IP traffic and requires some configuration on the client workstation.

server — A computer on the network that manages shared resources. Servers usually have more processing power, memory, and hard disk space than clients. They run network operating software that can manage not only data, but also users, groups, security, and applications on the network.

server console — The network administrator's primary interface to a NetWare server. Unlike Windows NT, the NetWare server interface is not entirely graphical. NetWare 4.x offers only text-based server menus at the console. NetWare 5.0 allows you to access commands through either a text-based or graphical menu system.

server mirroring — A fault-tolerance technique in which one server duplicates the transactions and data storage of another, identical server. Server mirroring requires a link between the servers and software running on both servers so that the servers can continually synchronize their actions and take over in case the other fails.

session — A connection for data exchange between two parties. The term "session" is most often used in the context of terminal and mainframe communications.

Session layer — The fifth layer in the OSI model. The Session layer establishes and maintains communication between two nodes on the network. It can be considered the "traffic cop" for network communications.

share-level security — A method of securing shared resources in which resources such as drives, files, printers, or CD-ROMs that are attached to a workstation or server are assigned passwords. Access to these resources may be read-only or full access (which includes read, erase, modify, and access rights).

sheath — The outer cover, or jacket, of a cable.

shell — Another term for command interpreter.

shielded twisted-pair (STP) — A type of cable containing twisted wire pairs that are not only individually insulated, but also surrounded by a shielding made of a metallic substance such as foil. The shielding acts as an antenna, converting the noise into current (assuming that the wire is properly grounded). This current induces an equal yet opposite current in the twisted pairs it surrounds. The noise on the shielding mirrors the noise on the twisted pairs, and the two cancel each other out.

signal bounce — A phenomenon in which signals travel endlessly between the two ends of a bus network. Using 50-ohm resistors at either end of the network prevents signal bounce.

signature scanning — The comparison of a file's content with known virus signatures (unique identifying characteristics in the code) in a signature database to determine whether the file is a virus.

Simple Mail Transfer Protocol (SMTP) — The TCP/IP subprotocol responsible for moving messages from one e-mail server to another.

Simple Network Management Protocol (SNMP) — A communication protocol used to manage devices on a TCP/IP network.

simplex — A form of data transmission in which data can only flow in one direction. Radio broadcasts are examples of simplex transmission.

single-mode fiber — A type of fiber-optic cable that carries a single frequency of light to transmit data from one end of the cable to the other end. Data can be transmitted faster and for longer distances on single-mode fiber than on multimode fiber. Single-mode fiber is extremely expensive.

Small Computer System Interface (SCSI) — An interface used to connect external devices such as hard disks or CD-ROM drives to computers. SCSI connectors come in many different varieties, depending on their transmission speed and type.

socket — A logical address assigned to a specific process running on a host computer. It forms a virtual connection between the host and client.

Standard Operating Procedures (SOPs) — Guidelines that establish standards for how to best accomplish something.

standby UPS — A power supply that provides continuous voltage to a device by switching instantaneously to the battery when it detects a loss of power from the wall outlet. Upon restoration of the power, the standby UPS switches the device to use A/C power again.

star topology — A physical topology in which every node on the network is connected through a central device, such as a hub. Any single physical wire on a star network connects only two devices, so a cabling problem will affect only two nodes. Nodes transmit data to the hub, which then retransmits the data to the rest of the network segment where the destination node can pick it up.

static routing — A routing technique in which a network administrator programs a router to use specific paths between nodes. Since it does not account for occasional network congestion, failed connections, or device moves, static routing is not optimal.

subnet mask — A special 32-bit number that, when combined with a device's IP address, informs the rest of the network as to what kind of subnet the device is on.

subnetting — The process of subdividing a single class of network into multiple, smaller networks.

subnetwork — Groupings of devices on a LAN that share some portion of their logical address.

subprotocols — Small, specialized protocols that work together and belong to a protocol suite.

switching hub — A hub that can interpret the addresses of incoming data and, based on those addresses, forward data to the appropriate port on the hub.

synchronous — A transmission method in which data being transmitted and received by nodes must conform to a timing scheme.

tape backups — A duplicate copy of data or program files kept on magnetic tape media for archiving or safekeeping.

Telnet — A terminal emulation protocol used to log on to remote hosts using the TCP/IP protocol. Telnet resides in the Application layer of the TCP/IP suite.

terminator — A resistor at the end of a bus network used to stop signals after they have reached their destination.

Thicknet — A type of coaxial cable, also known as thickwire Ethernet, that is a rigid cable approximately 1 cm thick. Thicknet was used for the original Ethernet networks. Because it is often covered with a yellow sheath, Thicknet is also called "yellow Ethernet." IEEE has designated Thicknet as 10Base5 Ethernet, with the "10" representing its throughput of 10 Mbps, the "Base" standing for baseband transmission, and the "5" representing the maximum segment length of a Thicknet cable, 500 m.

Thinnet — A type of coaxial cable, also known as Thin Ethernet, that was the most popular medium for Ethernet LANs in the 1980s. Like Thicknet, Thinnet is rarely used on modern networks. IEEE has designated Thinnet as 10Base2 Ethernet, with the "10" representing its data transmission rate of 10 Mbps, the "Base" standing for baseband transmission, and the "2" roughly representing its maximum segment length of 185 m.

token passing — A means of data transmission in which a 3-byte packet, called a token, is passed around the network in a round-robin fashion.

Token ring media filters — Small devices that allow token ring NICs to use UTP or STP cabling. A token ring media filter consists of a DB9-pin connector on one end (that plugs into the token ring NIC) with an RJ-45 receptacle on the other end to accept STP or UTP cables.

tone locator — A tool that uses a tone generator to apply an electrical tone to a wire or wire pair, and then uses a probe to identify the wire in a bundle, at a cross connect, or at a termination point. Tone locators and generators are used in both voice and data diagnostics.

top-level domain (TLD) — The highest-level category used to distinguish domain names—for example, .org, .com, .net. A TLD is also known as the domain suffix.

topology — The physical layout of a computer network.

traceroute (or tracert) — A TCP/IP troubleshooting utility that uses ICMP to trace the path from one networked node to another, identifying all intermediate hops between the two nodes. Traceroute is useful for determining router or subnet connectivity problems.

Transport Control Protocol (TCP) — A core protocol of the TCP/IP suite. TCP belongs to the Transport layer and provides reliable data delivery services.

Transport layer — The fourth layer of the OSI model. The Transport layer is primarily responsible for ensuring that data are transferred from point A to point B (which may or may not be on the same network segment) reliably and without errors.

transceiver — A device that receives and transmits signals. In most modern networks, a transceiver can only be found in NICs. Transceivers belong to the Physical layer of the OSI model.

tunneling — The process of encapsulating one protocol to make it appear as another type of protocol.

twist ratio — The number of twists per meter or foot in a twisted-pair cable.

uninterruptible power supply (UPS) — A battery-operated power source directly attached to one or more devices and to a power supply (such as a wall outlet), which prevents undesired features of the power source from harming the device or interrupting its services.

unshielded twisted-pair (UTP) — A type of cabling that consists of one or more insulated wire pairs encased in a plastic sheath. As its name implies, UTP does not contain additional shielding for the twisted pairs. As a result, UTP is both less expensive and less resistant to noise than STP.

upgrade — A major change to the existing code in a software program, which may or may not be offered free from a vendor and may or may not be comprehensive enough to substitute for the original program.

uplink port — A receptacle connecting one hub to another hub in a daisy-chain or hierarchical fashion. An uplink port may look like any other port, but it should only be used to interconnect hubs.

User Datagram Protocol (UDP) — A core protocol in the TCP/IP suite that sits in the Transport layer, between the Internet layer and the Application layer of the TCP/IP model. UDP is a connectionless transport service.

user-level security — A method of securing shared resources in which access to resources is assigned according to users or groups of users. A centralized server authorizes users to access the network and then validates users' permission to access resources.

Volume — A logically assigned amount of space on a physical disk. Volumes are created when the server NOS is installed, but may be modified later for size and type.

wide-area network (WAN) — A network connecting geographically distinct locations, which may or may not belong to the same organization.

Windows Internet Naming Service (WINS) — A service that resolves NetBIOS names with IP addresses. WINS is used exclusively with systems that use NetBIOS—therefore, it is usually found on Windows-based systems.

winipcfg — A utility in Microsoft's Windows 9x operating systems that supplies information about a computer's TCP/IP configuration.

workstation — A computer that typically runs a desktop operating system and connects to a network.

zone — The group of machines managed by a DNS server.

route, defined, 76
routers, 156. *see also* bridges
  bridge router (brouter), 76, 156
  compared to bridges, 70, 76, 156
  configuration and management, 54
  defined, 54, 76
  as gateway, 58, 78, 88
  modular router, 156
  packet filtering firewall, 144
  routable protocols, 16
    compared to nonroutable, 78
  routing protocols, 76, 82
routing
  dynamic, 82
  static, 82
routing protocols, 76, 82. *see also*
  routable protocols
  bandwidth overhead, 82
  convergence time, 82
routing table, 88
RS232. *see* Recommended
  Standard-232

S

SCSI. *see* Small Computer System
  Interface
Secure Sockets Layer (SSL). *see also*
  security; socket
  encryption and, 142
  in HTTP, 102
security. *see also* administrative
  account; encryption; filtering;
  firewalls; passwords; Secure
  Sockets Layer
  environmental factors effecting, 150
  models
    group, 138
    share-level, 138
    user-level, 138
  with proxy server, 112
  with PSTN, 132
  virus scanning, 168

segments
  characteristics, 6
    length, 6, 40
  connected with bridges, 70
  fiber-optic, 40
  separating, 70
Serial Line Internet Protocol
  (SLIP), 126
  compared to PPP, 126
serial port, RS232 standard, 152
server
  defined, 52
  as gateway, 58
  name server, 92, 106
  print server, 154
  proxy server, 112, 114
  remote access server, 128
  root server, 106
server console
  Novell NetWare, 12
    ConsoleOne, 12
server selection, network operating
  system and, 8
server-based network. *see also*
  network
  compared to peer-to-peer net-
    work, 52
Session layer, OSI, 34
shell, UNIX, 14
signal bounce, bus topology, 2
signature scanning, for virus, 168
Simple Mail Transfer Protocol
  (SMTP), 98
Simple Network Management
  Protocol (SNMP), 100
  storage in management informa-
    tion base, 100
simplex, 48
SLIP. *see* Serial Line Internet
  Protocol
Small Computer System Interface
  (SCSI), 152

SMTP. *see* Simple Mail Transfer
  Protocol
SNMP. *see* Simple Network
  Management Protocol
socket
  address, 110
  defined, 110
  Secure Sockets Layer, 142
software
  patches, 164
  troubleshooting, 176
  upgrades, 164
  for virus protection, 168
SOPs. *see* Standard Operating
  Procedures
SPX. *see* Internet Packet
  Exchange/Sequenced Packet
  Exchange
SSL. *see* Secure Sockets Layer
Standard Operating Procedures
  (SOPs), administrative account, 148
star topology, 4
  characteristics, 4
    hybrid technologies, 4
  hubs, 66
  10BaseT networks, 44
stripping, 28
  parity, 28
  parity error checking, 28
  RAID levels, 28
subnetting, 108
  subnet mask, 108
subnetwork, 78. *see also* network
switching hubs, 68. *see also* hubs
synchronous data transmission, 126

T

tape backups, 30, 166. *see also*
  backup,
TCP. *see* Transmission Control
  Protocol

V

video feeds, 96

virus protection, 168. *see also* security

  modes

    heuristic scanning, 168

    integrity checking, 168

    signature scanning, 168

  software, 168

volumes, 30

W

walkie-talkies, 48

WAN. *see* wide-area network

wide-area network (WAN), 50. *see also* local-area network

  dedicated line, 50

  as point-to-point link, 50

  topology, 2

Windows 9x

  modem settings, 134

  NetBIOS name, 22

Windows Internet Naming Service (WINS), 94, 114. *see also* IP address

Windows NT, 10

  domain controllers, 10

  domain model, 10

  graphical user interface, 10

  Hardware Compatibility List, 10

  member servers, 10

file system, 30

IPX/SPX server connection, 10, 18

network operating system, 8

WINIPCFG, 120

  viewing MAC address, 74

WINS. *see* Windows Internet Naming Service

workstations

  defined, 52

  moving and relocating, 90

  security, 138

Z

zones, 106